The Upper Room

*D*isciplines

1995

The Upper Room

*D*isciplines
1995

Coordinating Editor
Glenda Webb

Consulting Editors
Lynne M. Deming
Lynn W. Gilliam
Charla H. Honea
Janet R. Knight
John S. Mogabgab
Tom Page
Robin Philpo Pippin
Mary Lou Redding
Karen F. Williams

Editorial Secretary
Betty Estes

UPPER
ROOM BOOKS
NASHVILLE

The Upper Room Disciplines 1995

Cover photo © 1993 Frances Dorris
Cover design: Jim Bateman
Typesetting: Nancy Cole;
and E. T. Lowe Publishing Co.

ISBN 0-8358-0692-8
Printed in the United States of America

CONTENTS

FOREWORD

The apostles gathered around Jesus, and told him all that they had done and taught. He said to them, "Come away to a deserted place all by yourselves and rest a while."

—Mark 6:30-31

It would be difficult to accuse Jesus of being an escapist, of fleeing the world, of avoiding the hard realities of life. And yet, these are charges that are often leveled at the person who takes seriously the discipline and the rhythm in the life of Jesus: vigorous involvement in the needs of persons and the world, and unparalleled commitment to the time and space required for the practice of a life of prayer. The crowds were met, ministered to, and on occasion left behind with some needs still unanswered. For Jesus, his leaving was not a running away or an escape; rather, it was an essential element in his life and ministry.

For Jesus, prayer was the source of insight, wisdom, identity, strength, power, and direction. It would have been unthinkable—impossible—for Jesus to continue in ministry without going aside, without solitude, without prayer and reflection, without communion with God. Jesus really did live a life of prayer.

Sometimes we tell ourselves that our deeds are so important that they take the place of prayer. At other times we tell ourselves that the needs of the world are too great for us to spend time in prayer. Sometimes we say that we are too busy and do not have a moment's leisure, let alone time for prayer. There are even those occasions when we tell ourselves that we walk with God all day long and do not need the concentrated time of reflection, prayer, meditation, and waiting in God's presence. But even a casual observance of the life of Jesus

11

points out the foolishness of such responses. For Jesus, the ultimate value in heaven and earth was relationship with God. That relationship was forged and nurtured through the avenue of prayer.

The Upper Room Disciplines is designed to assist you in discovering and establishing that rhythm, balance, integration, and wholeness within your own life that was reflected so clearly in the life of our Lord. The scripture passages, the meditations—all are intended to lead you to the Creator God, who alone has the power to transform and make of your life more than it is.

Disciplines is designed to help you in establishing a creative and growing relationship with God. It is also designed to lead you to the world and to involvement with God in redemptive and healing activities.

Jesus demonstrated wholeness so perfectly; we do it so poorly. And yet, we are invited to continue on and are promised the presence and power of the only One who can lead us in the direction of the wholeness we yearn for.

RUEBEN P. JOB
Bishop (Retired), UMC

*Director, An International Center
for Christian Spirituality
and Dean of The Upper Room*

January 1, 1995   **Phyllis Tickle**✤
Sunday, January 1   Read Ecclesiastes 3:9-13.

One year ends; another begins. One measuring of days reaches closure. A new accounting of our time together begins— measured in such units as time's days and years.

Indeed, according to "the Preacher" in Ecclesiastes, time is the armature of the world as we know it, the capsule in which all beauty has been delivered to us, and the great obscuring scrim behind which Being flirts with us. And in the end, because we must, we all live out the Preacher's wisdom. We accept time's dominion over us; we adhere, however reluctantly, to its constrictions; we bow to its befuddlements.

Yet there is no spiritual virtue in mere compliance. The hallowedness of a New Year's Day for Christians lies instead in a certain scarcely suppressed, faith-filled excitement over the fact that the scrim is there at all. Children on Christmas Eve are driven by sure hope and absolute faith to upturn and shake their packages mercilessly, tirelessly. So too, we on New Year's Day are allowed to toy with time, to puzzle over it, to rediscover it in our scriptures as the wrapping paper of God's great gifts to us.

Half the exhilaration of not knowing what's inside a present is the not knowing itself, at least when one is very sure of the giver. Since we are, let us today greet one another with "Happy New Year" as a sacred blessing and a shared thanksgiving.

Suggestion for meditation: *Bring to mind those people who are dear to you. Wish each one a "Happy New Year" knowing that the new year and its events and all who live those events belong to God.*

✤Writer; Religion Editor, *Publishers Weekly*; lector and vestry member in the Episcopal Church, Millington, Tennessee.

13

THE VOICE OF THE LORD

January 2-8, 1995 **Walter Harrelson✤**

Monday, January 2 Read Psalm 29:1-2.

The opening verses of this psalm well disclose the mystery of worship. Our worship *affirms* the reality of God's love and power and justice as we acknowledge the glory of God, as we acknowledge God's splendor and might and just dealings with us and with all of the creation. Yet, our worship also *gives* something to God, something that God is pleased to receive, according to the Bible. God wants to hear our praises, wants to receive our petitions, and wants to be in conversation with us. Psalm 29 uses the verb *yahav*, "to give," as its opening word. When we translate "ascribe," as in the New Revised Standard Version, we are saying that God is worthy of praise, and we should join our voices with the whole cosmic chorus in praising God.

When we translate "give," as in the New American Bible, we are affirming another truth about worship. Our worship gives something that God is pleased to have. We could almost say that our worship enlarges the divine glory, spreads abroad the love and power and justice and beauty of God.

Worship thus counts for much. God *is* glorious; and, therefore, we "ascribe" glory to God. But God seeks us out and desires to be in conversation with us; thus in our worship we also "give" God glory. How marvelous it is, and how humbling, to recognize that God counts on us to *give back* love through our prayers and praises!

Prayer: *We glorify your name, O God, and we thank you that you invite us to address you in prayer. May our lives and also our prayers give you glory throughout the world. Amen.*

✤Professor of Hebrew Bible, emeritus, Vanderbilt University Divinity School; minister, American Baptist Churches; Nashville, Tennessee.

Tuesday, January 3   Read Psalm 29:3-11.

Psalm 29 is held together by the sevenfold "voice" of the Lord. The hymn has as its background the crashing thunder of the storm, causing waters of the seas to rage, the trees of the forests to bend and sway, and even the mountains to shake and bend before God's power. The poet causes our imagination to carry us to the high mountains of the Lebanon in the north and also to the wilderness of the south, to Kadesh, where the people of God encamped for most of the forty wilderness years. Throughout the entire land of promise, God's voice causes all to take notice and to tremble.

But it is not with fear that we tremble. We tremble at the thought that this majestic Creator and Controller of the universe also comes to us, in our places of worship, causing us to quake and to shake, as we offer our prayers and praises.

Gods of the storm are present in most religions. The sheer power of wind and wave and lightning strike awe, or even terror. Psalm 29 does not tell us directly what sort of voice this is. But the reference to Kadesh reminds us that the Lord, whose voice is heard in the storm, also spoke to Moses and called him to lead oppressed slaves from Egypt, called him to receive God's commandments, and graciously made a loving covenant with Israel.

The psalm says that in God's Temple everyone cries out "Glory!" Those who gather there *know* God's name. They can declare God's glory, for they have *seen* God's glory. Christians know that glory in its fullness in the face of Christ.

Prayer: *Make us attentive, O God, to your voice in the whole of your creation. Help us to honor your creation as we work to sustain it in health and safety for all. And give us the will and the strength to glorify you, both in our places of worship and in your temple, the earth. Amen.*

Wednesday, January 4   Read Isaiah 43:1-2.

The prophet's words of consolation are for a people in Babylonian exile, wondering if God any longer cares for them at all. Some of their prophets told them that they were in exile because their ancestors, and they themselves, had broken God's covenant with them. Was exile, then, the end? Or did God still call them "my people"?

Over and again in Isaiah chapters 40 – 55, the prophet passionately cries out that God has not forsaken them. No matter what the trial they face, no matter what the humiliation, no matter what they themselves have done to dishonor God's name, God is still their God and they are God's people.

The prophet sometimes stresses that God *can* save, for is not God the Creator of the ends of the earth, with limitless power, and before whom other powers count for nothing? At other times, like here, the prophet confidently asserts that God *will* save. It is God's character, God's nature, to be the Savior of the oppressed and the scattered and the lonely—the exiles of earth. God's love is not quenched when the people of God bring disappointment or sadness to their Lord. God's love reaches out and will not finally be denied.

It is that love that Christians know in Jesus Christ—self-giving and self-sacrificing, but also life-giving and life-transforming. We have passed through the waters of baptism and we know that we are secure in the face of mighty waters. We have known the fire of the Holy Spirit's love, and the flame holds no terror for us.

Prayer: *We praise you, O God, for the promises of scripture that you are indeed our God and Savior in all times of danger or despondency or grief. Forgive us when we find it hard to trust in you and to yield our lives into your constant care. Amen.*

Thursday, January 5   Read Isaiah 43:3-7.

Few passages in the Hebrew scriptures underscore God's love for Israel more powerfully than this one. Exodus 19:3-6 makes clear that Israel is a "special treasure" to God, loved and cared for, brought to freedom and given care and protection through the centuries, as dangers from outside and from inside the community occurred over and again. But many in Babylonian exile, where this text is set, must surely have found it bitter irony to talk any more about God's love and care.

The prophet of the Exile, however, saw things differently. Israel remains special in God's sight. All the peoples of the earth are God's people (see Exodus 19:5), and God cares for them all. But sheer love, love that cannot really be explained, is what God's people know—and they know it in times of exile and danger just as they know it in times of security and prosperity.

The prophet uses a bold image to try to explain God's special love for Israel. God was ready to give up the rich treasures of Egypt and the fabled gold of Ethiopia in order to claim Israel as this special treasure. And what should Israel do in return? Love and trust God, hold fast and believe in God's promise to save. Soon, very soon, the prophet says, God will bring the people of God from all the lands of earth, returning them to their homeland.

Israel is to do one other thing: live in such a way as to display God's glory. Let the nations see just how God wants all people to live: responsibly, with love for God and for all.

Prayer: *Loving God, help all your people to display your glory, in work and worship and in play. We love you and know that you love us too. Amen.*

Friday, January 6   Read Luke 3:15-17.

Clearly, John the Baptist was a powerful and popular figure in Jesus' day. He could hardly avoid being compared with Jesus, but all the Gospels make it clear that John did not see himself as a rival to Jesus. And Jesus did not see himself as a rival to John. Their ministries were very similar, for both called the community of Israel to repentance, both gave counsel and aid to non-Jews, and both had loyal disciples. They both knew that they were living in critical and decisive ways.

The remarkable thing is that each one was quite ready to be identified as a disciple of the other. Jesus came to John to be baptized, and John continually pointed to Jesus as the messenger of God who would bring God's saving purposes to fulfillment. What a lesson this is for religious leaders! It is so hard for any of us to be comfortable with someone in our line of work who does what we do, and does it better! We hear a bit about rivalry between the disciples of John and those of Jesus, and small wonder. But our text shows no rivalry at all between John and Jesus. John looks forward to the coming of Jesus as Messiah. He anticipates a Day of the Holy Spirit.

The text has one disturbing element. John is deeply convinced that the coming Day of fulfillment will separate people, bringing divine judgment to some and salvation to many. Some New Testament texts suggest that Jesus believed the same, but many of them show Jesus refusing to be a judge and a condemning voice. For Jesus, the Day of the Spirit is a day of decision, indeed. But it is a day of joy and delight in God's forgiving love and presence—extended to all and intended for all.

Prayer: *Loving God, open our hearts to receive your love and forgiveness as the Holy Spirit takes possession of us. Amen.*

Saturday, January 7   Read Luke 3:21-22.

Baptism is given enormous prominence in the Gospels. All the Gospels tell of Jesus' baptism by John, and all of them see it as an essential first step in his ministry. By baptism, believers affirm their commitment to God the Savior and their readiness to be identified before the world as Christians. Almost all Christians recognize that baptism is a once-for-all act, not to be repeated. From earliest times, baptism was done "in the name of the Father, the Son, and the Holy Spirit."

Jesus' baptism was accompanied by a voice from heaven and by the Holy Spirit in the form of a dove. For early Christians, these two signs assured that Jesus was both Israel's Messiah and God's agent of salvation for all the earth. The man Jesus, fully human as all mortals are, is also incarnate Word and divine wisdom, one in and with God and also one with all human beings.* This is why Christians see Jesus as friend and confidant, one who shares our pain and joys fully, and also the one we praise and to whom we direct our petitions. Jesus shares our life, Jesus prays to God as we do, suffers as we suffer, and is unmistakably one who loves and cares for us. But Jesus is equally the one we call Holy, Lord, Savior—one with Creator and Holy Spirit in the mystery of the Holy Trinity. Jesus' baptism says *so much*! Our baptism also grounds us in both earth and heaven, for we are baptized into Christ's death and raised with him to newness of life.

Prayer: *Christ our Savior: Teach us to remember our baptism in times of sorrow or despair or temptation. Teach us to listen for your voice, even as we open ourselves to the coming of the Holy Spirit. Amen.*

---

*Incarnate Word - John 1:1-4, 14. *Divine wisdom* - See 1 Corinthians 1:24; Luke 7:35, 11:49; (compare Proverbs 8).

Sunday, January 8   Read Acts 8:14-17.

Today's verses remind us that from earliest times in the first century there were different ways of becoming and of being Christians. As the message of Christianity spread, the community organized, adopted fixed practices, and arranged its life for the common good. But freedom always remained, often symbolized by the presence and power of the Holy Spirit. At Samaria, the coming of the Holy Spirit completed the lives of those Christians who had not yet heard and received the fullness of the gospel. When it was heard and received, new freedom came.

The story that follows our verses reminds us of the dangers of Christian freedom. Simon Magus, a worker of magic, wanted to buy the power that Peter and John had so that he could make a fortune by "selling" the gospel. The apostles had to rebuke him, telling him that the good news of the gospel came to all freely, without price. They also had to remind Simon that God's spirit claims human beings when and where and how *God chooses*.

We know this from our own experience. While our parents and relatives and congregation may prepare the way for us to claim God's love and forgiveness and new life in Christ, we know that *God's claiming us* is a miracle of divine love and grace. God comes to us, even as we turn and move toward God. The Spirit claims us, and we are left stunned and gladdened that God has done for us what we could never have done for ourselves. Sometimes we can hardly wait for that joy to come to those we love. But the Spirit moves freely to do *God's* will in *God's* time.

Prayer: *O God, Creator and Word and Spirit, come again and again to us, freeing us to follow you and to live freely in the power and discipline of your word. Amen.*

GOD'S GIFTS ARE FOR ALL

January 9-15, 1995   Jorge A. González✤
Monday, January 9   Read Isaiah 62:1-5.

God's action is for all

Three days ago we celebrated the feast of Epiphany, an important observance in the life of the church. In the Eastern church it is the festival of the baptism of Jesus and of the miracle in Cana of Galilee. In the Western church, ever since the fifth century, it celebrates the coming of the Magi or "wise men from the East" to worship Jesus (Matt. 2:1). As such, it is the feast of the manifestation* of Christ to the Gentiles.

With slight variations these themes have been incorporated into our lectionary for the Sundays after Epiphany. Last Sunday we celebrated the baptism of Jesus. The Gospel lesson for next Sunday is the story of the wedding at Cana of Galilee. Evident in this season of "common time" is our desire to remember still the glorious news of Christ's manifestation to the Gentiles.

This theme resounds in the words of the prophet of the Babylonian exile: "The nations shall see your vindication, and all the kings your glory." Here again is the powerful message that God's acts for deliverance of the Holy City shall be made manifest to all. God's great acts are not to be hidden from the world; rather, the divine action for Israel's sake is to be shared abroad.

Prayer: *Lord, help me understand and experience that your redemptive acts are to be announced to all who stand in need of your saving grace. Amen.*

---

*In Greek *epiphanes*, "coming to light."
✤Fuller E. Callaway Professor of Religion, Berry College, Mt. Berry, Georgia; member of North Georgia Annual Conference of The United Methodist Church.

Tuesday, January 10   Read Psalm 36:5-10.

God's refuge is for all

There are two very different perspectives in the Old Testament. One is exclusive and isolationist and presents the people of Israel as holding a special, privileged place in their relationship with God. Ezra, Nehemiah, and Esther, among others, represent this understanding. The other perspective, represented by books such as Ruth, Jonah, Job, and others, offers a more universal view. For these authors, the doctrine of election speaks not of Israel's privileges but of its responsibilities. The author of Psalm 36 evidently was a representative of this second line of thought.

The psalmist celebrates the magnitude of God's "steadfast love" (Hebrew *hesed*). No ordinary love, this love is one of God's most distinctive features. It is boundless, as deep as the deepest ocean, as high as the highest sky. No creature in the universe is left out of its grasp. This love is addressed not just to Israel: "All people may take refuge in the shadow of your wings."

We in the church claim to be successors and heirs to the promises and blessings given to Israel. Let us therefore remember that we, just as they, are called not to privileges but to responsibilities and that God's steadfast love is extended to all, not just to those of us who are part of the church. Refuge under the divine wings is available to all who seek it. Let us learn to accept as our brothers and sisters all those who seek refuge in God, united under the protection of this divine love which offers us the comfort of an everlasting refuge.

Prayer: *God, may your steadfast love, which knows no boundaries, inspire in me the same lovingkindness towards my sisters and brothers who with me seek refuge under your protecting wings. Amen.*

Wednesday, January 11   Read 1 Corinthians 12:1-6.

God's empowerment is for all

The Apostle Paul wrote to the church in Corinth in order to address the many problems that had developed there. One was the constant argument among its members as to which one of them was empowered by God with the greatest gift. Paul responded by admonishing them: "There are varieties of gifts, but the same Spirit; and there are varieties of services, but the same Lord; and there are varieties of activities, but it is the same God who activates all of them in everyone." In this manner Paul established the principle of unity in the midst of diversity.

Paul says that there are "varieties of gifts" (*charísmata*) of the Holy Spirit, and that not everyone has them. Those who do, receive them from one and the same Spirit for the edification of the church. Even though not all members of the Christian community have such gifts, they all share in "varieties of service" (*diakoníai*). This "service" is what a servant does for the master/lord. As servants of Christ, all that we do for him and for his sake is our service to him. Finally, all Christians participate in "varieties of activities" through which we do the work of the Lord. And the point of the whole thing is this: whether we have gifts of the Spirit, share in the services of Christ, or engage in the activities of the church, these are all the work of "the same God who activates all of them in everyone."

Whatever gifts I do have, in whatever service I am engaged to the glory of Christ, whatever the activity in which I take part in doing God's work—all are part of the harmony of our praise.

Prayer: *Guide me, O God, that I may use the gifts of your Spirit to your glory and my services to your praise. May the work of my activities accomplish your tasks. I ask all this through the power of your presence in my life. Amen.*

Thursday, January 12   Read 1 Corinthians 12:7-11.

God's manifestations of the Spirit are for all

We began this series of meditations by considering some of the "manifestations," or revelations, of divine activity. Today's reading once again brings into focus the same word as it speaks of "the manifestation of the Spirit," that is, the ways in which the spirit of God reveals its presence in the life of the Church.

First we must note the itemized listing of the manifestations of the Spirit found in verses 7-10. It is representative not only of the gifts alluded to in verse 4 but also of the services referred to in verse 5 and of the activities mentioned in verse 6. All of these gifts, services, and activities are manifestations of the workings of God's spirit .

Secondly, none of these manifestations takes place for the sake of the individual. Rather, they all take place "for the common good," so that it is evident that the Christian faith is not some form of personal, individualistic "good feeling." On the contrary, the Christian faith can find expression and meaning only within the context of a community of faith.

Finally, no one should think even for an instant that whatever manifestation of the Spirit finds expression through our lives makes us the recipient of a gift from God better than someone else's gift. The fact is that "all these are activated by one and the same Spirit, who allots to each one individually just as the Spirit chooses."

Prayer: *O God, bestower of gifts, in whatever gifts you have granted me, whatever service you have called me to do, whatever activity you have charged me with, let your grace inspire and your spirit perfect me to your honor and glory. Amen.*

Friday, January 13   Read John 2:1-7.

God's freedom is for all

This is the well-known story of the wedding at Cana of Galilee. Most of the time we refer to it as the occasion when our Lord performed the miracle of the changing of water into wine. What we fail to observe is that this was no plain, common, everyday water. The evangelist makes the point that this was very special water, for it was collected in "six stone water jars for the Jewish rites of purification, each holding twenty or thirty gallons," that is, a total of 120 to 180 gallons of ritually pure water.

According to Jewish law, vessels used for the Jewish rites of purification had to be ritually clean and could contain only ritually pure water. Therefore, in John's Gospel, permeated as it is with rich symbolism and imagery, this miracle story is not just about the transformation of water into wine but about the changing of the restrictive water of the law into the free wine of the gospel.

At that time religion was encumbered by legalistic prescriptions. Jesus had to break those bonds which had become burdensome for those seeking to conform their lives to the divine will. By doing so Jesus could offer them the freedom to find the joy of a living relationship with God. The Law was not a burden at the beginning but a source of spiritual guidance in the life of Israel. But when the Law became a legalistic means of approaching God, it became a shackle to the human spirit.

Let us remember this lesson, so that we may eagerly accept the freedom which we are given through Christ.

Prayer: *Dear God, help me to remember that the freedom that Christ imparts is available to all. Amen.*

Saturday, January 14   Read John 2:1-11.

God's revelation is for all

It is well known that John's Gospel is very different from the other canonical Gospels, the Synoptic Gospels. Perhaps the most striking difference is that in John's Gospel Jesus freely and openly discloses who he is, whereas there is in the Synoptics, particularly in Mark, an emphasis on the "Messianic secret"— Jesus urging his disciples and others not to tell who he is. This shift from "the Revealer" of the Synoptics to "the Revealed" in John (which marks the witness of this evangelist) is evident in the final verse of today's reading: "Jesus did this, the first of his signs, in Cana of Galilee, and revealed his glory."

In the first meditation of this series we focused on the words "And all the kings (shall see) your glory" and dealt with the epiphany, or manifestation, of God's redemptive activity. And now, here in the Gospel lesson, we return once again to the same theme as we read at the conclusion of the story, the summary statement that "Jesus . . . revealed his glory." It is in this revelation of the glory of Christ that the message of the whole Bible finds its fullness. Of course, in the most precise sense the glory of Christ is not completely revealed until it is made manifest in the Resurrection. But in John's Gospel there are numerous occasions when the stories it tells reflect rather clearly the post-resurrection faith of the Christian community.

This divine revelation is neither a secret to be guarded and shared with the few nor an exclusive inheritance of those who are part of the church. This is not the secret knowledge of the elect. On the contrary, this divine revelation of the power and glory of Christ is made available to all (John 3:16, for example).

Prayer: *Help me to share with all, O God, the wonders of the glory of Christ. Amen.*

Sunday, January 15   Read John 2:11.

God's gift of faith is for all

This beautiful story ends with a powerful summary statement: "And his disciples believed in him." Their participation in those events at the wedding in Cana so inspired them that they responded by believing in Jesus. Such belief was neither mere intellectual assent given to doctrine nor the acceptance of what was being said on the basis of authority. This belief is indeed the same thing as faith, that is, trust and confidence, which springs forth from the encounter with the glory revealed in the person of Christ.

But this faith is not limited to those who were there, who were eyewitnesses to the events. This faith is a divine gift available to all who are willing to accept it, even today. After all the centuries since his life on earth, there are still faithful disciples of Christ. *We* are his disciples, just as is anyone who makes his or her own the bounty of "God's gifts [which] are for all." God is not measuring blessings drop by drop, ounce by ounce. The immensity of the divine love makes all those gifts available to all who are willing to receive them with grateful hearts.

Prayer: *Lord, help me so to accept*
the power of your actions,
the protection of your refuge,
the empowerment of your grace,
the manifestations of your Spirit,
the freedom of your gospel,
the revelation of your glory,
and the gift of your faith,
that I may truly be counted as your disciple. Amen.

January 16-22, 1995
Monday, January 16

Esther de Waal♣
Read Nehemiah 8:1-3,
5-6, 8-10.

We can imagine the scene vividly—a crowd of people, a man reading, the people attentive as he reads distinctly, giving an interpretation, expanding the text; and the people say, "Amen. Amen." (So be it.)

For me the message which this passage brings lies in that word *attentive*. It is only when I stay with the text, when I pay attention, when I go below the surface of the text that it can become a living force in my life. Far too often my reading is the sort of reading that stays with the head but does not touch the heart.

When I first read the Rule of Saint Benedict, a sixth-century monastic text, I was struck by its idea of listening "with your heart," that is, total listening, listening with the whole of myself, listening which engages my feelings and my senses (for that is what the ancient understanding of the heart implied). I should expect such listening to touch me and to change me.

Suggestion for meditation:

What is more delightful than the voice of the Lord calling to us? See how the Lord in his love shows us the way of life.*

♣Anglican laywoman; writer and teacher; Hereford, England.
*Prologue to the Rule of Saint Benedict.

Tuesday, January 17   Read Psalm 19:1-6.

And now here is another sort of word, one that goes beyond language. The whole universe makes a statement about its Creator. The pattern of the coming of light and dark, the changing seasons, the rhythm of birth and death and new life—the never-ending cycle of creation—is lived out year by year. In all of this we can see, if we are willing, the handiwork of God. There is nothing more powerful than the sun, and the daily rising of the sun has always been something which early people acknowledged with respect. This is something we sophisticated, modern, often urbane people should learn from. We should never take for granted this daily gift of God to us. Although we live with the assumption that the sun will rise daily, we should never allow ourselves to take this daily miracle for granted.

Perhaps we might think for a moment of what the sun will see on its daily circuit, that tabernacle (v. 4c) that God has made for it to run its course, the whole world, human and nonhuman alike, created just for this one thing: to give endless glory, praise, and thanksgiving to the generosity of the living creator God.

Here is how Thomas Merton described the start of his day in *Day of a Stranger*: "It is necessary to be present alone at the resurrection of the Day, in the blank silence when the sun appears." It is at this point, as Merton describes it, that he receives "the one word 'Day,' which is never the same. It is never spoken in any known language."*

Suggestion for meditation:
"There is no speech, nor are there words."
Let the wonders of God's creation summon you to praise God.

---

*From *A Thomas Merton Reader*, ed. Thomas P. McDonnell (New York: Image, Doubleday, rev. ed. 1989), 435.

Wednesday, January 18　　　　　Read Psalm 19:7-11.

We are shown here the law, the way of the Lord, as something active in our lives, something that asks of us a positive cooperation. Here is something powerful that will convert us, literally change us around to go in another direction. It will make us wise; it will open our eyes and help us to see anew.

The psalm goes on to speak of walking upright, of walking free from sin. I think I know, in my own experience, how crippling and how life-denying it can be to be entangled in my own self-centered, self-directed thoughts which point me away from God. But to carry all the time the way of the Lord in my heart, to let that be the center of my world, of my thoughts and of my feelings, is really what I most deeply desire. It is as precious as gold or as honey.

The psalms always address the whole of ourselves; that is why their authors will speak so often of the heart, which was taken in earliest time to be the center of one's being, the own true innermost self. In today's section the law is described in a variety of ways—as commandment, precept, decree, ordinance; and it is described by the way it touches me also: it revives my soul and enlightens my eyes. But the phrase that touches me most, because it brings me back to the excitement and happiness experienced by the crowd which I read about on Monday, is that the law of the Lord will rejoice my heart.

Suggestion for meditation:

> *The precepts of the LORD are right,*
> *rejoicing the heart.*

Thursday, January 19   Read Psalm 19:12-14.

Inserted into this most glorious psalm, full of praise and rejoicing, comes a reminder of our humanness. It is often tempting to stay with the celebration of creation which may be too simplistic and one-sided. Here we see the psalmist refusing to do this. As we enjoy creation, we must not forget sin, evil, failure, and thus our need for repentance, for conversion, for redemption.

In the pattern of this week as we reflect on the law at work in our hearts, we must at some point find time to think of our failures, our weaknesses, and our need for support. This is not to brood over our sins or to dwell on them but simply to admit that we need help, particularly with our hidden, secret faults which lie buried deep down within us.

The picture of a person walking free and upright instead of bowed down is one that appeals to me. We were made to walk free, unshackled. In the end, this freedom is an inner freedom. Its foundation is in my innermost heart, in my interiority, in my most private thoughts. So this psalm draws to its end with one of the most familiar verses of all, addressed to God, who is Savior and Redeemer; who will guide, strengthen, and support me along life's way

I invite you to join me in praying the verse below. Just as I have prayed it many times, I say it again today with new conviction.

Prayer:

> *Let the words of my mouth and*
> *the meditation of my heart*
> *be acceptable to you,*
> *O Lord, my rock and my redeemer. Amen.*

Friday, January 20   Read 1 Corinthians 12:12-26.

Christ came to break down all the barriers, barriers of race and of color, barriers of free and of unfree. Christ came to end all those labels by which we separate, discriminate, and make judgments. We live in a critical age, and we are encouraged by our society that values individualism and competition to put people on the scales to decide if they are unworthy or if they are of greater or lesser importance. The criterion is nearly always the extent to which they are useful or not. And now here is a world turned upside down. Those perceived as the lower, the less interesting, the less honorable—we are told, are to be respected. They have their role to play. Each one is called and chosen, a unique son or daughter of a loving Father, who accepts each without any sort of qualification and with unconditional love, which does not sort people out and label them as superior or inferior.

We are coming more and more to see that what the Apostle Paul is telling us here is age-old wisdom. The idea of interdependence, of the unity, or bonding, of the parts and the whole, of the relationship through which the individual elements contribute to the harmonious working of the whole is as old as creation itself. As we deny or hide away the parts of ourselves and the parts of our society which distress us (for example, the aging, those with handicapping conditions, those with a mental illness), we are forgetting the gospel teaching of the Sermon on the Mount, that Jesus speaks with love and reverence of those whom society deems the least—the broken, the small, the damaged. These people are given to us to be part of the whole, and nothing or nobody is to be despised.

Suggestion for meditation: *"God arranged the members in the body, each one of them," so that all may work together as one.*

Saturday, January 21   Read 1 Corinthians 12:27-31*a*.

I have now to make yesterday's reflection refer not only to the wider world of the community in which I live and work (family, colleagues, parish) but to my own self as well. For I must see myself also as being made up of separate and disparate elements, all of which are God-given. I have been given my own particular skills and talents, gifts which I must handle seriously and responsibly.

In 1 Peter 4:10 there is a clear reminder of the responsibility that the handling of these gifts is for the good of all. God made men and women to be intricate, beautiful, delicate beings to be handled with love and with reverence. To live as a person who is no more than half alive is a tragic waste. I remember reading about a woman with a beautiful voice who, in her fifties, suddenly realized that her beautiful singing voice was God-given for a purpose, that God had given her this voice for herself, as the gift of a generous Creator. The gift was to be acclaimed and enjoyed. The implication that followed was that if she rejoiced in it for herself, she would cherish it and cultivate it, and others, too, would gain from what she had been given.

This is not self-discovery and self-fulfillment for the sake of one's own selfish development. It is my—indeed our—response to the talents and gifts which have been given to us (perhaps it is better to say "lent" to us) and for which we are responsible. And the best return that any of us can offer to God is to rejoice in our God-bestowed gifts, to use them, and to share them.

Suggestion for meditation:
> *"Like good stewards of the manifold grace of God,*
> *serve one another with whatever gift you have received."* *

---

*1 Peter 4:10.

Sunday, January 22   Read Luke 4:14-21.

There is a parallel here with the opening passage of the week: a man standing up in front of a crowd and declaring to them what is written in the book. Both men expound upon the text in such a way that it becomes alive and practical for daily living.

Here is Jesus preaching, taking his text from the Hebrew scriptures, showing us the continuity of the old and the new and showing us also the connectedness of the inner and the outer. The return to the heart, the acceptance of my whole self, the carrying of the law of the Lord in my innermost thoughts—all are necessary to live out God's law of love. Jesus, just as the prophets of old, has no time for abstract idealism.

To have the law of the Lord written in my heart first of all brings fullness of life, freedom from being blind and deaf and lost to what is an offer to those who listen and who are truly attentive to the word of God. It is spoken to each one of us, in our own hearts. But it is not to stop there. To live by the gospel and its teachings can never be only inward-looking. This is good news to be shared, to be proclaimed!

In his earthly ministry Jesus went about bringing "sight to the blind" and "release to the captives" and letting "the oppressed go free." That is the image of what is given to me, and of what I hope, with God's grace, to share with others.

Suggestion for meditation:

> *"Release to the captives and recovery of sight to the blind."*
>
> *What do these words mean to you?*

LISTENING TO YOUR LIFE

January 23-29, 1995   James A. Harnish♣
Monday, January 23   Read Psalm 71:1-6.

If he had lived six more months, Admiral Joe Fowler would have been 100 years old. The oldest graduate of the U.S. Naval Academy, he was a World War I navigator, a World War II shipbuilder, and the master builder of Walt Disney's empire. Even as his body weakened and his eyesight dimmed, his mind continued to be alert, his imagination dancing with new ideas. Past experience was the framework through which he viewed the future. He confronted new challenges with a cheerful, "Can do!"

Like Joe, the writer of Psalm 71 was of advanced years. The psalm is a lament, a cry of deliverance in which the psalmist prays not to be forgotten or to be put to shame, and pleads with God to be present. The very real fears of people are reflected in the psalm's words. But they also reverberate with a profound note of joyful gratitude and praise. On the basis of God's goodness in the past, the psalmist finds joyful strength and confident hope to face difficult days ahead.

In much the same way, Frederick Buechner invites us to listen to our lives and there see God's presence: "If God speaks anywhere, it is into our personal lives."* Further, Buechner writes that to live a life of listening is to live "to the fullness of the music."*

Prayer: *God of all ages, help us see your faithfulness in our past, that we may have hope for our future. Amen.*

♣Senior Pastor, Hyde Park United Methodist Church, Tampa, Florida.
Listening to Your Life (San Francisco: HarperCollins Publishers, 1992), 2, 4.

Tuesday, January 24   Read Jeremiah 1:4-10.

Jeremiah had been chosen before he was born. God's purpose was carved into his very being. But Jeremiah protested that he was too young, too inexperienced for the task. Yet, when he honored God's purpose, he was given strength to face persecution with courageous determination and prophetic hope.

Like Jeremiah, Eric Liddell, the hero of the award-winning movie *Chariots of Fire*, was young—only 22 years old—when he sensed that he had been chosen to fulfill God's purpose. "God made me fast," he said, "and when I run I feel his pleasure."

But running fast wasn't enough. His loyalty to God was tested in the 1924 Paris Olympics when his heat was scheduled for Sunday. He refused to run. He could not honor God's purpose if he broke the Sabbath. Officials even appealed to his loyalty to the British crown; still he refused. Instead of running the 100-meter, for which he had trained, he had to run the 400-meter—for the first time. God, whom I believe chose Liddell before his birth, gave him unusual strength to win that race. Liddell then followed God's call as a missionary to China. At 43, he died in a Japanese internment camp, where fellow prisoners drew strength for their struggle from his deep faith and Christlike joy.

Few of us are or could be Olympic athletes. Our stories will probably not be made into Academy Award-winning movies. But each of us can know an abiding sense that we have been chosen by God for a special purpose, or for a particular task.

Listen to your life. Do you sense that God has chosen you for some particular purpose? Where do you "feel his pleasure"? What would it mean for you to honor that purpose in your life?

Prayer: *Lord of all, enable us to honor your purpose in our lives that we may also feel your pleasure. Amen.*

Wednesday, January 25   Read Luke 4:21-30.

What went wrong? Why was Jesus rejected in his hometown?

The answer may be rooted in the prophetic tradition to which Jesus referred (1 Kings 17:8–18:1). Many widows of Israel suffered in the drought, but Elijah helped a foreigner in Sidon. Israel had many lepers, but Elisha healed a Syrian named Naaman (2 Kings 5). By their actions, the prophets shattered the illusion of particularity. They waged a frontal assault on racial, ethnic, and religious provincialism, expressing God's universal love. Jesus, too, pushed against the conventional boundaries of actions and beliefs. At Nazareth he proclaimed good news to the poor, release to the captives, recovery of sight to the blind, and freedom for the oppressed. His listeners, at first, were pleased by his words. But when the implications reached their souls, they rose in anger to throw Jesus out of town.

I grew up in a homogeneous community, much like Nazareth I suspect. We knew that there were people in the world who were different from us, but we suspected they were wrong. One of my first mentors to assault the provincialism of my life was a seminary professor named Gilbert James, who figured that people had not really heard the gospel until it made them angry. When we find the place where Jesus offends us, we have probably found the point at which the gospel can transform our lives.

Listen to your life. Where does Jesus make you angry? Where does the gospel push against the comfortable boundaries of your experience? Where does God's love stretch your acceptance of people who are beyond your normal comfort zone?

Prayer: *God of all creation, stretch our souls with your universal love until we desire to love all your children. Help us to be open to the miracles that only you can perform. Amen.*

Thursday, January 26   Read Jeremiah 1:8-19.

The prophetic life is tough. Like salt in an open wound, its message can bring healing but rarely without pain. Jeremiah didn't set out to create opposition, but it was the inevitable reaction to his faithfulness to God's call. God promised Jeremiah the word to speak and the power of God's presence to sustain him.

Central Methodist Church in Johannesburg, South Africa, was a powerful, white congregation in a nation divided by apartheid when Peter Storey was named its pastor. Like Jeremiah, Peter was called to be a prophet in a troubled land. Peter could not be faithful to God's call and to God's purpose for him while ignoring the sin of racism. When he opened the church doors to non-whites, 200 members left. Once, armed soldiers circled the chancel as Peter prayed. Through those difficult years, the church's witness grew around a profound commitment to God's word and a lively sense of God's presence.

Central Methodist is now a visible expression of the kingdom of God: a multiracial family touching the city with compassion, justice, and peace; a place where God's spirit is at work to release the captive, to set the oppressed free. Bishop Peter Storey led the training of 6,000 peace monitors to watch over the voting stations during South Africa's first interracial elections. He continues, with confidence and hope-filled faith, to help shape a new future for his nation.

Listen to *your* life. Where is God calling you to be a prophetic witness? Will you allow God to transform the tough places in your life into places of new life and hope?

Prayer: *God of the prophets, give us the word to speak amidst the promise of your presence, that we may fearlessly live and faithfully serve you. Amen.*

Friday, January 27   Read 1 Corinthians 13:8-13.

Life is a mystery. The little we understand is surrounded by the huge expanse of that which we can never fully comprehend. No matter how well we understand ourselves, there are unexplored continents in our personalities which can frighten, thrill, or surprise us. Our best hope is that the infinite God, whose purpose is carved into our creation, knows us better than we know ourselves.

In reflecting on listening to his own life, Thomas Merton, Trappist monk, author, and visionary wrote: "I have become convinced that the very contradictions in my life are in some ways signs of God's mercy to me."*

Paul acknowledges that we spend our lives "looking at puzzling reflections in a mirror" (Phillips).** But we live with the promise that one day we will "see reality whole and face to face." One day we will understand fully. In the meantime, we rest in the good news that we have been fully understood by God.

Listen to your life. Are there parts of your personality that frighten or surprise you? Where do you see God's spirit at work in unexpected ways? Allow yourself to acknowledge the mystery of your life, knowing that you are loved by God, who understands you better than you can understand yourself.

Prayer: *O loving God, within the mystery of our lives may we find the assurance of your unending love. Amen.*

A Thomas Merton Reader, Thomas P. McDonnell, ed. (New York: Image, Doubleday, rev. ed. 1989), 16.
**From THE NEW TESTAMENT IN MODERN ENGLISH © J. B. Phillips 1958, 1960, 1972. Used by permission of Macmillan Company.

Saturday, January 28   Read Psalm 71:17-24.

How will your story end? What sounds will accompany your transition from life, through death, to life eternal? The psalmist comes to life's end and the conclusion of this psalm with a great shout of joyful confidence in the God who had been both refuge and strength in life and who was able to overcome even death.

I was working on these meditations when the call came. A 39-year-old attorney, father of three and a former star athlete for the University of Florida football team, had died after a long, difficult battle with cancer. During the final hours of his life, the drugs he was taking caused him to hallucinate. His wife realized that he was playing football again, calling the plays, shouting to friends along the sidelines. He and his wife began laughing together, just the way they had laughed then. The vision passed. In a little while, he was gone.

This reminded me of a line from Thomas Merton: "Love laughs at the end of the world because love is the door to eternity." * As a witness to our faith in the God who raises us to new life, we began the memorial service by singing "Christ the Lord Is Risen Today." In spite of suffering and pain, the psalm of his life ended and his resurrected life began with a shout of joy.

Listen to your life. Are you building the kind of memories that can fill the final days of your life with joy? Are you nurturing the kind of faith in God that becomes a refuge and strength in life—and a shout of hope in death?

Prayer: *God of resurrection, may my life culminate in a shout of joy because of your presence and power at work in me. Amen.*

---

*A Thomas Merton Reader, Thomas P. McDonnell, ed. (New York: Image, Doubleday, rev. ed. 1989), 191.

Sunday, January 29   Read 1 Corinthians 13.

We live in a time of dizzying change when all of us, sooner or later, find ourselves asking, *Is there* anything *we can depend on? Is there anything that really lasts?* Paul said that faith lasts. Faith is the absolute trust that one of our earliest prayers is actually true: God is great and God is good. This reflects a solid confidence deep within the marrow of our bones, a confidence that when everything seems to be coming apart around us we can still be sure of the greatness and goodness of God.

The bronze figure of a young soldier stands at the foot of Stone Mountain in Georgia. The shirt has been torn off his back; his pants legs hang in shreds above bare feet. In his hand he holds a broken sword. His face is lifted toward the sky. The inscription reads, "Men who saw night coming down about them could somehow act as if they stood at the edge of dawn." People of biblical hope are like that. Even when darkness seems to be closing around them, still they act as if they can see the coming of God's dawn of wholeness and life. *That* kind of hope lasts.

"But the greatest of these"—that which can outlast everything—"is love." Martin Luther King, Jr., said that instead of hatred he had decided to adhere to "a strong, demanding love"*—the love of God.

Listen to your life. Where have you experienced the strength of faith? Where the courage of hope? Where have you known the power of love? What is there about your life of faith that will really last? What will it mean for you to stick with love?

Prayer: *O God, give us faith, hope, and love that can outlast anything.*

A Testament of Hope: The Essential Writings of Martin Luther King, Jr.; James Melvin Washington, ed. (San Francisco: Harper & Row, Publishers:, 1986), 250.

WORSHIP AND WORK

January 30–February 5, 1995   **John Ed Mathison**�֍
Monday, January 30   Read Isaiah 6:1-4.

There are many different ways to worship. Some worship in great Gothic cathedrals, while others worship outdoors under trees. Some sing accompanied by magnificent pipe organs, while others sing to the music of guitars and indigenous instruments.

Some worship experiences are extremely solemn, while others are less formal and include hand-clapping and bodily movement. The *form* of worship is not nearly as important as the *experience* of worship. Our lesson today relates the marvelous worship experience of Isaiah as he came into the Temple.

The first thing Isaiah experienced was the awesome presence of God. He described his vision of God's majesty: "the Lord sitting on a throne, high and lofty; and the hem of his robe filled the temple." His first focus was not on the other participants of worship or on the appointments of the worship setting but on the majestic presence of God.

We then see specific manifestations of God's presence in the seraphs and the shaking of the Temple's foundations. The manifestation was so dramatic that even the seraphs covered their faces.

What Isaiah experienced was not limited to him. The majesty of God was expressed in a magnitude that covered the whole earth. Isaiah saw that God's presence was with him, yet the whole earth was full of God's glory.

Real worship is not the outward setting but the inward experience of the presence of God.

Prayer: *O God, help me to worship today as Isaiah worshiped. Amen.*

✖Senior Minister, Frazer Memorial United Methodist Church, Montgomery, Alabama.

42

Tuesday, January 31   Read Isaiah 6:5-8.

Genuine worship causes us not only to look up and experience God but to look inward and sense our own condition. This happened to Isaiah. When he saw God, he also saw himself. In verse 5 he described himself as a man of unclean lips, living in the midst of a people of unclean lips.

Real worship can occur when we are honest enough to look at our real condition. The majesty of God makes evident the mess we have made of our life. Recognition of our condition leads to confession. I do not wallow in the mess of my condition, but I can confess my sins. That's what Isaiah did.

Confession leads to cleansing. Verse 7 announces that Isaiah's sin was blotted out. The whole message of the Bible is that God readily cleanses and forgives when we confess.

The last step of worship is our commission. Isaiah heard the voice of the Lord asking, "Whom shall I send, and who will go for us?" Isaiah committed himself with the words "Here am I, send me!"

Authentic worship helps us to look up and see God, to look in and see ourselves, and then to look out to the challenge and commission God has for us.

Prayer: *O God, show me today the areas in which change must occur and the places where you want to send me as your representative. Amen.*

Wednesday, February 1

Read Psalm 138.

Worship reminds us that God is accessible to us every moment of every day. Worship is not something reserved for a specific time at a specific place; we can experience it in all of life's activities.

In Psalm 138, David begins with gratitude for God's steadfast faithfulness. God always answers when we call. God is always ready to give us the strength we need to meet any situation. Whatever God calls us to do, God will provide us with the guidance, courage, and strength necessary to meet that situation. In verse 3, David experiences God's strength in his soul. In verse 7, he knows that even in the time of trouble, God will provide all that he needs. God stretches out a hand that delivers.

Verse 8 reminds us that our weakness is made perfect in God's strength. When we try to do things on our own, we often fail. Our greatest strength comes when we recognize our weakness and rely on God's strength.

Focus today on God's presence and God's power in every situation that you confront. Remember that the greatest power comes when we recognize our weakness.

Prayer: *O God, teach me to walk confidently, knowing that you walk with me through every circumstance of life. You provide everything to fulfill your purpose for me. Amen.*

Thursday, February 2   Read 1 Corinthians 15:1-4.

Coach Bear Bryant of the University of Alabama said that the most important part of coaching is to teach the fundamentals. He spent most of his time, effort, and energy keeping his team focused on the fundamentals.

Today's lesson centers on Paul's focus on the fundamentals of our faith. In verse 3, he states that of first importance is that Christ died for our sins according to the scriptures.

Paul goes on to remind us that Jesus was raised on the third day according to the scriptures. The resurrection became central to Paul's faith. All the principles on which his personal faith was built hinged upon the resurrection of Jesus Christ.

God created life not just to be lived in this world but to be lived for eternity. Through the death and resurrection of Jesus Christ, each of us has an opportunity for eternal life.

Paul emphasizes that these fundamentals are according to the scriptures. The scriptures were not some nice writings to which Paul sometimes referred; rather, the scriptures were fundamental to Paul's whole faith system.

As you read today's scripture passage, know that what we believe is based according to what the scriptures teach. The scriptures become our "playbook," for it is from the scriptures that we learn God's will and God's way for our lives.

Prayer: *O God, help me today to focus on the fundamentals of the Christian faith. Amen.*

Friday, February 3   Read 1 Corinthians 15:3-11.

Paul explains that he knows the Resurrection is true because of the testimony of several witnesses to that amazing event. The Resurrection was not just some theory that was being projected; Paul wanted everyone to know that there were witnesses to the resurrection. He begins by saying that Jesus appeared to Cephas and the twelve (v. 5).

Paul goes on to state that Jesus appeared to five hundred people and then to James and then to all the apostles. The number of witnesses makes a strong argument for the truth of Christ's resurrection.

But the real clincher for Paul is given in verse 8. He testifies that Jesus had appeared to him also. This makes the Resurrection personal. It is neither just a story from scripture nor just an event that other people have witnessed to; Paul himself has seen Jesus.

People can argue with theories and philosophies, but the unanswerable argument is personal experience. The thing that makes my faith solid is to know that the resurrection of Jesus Christ was for me and that I have the certainty of eternal life.

Paul reminds us that we are not worthy of what Christ has done for us. It is only by grace that we stand as recipients of a resurrection faith.

Suggestion for meditation: *What does Christ's resurrection mean in your life? Focus on your experience of and witness to the Resurrection.*

Saturday, February 4   Read Luke 5:1-5.

God was always confronting people as often at work as during worship. Such is the case in today's lesson.

Simon was fishing (he had not yet been named Peter). There were so many people who had gathered around to hear Jesus teach that he had to borrow one of Simon's boats and push out from the land. He then turned his attention to Simon and told him to put down his net for a catch.

Simon thought he would explain to Jesus the reality of fishing. He gave a very logical explanation of how he had worked all night and had caught nothing. Oftentimes when God asks us to do something, we are very adept at forming a good rationale as to why we should not do it.

The amazing thing is that God's thoughts are so far above our thoughts and that God is always right. The question is not whether or not God is right; the real question is whether or not we will be obedient.

After giving his argument, Simon concludes, "If you say so, I will let down the nets." Even though he had his own argument, Simon's response was obedience.

Prayer: *Lord, may I give you less argument and more obedience today. Amen.*

Sunday, February 5   Read Luke 5:6-11.

God's will for us is never wrong, and obedience to that will always brings good, and sometimes wonderfully surprising results.

Moses gave many excuses for why he should not be the one to lead the Hebrews out of bondage, yet when he obeyed God, the results were staggering (Exod. 3:13–4:17). Gideon could not believe God's command to cut his army by two-thirds (Judges 7:3), but he was willing to be obedient and God made good on every promise.

Simon obeyed Jesus and experienced tremendous results. He caught so many fish that the nets began to break. He had to ask other people to help him bring in the fish.

Seeing this tremendous catch, Simon felt very inadequate. Nevertheless, Jesus still called him to be one of his disciples. God is less interested in our ability than in our availability. God's real desire is to take us as we are and make us into the persons God wants us to be. Simon and his ministry are a beautiful example of what allowing God to work in our lives can bring about.

Doing God's will always results in good. My greatest desire is to be obedient to God.

Prayer: *Lord, the greatest calling in life for me is to be faithful to your will. May I be obedient to you today. May I present myself as I am and let you make me the person you want me to be. Like Simon Peter, may I be ready to leave everything and follow you. Amen.*

BENEFITS FROM GOD

February 6-12, 1995   **Juan G. Feliciano❖**
Monday, February 6   Read Jeremiah 17:5-8.

"They shall be like a tree planted by water"

In our busy lives and fast-changing world we have become used to paradigms, paradoxes, and conflicts. We are trained to choose among alternatives. This is never easy. It is like living in a constant dilemma.

The people of Judah experienced a similar situation. Jeremiah witnessed one of the most troubled periods in the history of the Near East: the fall of a great empire (Assyria) and the rising of another even greater (Babylon). Meanwhile, the kingdom of Judah was ruled by deplorable kings, and its downfall was imminent.

Jeremiah's inclusion of wisdom literature in his prophetic word, as noted in today's passage, places emphasis on the dilemma. We learn to live in ambiguity and uncertainty, knowing that we live in an unstable world. We are called to choose between two options: either trust in God or trust in humans (Psalm 1; 118:8-9; 146:3-9). God calls us to trust in God; and God gives us the necessary faith to do so.

Prayer: *O God, thank you for holding it all together. Thank you for being with us when we do not know how or what to choose. We want to trust in you every day. Please add faith to our lives, as you pour water down the stream to nourish the trees. In Jesus' name. Amen.*

❖Clergy in the Methodist Church of Puerto Rico; pastor of United Methodist Hispanic Church–Kedyre Ave., Chicago, Illinois. Associate Professor of Christian Education and Director of the Center for Hispanic Ministries, Garrett Evangelical Seminary, Evanston, Illinois.

Tuesday, February 7   Read Jeremiah 17:9-10.

God's gift of God's self to us

We need to be able to believe that something is holding this unstable world together. Something does hold us together: the grace of God, and that is something in which we can trust. God's grace is more trustworthy than our "hearts." Indeed, God is our only refuge, for the human heart is the root of evil, according to this pericope from Jeremiah.

The scriptures are full of promises and blessings for all: strangers and children, old and young, women and men. We can all receive benefits from the reign of God. Jeremiah was called by God to be a prophet to Judah and other nations in the midst of political conflicts. The word of God was disclosed. This was God's self-disclosure. Praise God!

Yet, all benefits come with some strings attached to them. In contemporary society, we are trained in economics and technology. We use the term *cost-benefit*. We even use this concept in our homes when we teach our children that everything has a cost: "Nobody gets anything for free." We also teach them that "if it is too good to be true, then it probably isn't." That is our way of saying that everything has a just price.

Only God can give gratuitously. God's love is for free, and it is for all. We need only to accept the gift and act upon it.

Prayer: *O God, write your law and your justice on our hearts so that we may know you and be able to walk humbly with you. Thank you for your gifts. Amen.*

Wednesday, February 8   Read Psalm 1.

A way to happiness

Benefits bring joy. Sometimes they are expected; they may be astonishing; they are usually valued. Sometimes they surprise us. When we buy an article, we are eager to open it, use it, and find out if we have made a good buy. We expect others to like it, too. Sometimes we are frustrated because we realize we have been "taken for a ride." At other times we feel blessed and joyful with the benefits received. If we give a present to someone, we expect it will bring benefits to the recipient.

Happiness comes in all sizes and colors. It comes in all forms and shapes. Happiness is abundant for all ages—and it is free.

Psalm 1 is a wisdom hymn with the theme of happiness. It serves as a preface for all of Pslams. *Happy (Blessed)* is the first word expressed in this psalm. In searching for the meaning of *blessed*, we discover that *happy* has the following interpretations: cheerful, content, delighted, glad, pleased, fortuitous, fortunate, lucky, opportune, seasonable, timely.

In wisdom literature, the use of the word *happy* or *blessed* is characteristic. (See Proverbs 3:13; 8:32-33; Psalm 32:1; 34:8.) The "wicked" is its contrast. One is portrayed as a productive tree rooted near abundant waters; the other as chaff, as lifeless.

Happiness is abundant. What does attaining it require from us? That we look for it in the "just" place. The same is true with God, who calls us children and tells us how to find happiness: by following God's law.

Prayer: *Gracious God, grant us faith to trust your ways so that we may find happiness in them. In Jesus' name. Amen.*

Thursday, February 9   Read Luke 6:17-22.

Immanuel, God incarnate, is with us

We may wonder who are the persons who have produced what we see and buy in our stores; who are the ones who have grown the vegetables or baked the bread that we buy at the grocery. There was a time in almost all communities, even the communities within large cities, that people knew the shoe-maker, the baker, the florist, the kindly "grandma and grandpa" who ran the general store. The person behind the product or service was known to us. Knowing what kind of person he or she was led us to trust or distrust the quality of what we bought.

Today, in our global village, our worldwide economic market, we seldom can know anything about those people who help furnish the products and services we use day by day. Our world has indeed become extremely impersonal and, in turn, has often created an atmosphere of distrust, even cynicism and sometimes fear.

We find ourselves building walls between us and those we don't know or understand, simply because we have not had or taken the opportunity to build mutual trusting relationships.

We are called to remember that all persons are children of God, all have been created in the image of God, all are redeemed from many mistakes and sins—and all are being sustained by the same spirit of God.

That same God "came down with them and stood on a level place" (Luke 6:17) and taught a new way to live: in communion with God and with one another. God announced again the same message of benefits from God. And people from many places saw, received, and trusted in him.

Prayer: *Holy God, make us one. In Jesus' name. Amen.*

Friday, February 10   Read Luke 6:20-26.

Receive the blessing of God

One of the most marvelous benefits we receive when we come to Christ—to hear, to learn, to be healed, to trust in God's word—is that we become citizens of an "upside-down kingdom." This citizenship does not allow us to be "conformed to this world" (Rom. 12:2). Rather, it is a citizenship that calls us every day to be transformed by the renewing of our minds, thoughts, deeds, faith, and trust, if we want to know the will of our Creator, Redeemer, and Sustainer. God's will is proclaimed by Paul as that which is "good and acceptable and perfect" (Rom. 12:2).

The password in this reign is *trust*. No matter if we are poor, hungry, homeless, excluded, insulted, rejected; if our *trust* is in God, we are called "happy," "blessed." We become beneficiaries of the upside-down kingdom—due not to our royal merits but to the merits of the One who was obedient and gave himself for the ransom of all humanity.

"Blessing" comes from the Latin word *benediction*, which means to say good things of a person (*bene* = "good" and *dicere* = "to say of, to talk, to speak of"). The benefit of being called "blessed" is twofold. On the one hand, we feel delighted and happy at the promise of our redemption. On the other hand, we receive the benefit of an Advocate who is justifying us all the time.

Prayer: *Merciful Lord, allow us to walk with you and learn from you to be faithful citizens of your reign so that we may be transformed and renewed by your presence and guidance. I pray in Jesus' name. Amen.*

Saturday, February 11   Read 1 Corinthians 15:12-20.

A new life in Christ

When I accepted the assignment to write the meditations for this week, I was not aware of the correlation between this pericope and my own life journey. First, yesterday, February 10, I celebrated my birth day, 44 years ago. The opportunity to reflect on scripture in the midst of one's own life and faith journey is a blessing from God. This anniversary of the day of my birth confirms that I am spiritually alive, thanks to God.

Secondly, I am a Christian who believes in resurrection in its twofold dimension: resurrection as a new life in Jesus Christ, here and now, in the acts of conversion, transformation, and sanctification through grace; and the resurrection of the dead, of which Christ was the "first fruit." I live trusting God's promise of resurrection into a better life.

Thirdly, I am writing these meditations in the midst of my own preparation for Holy Week of 1994. The context from which I am reflecting is intimately affected by the endurance of the story of the resurrected One. I walk with God through Lent, knowing of the power of resurrection. I praise God for that.

I was born and reared in a religious home, in a religious culture. I went to parish school. I was an altar boy. I knew the liturgy in three languages; I was a religious, pious youngster. When I finished high school, I, like many, abandoned the church. It took me another twelve years to believe and experience resurrection. I praise God that I have come to believe.

Prayer: *Gracious God, as you journey with us in this new life you gave us in Jesus Christ, we acknowledge you and praise you for your kindness. Thank you, Lord, for your benefits. In Christ's name. Amen.*

Sunday, February 12   Read 1 Corinthians 15:12-20.

The promise of resurrection

Without Christ there was no hope in my life. Although I had fulfilled society's demands by earning a doctoral degree from Harvard, teaching at the state university, and presenting the status those provided, my life was empty. The promise of resurrection, of a new life in Jesus Christ, transformed my life from a hate-filled life to a life searching for peace, justice, and service to others. It was like the story of the Hebrew scriptures: one paradise lost (Eden) and another gained (the promised land). In Christ, there is no longer confusion: He was raised from the dead as an affirmation that the resurrection, a new life in Jesus Christ, is available to all of those who believe (John 11:25-26).

The problem with many of us Christians today, as it was when Paul wrote to the Corinthians, is that we are unable to imagine how any kind of existence can be possible after death. This problem poses a predicament for us, for if there is no resurrection, there is no reason for our faith. If that is the case, argues Paul, then there is no forgiveness of sins and salvation is an illusion. Thus, there is no transformation possible through grace, only through deeds.

The need to believe is clear. If God can transform an intellectual nonbeliever into a new creature (2 Cor. 5:17), then Resurrection took place and Jesus was the "first fruit." Look inside yourself: In how many ways has God transformed you? How is God transforming you right now?

Prayer: *Amazing God, our Divine Parent, you gave us life abundantly. You gave us your promise of resurrection. We believe it and accept it. We are grateful. Because of Calvary and Easter, we praise you. And we thank you, O Lord. Amen.*

THE GOD WE CAN TRUST

February 13-19, 1995   **Mildred Sullivan Lacour**✤
Monday, February 13   Read Genesis 43:1-11, 15.

Food was very important in Jacob's life. As a young man,
"the schemer" had given his brother Esau a mess of pottage in
exchange for Esau's birthright (Gen. 25:29-34). Then, Jacob
brought tasty game to his aged, sightless father as he pretended
to be Esau—to secure from Jacob the blessing rightfully Esau's
(27:1-29). In today's reading food becomes even more important
as famine continues in the land. Earlier, Jacob had sent his sons
to buy grain in Egypt. There they encountered Joseph, who
ordered them to bring their younger brother on their return.

With the depletion of those food supplies, hunger forces a
return visit to Egypt—and to Joseph. As Jacob realizes that he
must let his beloved Benjamin go, he collapses in fear and grief.
His situation is desperate. Where is God?

Like Jacob, many people have known desperation and have wondered, *Where is God?* A seminary student described such a situation. "One day, a bartender told my pastor of her tragic life—
her husband in jail, her two older children in trouble. 'That is
tough,' he said. 'But remember, God has a plan for your life.'

"Many nights, sometimes with her little son, this woman listened
to the pastor's meditations on TV. One day she met Jesus, and
God's plan for her began to unfold. I know this story well,
because that woman was my mother and I was that little boy."

Prayer: *Almighty God, "I will trust and will not be afraid."* * *Amen.*

✤Harpist, retired from the Colorado Springs Symphony; retreat leader;
active layperson, Boston Avenue United Methodist Church, Tulsa,
Oklahoma.
*Isaiah 12:2

Tuesday, February 14   Read Genesis 43:11, 15.

Clever, creative Jacob! He could always think of a way to appease an enemy, to buy goodwill. Once, hoping to pacify Esau, the brother whose blessing he had stolen years before, he had brought many gifts (Gen. 27:1-29). And now, to curry favor with the governor in Egypt who holds power over their lives, he instructs his sons to "carry [the choice fruits of the land] down to the man as a present."

In both instances Jacob's apprehension was ill-founded and his lavish gifts unnecessary. When the twin brothers finally reunited, Esau was gracious and forgiving. Likewise, there was no need to fear Joseph, the governor. In both cases God had gone before and was working out the divine purpose.

Are we sometimes part of Jacob's clan in our attempt to buy goodwill? Someone contributes to a politician's election fund in return for a favor. A speeder bribes an officer to tear up a ticket. A husband brings home a dozen roses to pacify his wife. Some parents, pursuing their own fulfillment, buy off their children with things rather than give them their time and attention.

Even with God, sometimes we try to "carry down a present" in an effort to gain God's goodwill. I am remembering all those years of trying to do "good" things so that a judgmental God wouldn't strike me down. When I was in my thirties, I faced a difficult personal struggle; and I was forced to search for who I was and who God is. Out of that struggle with guilt and depression, I learned that there is absolutely no need to try to buy God's goodness. God's compassion is there even before we seek it.

Prayer: *Gracious God, I trust your goodness and accept the love you freely offer. Amen.*

Wednesday, February 15   Read Psalm 37:1-11, 39-40.

In Psalm 37 David is speaking out of long experience and great wisdom. When he admonishes us not to worry ourselves about the wicked, no doubt he is remembering some of those who had done harm to him. He could not forget the hostile foreign armies or Saul, the king who tried to kill him in a fit of jealousy and rage (1 Sam. 18–20). Even more painful were the memories of people he had once trusted—Ahithophel, for instance, the boyhood friend and most trusted counselor who had deserted him and joined the conspiracy to dethrone him (2 Sam. 16:15–17:23); and Absalom, the beloved son who led the insurrection (2 Sam. 15*ff*). Over time, David would recall many painful experiences with evildoers.

But David also warns to "refrain from anger." Do not return evil for evil; that keeps the cycle going, it dissipates one's power. Evidently, this is a lesson David learned well. We do not know how he would have responded to Ahithophel, for he committed suicide before David regained his throne. We do know that David showed compassion to King Saul and the disloyal Absalom.

The devices of the evil will boomerang, says the psalmist, and "their sword shall enter their own heart" (v. 15). A nun who works with prisoners tells the story of parents who wanted their son's murderer to receive the death penalty. But when their wish was granted, that death did not heal their grief or help them feel that their need for justice had been satisfied. Settling the score is not our prerogative; we are to take refuge in God, trusting that God will help us in our grief so that the need for revenge is not the driving force in our lives.

Prayer: *Dear God, teach me how to forgive rather than to seek vengeance. Amen.*

Thursday, February 16   Read Psalm 37:1-7.

At some time most of us have a desire to possess something—a quality or a situation—that someone else has. The other person is thinner or is a better student or has a better job; makes more money, has more friends, is a better athlete, seems to come by things without struggle. *Envy* corrodes the soul and poisons our relationships. So the psalmist wisely instructs us to "not be envious."

Envy also keeps us from an intimate relationship with our Creator, for out of envy we question God's wisdom and justice. *If the Almighty really cared for me,* we think, *God would work out a better plan for my life.*

Fortunately, there is a cure for this dread disease; the cure is trust. "Commit your way to the LORD; trust in him, and he will act." Don't hold back any part of yourself, the psalmist is saying. Like a person completely relaxing into an easy chair, let your entire weight down on the Almighty. Then, having entrusted all, leave the results in God's hands and "wait patiently for him."

In our impatience, we want to see God act immediately, of course. But God's answer—never too early, never too late—is worth waiting for. And all the while we are waiting, this trust is producing greater peace and security. As we "take delight in the LORD" we are given the desires of our heart, all that is really good for us.

Prayer: *Loving God, help me not to envy another's advantages but to wait for the blessings you have prepared for me. Amen.*

Friday, February 17   Read Luke 6:27-36.

"Love your enemies," Jesus commands us, and we shrink back. "O Lord," we cry, "you ask the impossible. Maybe Mother Teresa might come close. But I can't even *like* some people, let alone *love* them."

But Jesus is not requiring that we like everyone. The word he is using for love is not *philia* (affection) or *eros* (sexual love). He is not asking us to love our enemies as we would our best friend or our spouse. The word here is *agape*—self-giving love, the love that Jesus demonstrated. It means that even if a person mistreats us, hates us, or curses us, we will always go out of our way to do good to her, to bless and pray for him. Jesus sums it up in the Golden Rule: "Treat others as you would like them to treat you" (NEB).

This kind of love does not require sentiment. Rather than something we *feel* like doing, it is something we *will* ourselves to do, by the grace of God. And we do it because it copies God, who is kind to the ungrateful and the selfish.

A young attorney was complaining about his unhappy work situation. "My boss makes my life miserable. Every night I pray that he'll die, or at least break his leg, so he won't be there in the morning." A friend suggested he begin pray for him and to go out of his way to do helpful things for his "enemy." In the process, both men were changed, and eventually, the attorney reported, "You know, my boss is really not such a bad fellow."

Suggestion for meditation: *Think of someone you do not like. Could you, by the grace of God, go out of your way today to show self-giving love to that person? Will you pray for that person?*

60

Saturday, February 18   Read Luke 6:37-38.

The scripture for today expands on the Golden Rule: "The measure you use for others is the one that God will use for you" (TEV). So Jesus commands us to be compassionate toward other people. If we judge or condemn, we will ourselves be judged and condemned. But if we forgive, we will be forgiven. How sad that so often we prefer to nurse an injury, letting it estrange us from another person and from God!

In addition to being compassionate, as copiers of God we are to be generous. "Give to others, and God will give to you. Indeed, you will receive a full measure, a generous helping, poured into your hands—all that you can hold" (TEV). Someone has said that there are only two kinds of people in the world— the givers and the takers. The takers, those guarded personalities, tend to get as much as possible—material things or responses that feed their self-importance—and then keep it for themselves. The givers, however, move in the other direction. Spending themselves in time, strength, and finances, these generous souls receive back more than they can hold.

During the children's hour, the pastor was giving an object lesson on God's generosity. As each child extended cupped hands, the pastor poured out as much wrapped candy as those little hands could hold. When she came to the last tiny girl, she gave the sack and all the candy that remained. Overwhelmed, the beaming child said to all of us, "Look! I got the *whole sack*!"

When we give, God gives us such a "generous helping."

Prayer: *Loving Christ, as I meet people today, may I model your compassion and generosity. Enlarge my capacity to receive your gifts. Amen.*

Sunday, February 19   Read 1 Corinthians 15:35-38, 42-50.

She wanted so much to stay alive for her three small children. But now Kristin was dying. As I stroked the small, thin body so ravaged by cancer, I thought about the shortness of her life and the limitations of our mortality. Our physical bodies are so imperfect, so subject to passion and impulse, so powerless to carry out all our dreams and plans. Eventually they sicken and die. How would Kristin's wasted body be changed after death?

When the Corinthians asked similar questions, Paul used the analogy of seed and plant. The seed which is sown dies in order that the plant (body) may live. Both the seed and the physical body are put in the ground, and something quite different appears. Because of Christ's own resurrection, Paul asserts, those who have put their faith in him will possess a glorious body similar to that of the risen Christ. As we once bore the image of the first Adam, we will now bear the image of the last Adam, the "man of heaven" who became for us a life-giving Spirit.

Paul contrasts the earthly and heavenly conditions of life. In our mortal life the natural body is "sown" in corruption, dishonor, and weakness. But our new spiritual body, suited to the spiritual conditions of the new life, will be imperishable, glorious, and powerful.

Kristin truly loved God in this life. I can see her now, in her glorious body, joining the angels in giving to God the perfect love and service that was impossible here on earth.

Prayer: *O Risen One, thank you for your gift of the glorious spiritual body and the possibility of one day worshiping you perfectly. Amen.*

HARD-TO-HIDE HOLINESS

February 20-26, 1995   Charles B. Simmons♣
Monday, February 20   Read Psalm 99.

The season of Epiphany concludes with a dazzling array of texts that illustrate its theme of God's self-revelation. Mysteriously, God makes Godself known to human beings in ways that make life so different that the change cannot be concealed. Faces light up, veils come down, and faith comes shining through when people experience God's presence. Mountaintop moments are hard to hide! They transfigure us and transport our private faith into the domain of public witness.

We begin with a psalm written for the enthronement festival held in Israel at the beginning of the New Year. This ceremony was an effective means of Temple instruction. It taught the present meaning and strategic worth of the faith that "the LORD is king!" Thus, every year, God's governance over Israel was lifted up to central significance.

The psalmist declares, "For the LORD our God is holy," implying that Israel is not holy and needs forgiveness. Still, the author's choice of verbs reveals the national belief since the Exodus. It is the role of the people to "cry," and it is the God-King's most faithful preoccupation to "answer."

As we start our week's devotions, ask yourself: Am I ready to meet with the Holy One as did Moses and others, knowing my life may be forever changed? When you "worship at [God's] holy mountain," the effect is hard to hide.

Prayer: *Answer my cry, Lord, to rule in my heart this day, that your glory may show forth in my life. Amen.*

♣Senior Minister, Broadmoor United Methodist Church, Baton Rouge, Louisiana.

Tuesday, February 21   Read Exodus 34:29-32.

Here we come to the climax of the narrative that began earlier with the story of the golden calf. Chapter 32 of Exodus related the breaking of the covenant, while chapter 34 recounts its restoration. In these verses, however, the emphasis is different than in the main body of tradition. The primary focus is not the covenant law, given by God and inscribed on stone tablets, but Moses, the intermediary.

The forty days Moses has spent with God atop Sinai is evidenced by a change in his physical appearance. The Hebrews barely notice his coming down the mountain with a second set of Commandments. They behold instead the now radiant face of their leader. His skin shone to the degree that "they were afraid to come near him." Yet Moses, so wrapped up in the wonder of his encounter with the Divine and so determined to deliver God's words to the people, is himself oblivious to having undergone a transformation.

The unawareness of Moses makes it clear that the divine glow on his face should not be understood as a metamorphosis. Moses, the leader, remains fully human; his countenance is but a reflection of heavenly glory. Still, the change wrought by Moses' intimate experience of God's presence is too dramatic to hide from others.

What does your face show about your relationship with God? Does your countenance reveal a mountaintop closeness? Can others see Christ in you? What testimony is there to the life-changing experience of God's presence in your life?

Prayer: *Master, so help me to reflect your presence in my life that others may see you in all I think, say, or do. Amen.*

Wednesday, February 22   Read Exodus 34:33-35.

The passage for today shifts from the past to the ongoing practice of Moses in his office as mediator between God and God's people.

Although the radiance of Moses' face so unnerves the Hebrews that it must be veiled, Moses hears the word of God in their stead and communicates God's will to them. The occurrences of the verb *speak* in this brief text give ample indication of the author's intention. We readers, like the Hebrews, are to *see* Moses' Sinai experience reflected in more than glowing skin. His encounter with the divine is too empowering to remain a matter of appearance alone. It bursts forth in concrete acts of ministry. Whenever Moses proclaims God's words to God's people, the experience of the mountaintop can also be *heard*. Those in the valley also encounter the High Holy One.

The discussion of when the veil is worn by Moses serves to enhance the portrait being painted. The message is about the ministry of the mediator between God and Israel. Moses continued to function as a mortal, yet in his office he bridged the enormous gap between the awesome and zealous God of Sinai and the fearful and sinful people of the Covenant. In him is foreshadowed the mediating work of Jesus, who in his person bridged the gap between God and the world.

Among our generation are many as far removed from God as those who bowed before the golden calf. There is yet a need for those who will act as mediators for God. When you speak and minister, are others made mountain bound?

Prayer: *Through my words and way, Lord, may paths be prepared for others to hear your word and follow your way. Amen.*

Thursday, February 23   Read 2 Corinthians 3:12-18.

Although Paul had founded this church, his leadership was under attack. A group of Judaizers were critical of his claim that Gentile believers were free from the need to obey the Law of Moses to be perfected in the faith. Paul penned a defense of his ministry in which he refuted all such legalism by showing the surpassing glory of the gospel of grace.

Paul illustrates from our Exodus text. The ministry of Moses, which is characterized by *concealment*, is contrasted with Paul's *openness* to prove the superiority of the new covenant. *He uses no veil.* His is not a message of fleeting hope that must be hidden behind threats of condemnation and death. Rather, he "boldly" preaches the permanence of grace and mercy to every sinner who repents and believes. The eye of faith may gaze upon the glory of Christ without interruption or fear it will fade away like the glow on Moses' face.

The image is helpful. Whenever religion teaches only rules of can do's and cannot do's, it blinds believers to the heart of things. Even when the focus is on things that matter, it obscures what matters most. It can prevent the faithful from face-to-face encounter with God. The trappings of religion are empty except where there is also love, joy, and freedom as found in Christ.

Paul says that when one turns to the Lord, the veil comes down. We are liberated and made more and more like Christ.

Prayer: *Lord, take away whatever would get in the way of my seeing you more clearly and serving you more nearly. Amen.*

Friday, February 24   Read 2 Corinthians 4:1-2.

Paul in his response to the Judaizers in Corinth argued that the gospel is superior to the Law of Moses in that through it the glory of God can shine "unveiled" (3:18). Only in Christ are the scriptures understood and hearts made free! Now the Apostle continues the defense of his ministry by updating the contrast between his openness and the deceptive practices of his critics.

Answering the charges of his opponents, Paul insists his actions are always aboveboard. Not for him the underhanded ways of the unscrupulous politician or the manipulation of the master salesperson! Unlike some, he has renounced such secret, "shameful" methods as inconsistent with his claim to be a minister of Christ. In Paul's model of ministry, there is no place for "cunning."

Can you name anything to which a Christian must say a decided NO in ministry? What about "falsifying" God's word? In teaching or preaching or talking with others, are you tempted to dilute the severity of the scripture to make the message more acceptable or yourself more popular with hearers? Conversing on the issues, do you ever play down the demands of discipleship or gloss over the "foolishness" of the gospel to make it sound more palatable?

The Apostle Paul argues such tampering empties the gospel of its power, and our witness and ministry of its effectiveness. While craftiness may draw a crowd and gain us accolades, only the "truth"—presented directly and faithfully—will commend itself to human hearts and build the church.

Prayer: *You give me my ministry, Lord. Give also the courage to live, to act, and to speak in ways that openly proclaim you. Amen.*

Saturday, February 25   Read Luke 9:28.

Peter, James, and John had accompanied Jesus for years. He was their chosen leader, the one they saw as the answer to their deepest questions. Upon this mountaintop, though, they would begin to see him in a powerful new way.

What was about to take place would make them realize there was so much more to their Lord than they had previously known. Not just a man of God but the Son of God. Not just a messenger preaching about the Kingdom but the Messiah ushering it in. There, in some strange and mysterious manner, Jesus would become the ultimate authority in their lives. They had gone up the mountain enamored with his ways; they would come down committed to his cause. Jesus would be *transfigured* before them; they would be *transformed* because of him!

Somewhere along the way all disciples need an experience like that. At some point everyone of us must encounter that same kind of undiluted epiphany where we realize that Jesus is as much our Savior as he was Peter's, James's, and John's.

Not all believers must undergo an emotional conversion, of course. But many Christians seem not to have had any kind of uplifting experience that impresses upon their heart that Jesus is *their* Redeemer and offers to *them* the power of the Kingdom. We need an experience that lifts us out of ourselves, that allows us to know the joy of being fully committed to Christ.

Have you ever been on the mountaintop, no matter if you've been in church all your life? Was it so long ago that you need to revisit the experience? The scripture says we are to begin in prayer.

Prayer: *Draw near, Lord, that I might carry a vision of your mountaintop in my heart even as I live in the valley. Amen.*

Sunday, February 26   Read Luke 9:29-36.

Similar versions of the Transfiguration story appear in the Gospels of Matthew and Mark. Noting what Luke adds to his account uncovers a unique message.

The evangelist puts his usual emphasis on Jesus' praying, but his major contribution comes when the content of the conversation between Moses, Elijah, and Jesus is reported. It is "his departure"—our Lord's upcoming suffering and death—that is being discussed. To make this more explicit, Luke borrows the Gethsemane motif of the disciples asleep. Snoozing, they see only the resulting glory of Jesus' changed appearance, just as Christ's actual resurrection goes unobserved. Another clue is furnished by the phrase, "behold, two men," which will appear verbatim in the Resurrection narrative (Luke 24:4). Clearly, the information Luke alone provides links this account with Jesus' Passion and Resurrection. The question is, Why?

One answer resonates with the reason Transfiguration Sunday comes immediately before Ash Wednesday. Luke wants his readers to learn what the church teaches all Christians in Lent: *To climb up to the mountaintop with Jesus we must also be willing to climb onto the cross with him.* The same glory offered our Lord comes from giving away our lives in service to others.

As the Epiphany emphasis on "God made manifest" ends, we need to ask, *What good is a heavenly encounter with Jesus without a corresponding encounter with sisters and brothers on earth?* If we take our faith as seriously as God offers it, the mountaintop experience will not be enough. We will find ourselves following Jesus into the valley where the *people* are whom we are called to serve in Christ's name.

Prayer: *Lord, lead me to a place beside you to serve others. Amen.*

February 27–March 5, 1995   **Stanley R. Copeland**✤
Monday, February 27   Read Deuteronomy 26:1-11.

Road of thanksgiving

This "Journey to Joy" begins with Moses, the preacher, who has a message of hope mixed with a word of instruction for the Hebrew children. The hope is for the possession of the promised land. The instruction is about what to do and say when they get there. Moses exhorts them that after they possess and settle in the land, they are to take the first fruits of the ground, place these in a basket, and hand the offering to the priest at the place that the Lord chooses. Then they are to make a creedal response that weds their ancient heritage as sons and daughters of the wandering Aramean Jacob to the future they will enjoy as inheritors of the land flowing with milk and honey. Moses, this preacher, stands at the crossroads of faith and points with a basket to the only road one can take to God, who has given so graciously. The "Journey to Joy" for *all* faithful wanderers begins on the road called thanksgiving.

At the baptism of a six-year-old Cambodian girl, her response was spontaneous. As she was baptized "In the name of the Father, and of the Son, and of the Holy Spirit," she joyously released from her smiling lips the first English words she had learned to say, "Thank you!" Her basket was full, and it spilled over to touch our hearts as we journeyed on together.

Prayer: *God of the journey, who fills our baskets to overflowing and promises places and times full of joy, make us thankful people willing to walk with you a lifelong while. Amen.*

✤Author; Pastor, Pollard United Methodist Church, Tyler, Texas.

Tuesday, February 28   Read Isaiah 58:1-12.

Road of compassion

The people find themselves preparing for a time of fasting, as do we, on this day that precedes Ash Wednesday. We call this day Shrove Tuesday, referring to the shriving or cleansing of sins. The French call it *Mardi Gras,* the Germans *Fasch Nacht,* both observing a day of feasting and carnival. What does this day before Lent mean to us? How do we enter and walk through this season of Lent as a preparation for Easter?

Isaiah's questions to the ancients are still pertinent today: "Why do we fast? "Why humble ourselves?" The answer is to line up behind our God, who stands before us on the road of compassion that is the way to justice. The fast that the Lord stands for is the one that loosens and breaks the "ball and chain" of injustice. The road of compassion leads the traveler to strive to meet the needs of the afflicted, to feed the hungry, to house the homeless, to clothe the naked, to befriend the lonely child, to visit the homebound adult, to dry the tears of those who grieve.

Marcus was diagnosed with multiple sclerosis in 1977. Over a period of years he has lost his job, his wife, and most of his ability to move. He lies in bed skirted by pictures of himself with his beloved Irish setter, Poko. When I visit him *my* day will be brightened; for he has a spiritual gift of talking about his faith, a gift that always uplifts me. I take him Holy Communion. In our fellowship with one another over the breaking of the bread and the drinking of the cup, we hear it—chains rattling and shackles breaking—and we realize we have partied together with our Lord on that road called compassion.

Prayer: *Author of justice, nudge us down the trail of compassion. Help us see those who hurt, and move us forward to tend their needs. Amen.*

71

March 1 (Ash Wednesday)
Read Psalm 51:1-17.

Road of forgiveness

Today we begin the season of Lent. This great psalm that heralds the heart and soul of Lent is one to be sung throughout our forty-day journey. Were Psalm 51 to be put to music, blues-style gospel with its tension between harmony and discord would be most appropriate; for it would express the tension in this psalm between sin and salvation. Thomas A. Dorsey, the great writer of jazz and blues, professed this tension. When mourning the death of his wife and newborn son he said, "God, you aren't worth a dime to me right now!" Later he wrote both the words and music to the hymn "Precious Lord, Take My Hand."

Our reading for today from the Psalms is a confession of sin that explores the deepest reaches of human guilt. It is also a prayer for joy, as the writer on the road of forgiveness walks on tiptoe to touch God's salvation. These words are uttered in the assurance of a God whose steadfast love cleanses us from any wrong. The psalmist proclaims a gracious God, who, like a master potter, remolds us, recreates us, and puts a right spirit within us.

Today, marked with ashes, we continue our journey. Our walk of faith is a sacred tension made into a spiritual reality. Our walk is toward a cross, yet our destination is the entrance to an empty tomb, beside which stands a large round stone that has been rolled aside.

Prayer: *Precious Lord, remind us of forgiveness. Keep us swaying to the rhythm of salvation, as we journey toward your joy. Amen.*

Thursday, March 2   Read Luke 4:1-13.

Road of wilderness

Jesus knew that the "Journey to Joy" needs to go through the wilderness. The wilderness in this passage has a spiritual dimension in which we deal with who we are in light of that which tempts us. The wilderness is where we deal with "what ifs" and make choices based on God's will for our lives.

Moses, in the wilderness, was on Mount Sinai following a forty-day fast. Like Moses, our Lord was led into the wilderness for forty days. Jesus had been baptized and had heard God's voice from heaven proclaim him Son of God, the one whom John foretold. Full of the Holy Spirit, Jesus was led into the wilderness to wrestle with his identity and was met there by the devil. Satan wanted Jesus to turn stone into bread, worship him in exchange for power, and jump from the Temple pinnacle to be rescued by angels. Jesus countered the temptations with God's word recorded in Deuteronomy, "One does not live by bread alone"; "Worship the LORD your God, and serve only him"; and "Do not put the LORD your God to the test" (8:3; 6:13, 16). The devil went away, and Jesus walked back into life.

Later he entered Gethsemane. He sensed a cross and perhaps thought of that rescue team of angels. Yet his prayer in Gethsemane was, "Father . . . not my will but yours be done" (22:42).

Perhaps the experience of a serious illness, a splintered family, the loss of a job or a loved one brings you to the wilderness. The only question here is, What is God's will for your life? By the power of the Spirit within you, you can make decisions, walk back into life, and continue the journey.

Prayer: *God of the wilderness, Lord of life, lead us to decisions that are in keeping with your will for us. Amen.*

Friday, March 3   Read 2 Corinthians 5:18–6:10.

Road of reconciliation

Paul has a name for those of us who "Journey to Joy." He calls us "ambassadors for Christ." An ambassador for Christ is a citizen of the kingdom of God with the responsibility of representing Christ in the world.

The road on which we walk is one of ministry. Paul calls it the "ministry of reconciliation," which is all about restoring broken relationships, healing deep hurts, sowing peace seeds— all in love, all for Christ's sake. There is a need for ambassadors for Christ to be engaged in the ministry of reconciliation *now*!

Over a year ago in our little city, a young man was abducted from a peaceful park and brutally murdered by a group of men. The reasons given by the abductors for this act of violence was that the man was homosexual. Months later a rally was staged in the same park under the slogan "Stop the Hate." It was a media event that attracted national publicity. Some people were there holding banners heralding gay rights. Politicians used the day as a platform to promote "hate crime" legislation. Some were there in business suits, others in faded, torn jeans; some were there alone and others with families; some were adults and some were children. I thought to myself, *Why are you here?*

Then one of my clergy colleagues approached the podium to speak and announced, "I have come to share with you my orientation. I am oriented toward the love of Christ and reconciliation." As ambassadors for Christ, with the love of Christ working in and through us, we are called to reconcile the world.

Prayer: *O God, whom we know as Love and as the One who reconciles us to yourself, make us ambassadors for Christ with the ministry of reconciliation in our hearts. Amen.*

Saturday, March 4   Read Matthew 6:1-6, 16-21.

Road of Spirit-cadence

Motivation is a big word today, and it is related to competition, "getting ahead," success. Jesus in this passage has just called his followers to Christlike love. He now addresses his disciples on a Christlike lifestyle, and the underlying matter at hand is motive. The subject is Jewish piety—almsgiving, prayer, and fasting. "How to?" and "Why?" become the focus questions of Christlike motivation. Each point embraces a formula beginning with "Whenever you," moving to the warning "Do not be like the hypocrites," followed by the instruction "in secret," and concluding with the promise "Your Father . . . will reward."

I had purchased a top-of-the-line day-planner system to enhance my motivation and success. On a weekend trip with my family we stopped to eat. Before getting back into the car, I placed my day planner on the roof. Back on the interstate we heard a bump. My new leather-bound day planner was smashed under the tire of an 18-wheeler. I was reminded of the words of Jesus: "Do not store up for yourselves treasures on earth, where moth and rust consume"—and 18-wheelers smash.

As followers of Christ, we have different treasures and motivations. Our motivation is not material; likewise, we are not ultimately driven by a slick day-planner system. We walk to a spiritual cadence driven by the Holy Spirit. Our success is measured not by how much we have but by how much we give away, not by how far ahead we get but by how careful we are not to leave others behind; not by whether the world calls us "winners" but by whether we know that Christ won the victory for us.

Prayer: *God, who through Christ presents us with a different drummer, direct our steps to march to your spiritual cadence. Amen.*

Sunday, March 5   Read Romans 10:8*b*-13.

Road of salvation

It seems appropriate that this "Journey of Joy" bid the Lenten traveler "farewell" and "happy continued journey," with Paul's pointing the way to God's salvation: "The word is near you; it is in your mouth and in your heart" (NIV). There is an overwhelming sense of companionship in knowing how near the Word is to us. Could anything be closer to us than the words on our lips and in our heart? It is here that we discover salvation, not at the end of a long and winding road but in Christ Jesus. Paul points to God's salvation as experienced now—within us—because God has drawn near to us in Christ Jesus.

Paul's message is assuring, stating that "if you . . . believe in your heart that God raised [Jesus] from the dead, you will be saved." Paul's "you" is all-inclusive and stresses that salvation is not restricted to a few; rather, it is offered to all. For Paul, the road to God's salvation is a crowded one, with Greek and Jew, slave and free, men and women—all walking hand in hand.

This road to God's salvation is one on which we are called to talk with fellow travelers about the one truth of which we are convinced: Jesus is Lord! We are called to talk with sojourners about the one truth ready on our lips: Jesus is risen! Along the way we are to call on the one name: Jesus Christ, our companion of salvation. These all-important steps move us from mere companionship to true relationship with Christ our Lord and Savior.

Prayer: *Faithful Companion, Word that is near, help us to see you in each step of life's journey, feeling the warmth of your nail-scarred hands as we walk together. Amen.*

TRUST IN GOD'S TRANSFORMING LOVE

March 6-12, 1995 **Judith Freeman Clark**✤
Monday, March 6 Read Genesis 15:1-3.

The family is a social structure common to virtually all human cultures. Since we are born into families, we can understand the despair that Abraham felt because he had no heirs. Living on through descendants was of utmost importance to Abraham; family lineage was the sole immortality his people knew.

In saying, "What can you give me, seeing that I am childless?" (REB) Abraham did two things. First, he voiced his anger, then he challenged God: "What can you give me?" In the question, we hear both belligerence and pain. It is easy to imagine Abraham flinging these words at God like a frustrated teenager shouting at his parents.

We are often like Abraham. We come to God empty, sometimes angry. Bereft of comfort, we want relief from the intense despair that devours us. We want hope for something better. In our pain, we may even want to hurt God, so we issue the challenge: "What can you give me?" To Abraham, the only right answer also seemed impossible: he wanted a child so he would not have to leave his legacy to a non related member of his household, a servant.* When Abraham asked God to fix his problem, he really wanted God to give him hope for the future.

Prayer: *Be near us, Lord, in our despair and in our hope. Draw us closer to you, that we may be able to see your love at work in our lives. Amen.*

✤Episcopal laywoman and author; Claremont, New Hampshire.
*See *Anchor Bible,* vol. 1, pp. 110-112.

Tuesday, March 7   Read Genesis 15:4-12, 17-18.

It is not hard to understand how hopeless Abraham felt when contemplating his childlessness. Like Abraham, we are often confronted with seemingly insurmountable challenges. Like him, we sometimes feel as if God is either blind to our needs or powerless to assist us. The more desperate the situation, the worse we feel. A sick and aging parent, a rift in our marriage, prolonged unemployment, a troubled child—why doesn't God see that we need help?

We are so much like Abraham that his words sound familiar. "What can you give me?" The question has a hollow, self-pitying ring. If we repeat it several times, we can fully grasp the bitterness and failure it expresses.

God's reply to the question was not meant only as a comfort to Abraham. It was also a foreshadowing, an example of God preparing the people for the Sinai covenant. "Look up at the sky, and count the stars. . . . So many will your descendants be" (REB). God wanted Abraham's people to know that they were chosen; he could not have used a better metaphor. To say to that childless man that he will have as many descendants as there are stars in the sky reveals God's understanding of Abraham's despair and God's desire to comfort Abraham.

In God's reassurance of Abraham, there is a message for us. God's response to "What can you give me?" recalls Abraham's deliverance. As God heard Abraham, so God hears us; and God will keep the covenant with us as well.

Prayer: *Dear God, help us to recognize the good things you give us. Make us mindful of your boundless love. Amen.*

Wednesday, March 8   Read Psalm 27:1-9.

With words expressing absolute trust in God, the psalmist stands in marked contrast to the despairing Abraham. As he faced God with fury and hopelessness, Abraham challenged God (Gen. 15:1-3). Unlike the psalmist, who placed himself in God's hands, Abraham in his continuing childlessness was reluctant to trust God and unwilling to praise God's loving power.

We are like Abraham in our anger, and like him we frequently turn to God in frustration. But in the psalmist's words, too, we hear familiar echoes. "Should an army encamp against me, my heart would have no fear," and "He will hide me in his shelter in the day of misfortune" (REB). These statements reveal a limitless trust in God. We are taught that God loves us. Psalm 27 reminds us of how confident—and thankful—we can be in that love.

How many times each week do we remember that "the LORD is the stronghold" of our lives? Do we remember to "acclaim him"? How often do we sing psalms "of praise to the LORD"? Are we thankful for a niece's accomplishments, a son's talents, a neighbor's helpfulness? Do we feel good about finishing a complex task at work? Have we found peace and comfort among family members? It is easy to take life for granted, but we know that each detail is the work of God's love. Like the psalmist, we know that it is from God that our life's blessings flow.

Prayer: *Lord, teach us to remember you in all of our prayers and to praise you in everything we do. Amen.*

Thursday, March 9   Read Psalm 27:10-14.

Life would be lonely if we did not have confidence in those around us. Because we naturally enjoy spending time with those we love, it is usually to them that we look as we seek reassurance. These are the people who make us feel less alone when we are worried or frightened.

The significance of family is underscored in the passage "Though my father and my mother forsake me, the LORD will take me into his care" (REB). We place great importance on our relationship with our parents, or on those whom we see as our parents. For them to "give up" on us would be for us to feel separated from all human support and love.

In asking God to take over for absent parents, the psalmist reveals absolute trust in God. The words *Teach me, show me,* and *lead me* emphasize how complete is that confidence in God. These words remind us that others may look to us to be helpers or mentors in our common struggle. When we offer encouragement or hope, we reflect God's love.

As children we relied on our parents; as adults, leaving childhood behind us, we depend on each other. We look for God to take us under wing and "into his care" (REB). One of the ways God does this is by providing us with each other. Among those who love God, there is an abundance of strength and caring. Our community of faith leads us closer to God.

Prayer: *Reveal to us, Lord, new opportunities for sharing your love. Help us live up to the trust others have in us. Amen.*

Friday, March 10   Read Luke 9:28-32.

It was undoubtedly both mystifying and uplifting for Peter, John, and James to see Jesus transfigured. They had probably not expected anything extraordinary to happen when they accompanied Jesus to the mountain to pray. Perhaps they had hoped to dissuade him from traveling later to Jerusalem, for the disciples were afraid of what would occur there. They were afraid of losing Jesus, and they may have anticipated a quiet time alone with him on the mountain. They were unprepared for what happened as he began to pray.

As Jesus was praying alone, the disciples were shocked into attentiveness. His glory was revealed to them in a wholly unexpected, unforgettable manifestation. "The appearance of his face changed and his clothes became dazzling white" (REB). The disciples could not understand all that it meant at the time, but they knew the change in Jesus was an important sign from God. They came away from their mountain episode chastened and thoughtful, once more aware that Jesus was no ordinary man.

Jesus' transfiguration was meant to be for the disciples a guidepost, an emphasis, a reminder. Because God's will for us is seldom clear, like the disciples we also need to watch and listen for signs. We need to be attentive to God's will and attentive to the ways open to us to serve—ways to heal the sick, feed the hungry, comfort the lonely, shelter the homeless. We must find opportunities to help transform the world with love.

Prayer: *Lord, guide us to the people and places that can benefit from our loving efforts. Amen.*

Saturday, March 11   Read Luke 9:33-36.

In speaking to the disciples at the Transfiguration of Jesus, God said, "This is my Son, my Chosen; listen to him" (REB). Following this event, there could have been little doubt in their minds about what they were to do. The disciples were in an enviable position. Peter, John, and James had clear instructions from God: they were to listen to Jesus, and they were to follow him. Because they lived with Jesus, it was, perhaps, easier for them than for us to listen and follow.

Compare the disciples' situation to our own. We believe that Jesus' life presents a good example of how we are to live. We may try to follow his example, but in many instances it is unclear how we should act. Often, the circumstances we encounter are far removed from those facing the disciples many centuries ago. Consider the ethical dilemma someone confronts when a loved one is terminally ill. A life-support system is an available means of extending the patient's life. Should it be used? Imagine the anguish of a pregnant teenager who comes to you for counsel: what can you say to her?

At the Transfiguration, the disciples learned that God had chosen Jesus to carry pain, fear, and sorrow for all. This means that no matter how perplexing our problems, no matter how overwhelmed we feel, we are assured of God's mercy. God's love transfigured Jesus. If we allow it, God can transform our lives, as God transformed the lives of the early disciples.

Prayer: *Be close to us, Lord, as we struggle. Help us to reconcile ourselves to your holy will for each of us. Amen.*

Sunday, March 12   Read Philippians 3:17–4:1.

In this portion of his letter to the church at Philippi, Paul both warns and reassures. He acknowledges that the church has enemies and that their physical appetites are destructive. He then offers himself and others of the faith as models of good Christian behavior: "You have us for a model; imitate those whose way of life conforms to it" (REB). Paul urges the Philippian Christians to pay attention to their lifestyle choices.

In his letter, Paul stresses the importance of looking to heaven for guidance and for deliverance, which, he says, will come indeed: "We are expecting a savior." Paul says that God will "transfigure our humble bodies, and give them a form like that of his own" (REB). Paul emphasizes the point that real transformation is possible through God's redeeming love. His words also recall Luke 9:28-36, in which the disciples witnessed Jesus transfigured by the Holy Spirit.

For Christians today, just as for those in the early church at Philippi, Paul's words are comforting. They underscore the fact that we need not wait for future salvation. God's love is available to us now. The choice is ours. This message was important when the first Christians spread the word about Jesus. It is just as important in the late-twentieth century. The miracle of God's healing love is that it requires no waiting.

Prayer: *Dear God, show us that we do not have to wait to see your kingdom. Help us to recognize it here among us now. Amen.*

THIRSTING FOR GOD

Betsy Schwarzentraub✤
Monday, March 13   Read Psalm 63:1-5.

The gift of longing

"O God, you are my God, I seek you, my soul thirsts for you;
. . . as in a dry and weary land."

Fierce landscapes sometimes loom in our lives, where arid
winds blow across our bleak, sandy soil. Events have robbed us
of hope. Our ability to love has withered away. Our joy in living
has been scorched out of us, until we long for God like the
parched earth yearns for shimmering droplets of rain.

Could our very thirst for God—our longing for a sense of
God's living presence—be a gift in itself and not just a terrible
inner desolation? Could our sense of God's absence be more
than personal torment? Could it be something God has placed
within us, driving us to seek communion with our Creator?

Psalm 63 gives us hope in wilderness times. Centuries ago,
the psalmist sang out his personal anguish, isolation, and
betrayal. Yet even as he sang, he realized that there is something
even more precious than life itself. It is knowing God's *hesed*,
the steadfast love or covenant loyalty of God.

This eternal faithfulness on God's part holds us up in the
times when we cannot see or touch God. Even when our lives
seem arid of meaning and bereft of love, there is One who loves
us, who walks with us in our desert wastes. It is this One whose
longing for union with us has been placed deep in our souls.

Prayer: *God of my heart, I will praise and bless you as long as I live.
Your steadfast love brings the waters of life to my wilderness. Amen.*

✤Church consultant; clergy member of the California-Nevada Conference of The United Methodist Church; Davis, California.

Tuesday, March 14   Read Psalm 63:6-8.

Singing God's grace

In the silence of the night, all our roles and pretenses slip away, leaving us vulnerable and alone. Occasionally tears, regrets, or anxieties can creep into our beds as we lie awake trying to sort through a jumble of loneliness, confusion, or shame.

The psalms give us a language for such times of anguish and for the grace that shines through them. It is precisely in these moments of weakness or worry that God's life-giving presence upholds us and gives us hope. In the darkest nights of our soul's need, God can turn our tears into joy.

"I think of you on my bed, and meditate on you in the watches of the night," says Psalm 63. As we lie awake in the dark with all masks stripped away, God's sheer grace upholds us. Like a newborn clutching its mother, we cling for life to God's love for us, as we are, no matter what our failures or faults.

"You have been my help. In the shadow of your wings, I sing for joy!" As shade is welcome in an arid land, so do we find the shadow of God's presence in our self-scorched souls (Psalm 121:5). As a hen gathers helpless chicks under her wings for protection and comfort, so God seeks to gather us (Matt. 23:37).

"My soul clings to you," we cry out in the middle of our own deepest nights. And we sing, "Your right hand upholds me!"

In our sleepless times of mortality and unknowing, the uncertainty or woundedness in our lives causes us to admit our creatureliness. It is in such a "dark night of the soul" that God's loving presence enfolds us, and we can sing for joy.

Suggestion for meditation: *When has my public self been stripped away, showing my deep need for God? How have I experienced the sheer grace of God's presence amid near despair? In what greater ways can I sing for joy?*

Wednesday, March 15   Read Isaiah 55:1-5.

Priceless water

"Come get water! Buy and eat!" The raucous voices of water-sellers and food vendors in the Babylonian marketplace were common as they wove their way through the Jewish crowds.

Yet the community lived in exile under foreign rule, far east of their homeland. Even for those born in this captive generation, it was hard to be hopeful so far away from the birthplace of their own people, the land of their God.

So the prophet took up the cry to shout out God's remarkable message. "Ho, everyone who thirsts, come to the waters." The people had thirsted for God's presence for so long! At one time they had felt a close communion with God, joyfully receiving God's promise of covenant relationship with their king, David. But those days were decades behind them now, their covenant broken irreparably by infidelity.

So what glorious news Isaiah now could tell them! Although they felt lost in a foreign land, God was about to save them. The God of their homeland was with them even here and would extend the promises made earlier to David to the entire people in an everlasting covenant which could not be broken. In the next year, God would allow Cyrus, the Persian king, to conquer Babylon and release Israel to return home. In this way, Israel would witness to God's presence and power as surely as the Christ, God's new David, would witness to God's rule over all people in an age yet to come.

Sheer grace! The promise of relationship with God is as essential to our life as are water and bread to our bodies. God offers us an everlasting covenant.

Prayer: *Merciful God, I thirst for your presence. Help me come to you for the life-giving water of your word. Amen.*

Thursday, March 16   Read Isaiah 55:6-11.

As sure as the rain

God's word accomplishes what God sends it to do. We can trust that God's love will not reach out to us in vain: "For as the rain and the snow come down from heaven," says God, "so shall my word be . . . ; it shall not return to me empty!"

Isaiah's listeners were an agrarian people. They knew the cycle of the seasons and that rain and snow usually meant a fruitful harvest. Isaiah was not giving them a farming lesson; he was reminding them that they could depend upon God's word to get out to all creation and to produce astounding abundance.

Sometimes we would rather not have to think about effectiveness. We would prefer to keep the gospel at the level of speech, not action. That way we can feel we have done something if we merely talk about food for the hungry, shelter for the homeless, and countless other justice issues too close to home.

God's word is the message of who God is through what God does in our midst. For God, word *is* action. It changes events and people. Whenever God speaks, life is transformed.

"For my thoughts are not your thoughts, nor are your ways my ways, says the LORD. . . . [My word] shall not return to me empty, but it shall accomplish that which I purpose, and succeed in the thing for which I sent it." What reassurance! We may muddle through good intentions and unfinished dreams with prayers that fizzle on the follow-through. But God's word endures, transforms us and all creation, and ultimately accomplishes its purpose!

Suggestion for meditation: *How can I act on God's word today to accomplish what God wants to do through me? Where are the newly-sprouted shoots of God's word around me? How can I nourish them?*

Friday, March 17   Read 1 Corinthians 10:1-11.

Water from the rock

Here he was back in the wilderness! Moses must have grumbled under his breath. This is where his unwilling adventure had begun, at the burning bush. That was before his mission for God in Egypt and then his crazy flight back over the border by night after killing an Egyptian. Would God's unreasonable expectations ever end?

And this time he didn't have just himself to worry about. He had a whole people with him, an unruly bunch of ex-slaves, from toddlers to grandparents. They were used to structure and punishment and filled with a hatred of authority which had been born of the whip. So they "murmured" against Moses. Earlier, they had staged a protest over getting meat and bread. Now they talked openly of killing him if he didn't find water soon.

So when Moses brought their demands back to God (not complaining, you understand), God told him to strike the rock at Horeb and water would come out of it, that the people and livestock might drink.

God's response required real faith on Moses' part: first to walk in the midst of his near-to-mutiny people and then to risk looking like a fool in their eyes as he searched for water amidst the rocks in that parched wilderness. Yet God's patience was greater than the people's rebellion. Moses struck that rock as if his life depended upon it (which, of course, it did). The rock split open, and a wellspring gushed forth. Moses' story proves that we may have our limits, but God's love for us does not.

Prayer: *God of infinite mercy, you provide the water of abundant life to our thirsty, self-parched souls. Help us stop complaining long enough to look to your living water upon which we all depend and to trust you with our lives. Amen.*

Saturday, March 18   Read 1 Corinthians 10:12-13.

The way out is through

"The center of God's will is our only safety," said Betsie ten Boom, Christian rescuer of Jews from Nazi concentration camps and herself a casualty of one of those camps. Her own experience in those camps told her that having faith in God does not protect us from terrors in life.

Leslie Weatherhead, English pastor and author, knew this too. During that same war, he warned his congregation not to mix the myth of God's protection with their life-tested faith. Some people did, however, and then when their London homes were bombed, their entire faith went up in smoke.

Paul reminds potentially overconfident Christians in Corinth of this point as well. God has given them many spiritual gifts for the good of the church; but if even some Israelites of the Exodus, gifted with God's glory in the pillar and the cloud, fell into idolatry and disobedience toward God, why should the Corinthians be exempt?

Paul doesn't say who does the tempting that tests us. Sometimes it is evil, intending to destroy our love of God. Sometimes it is our inner desires warring inside us. Other times it is people whose blindness to God's presence causes them to murder God's messengers. Regardless of the source of our suffering, terrible trials do come. Paul's good news is that God is faithful toward us in the midst of our temptations and gives us the resources to endure; we need only to accept those resources.

The "way out" which God offers us is not *around* our troubles but *through* them.

Suggestion for meditation: *How am I being tempted right now? Where is the high ground on which I can stand, fight, and win, with God's help?*

Sunday, March 19   Read Luke 13:1-9.

Rooted in the living waters

It is easy to worry about other people's faith journeys and not question our own. Jesus sensed that tendency among his followers and warned them to check the depth of their own spiritual roots. Think of a fig tree planted in the vineyard, he said. Its purpose was to shade the workers and give them fruit in season. It was leafy and beautiful from a distance, but for three years running, it hadn't produced a single fruit.

"Cut it down," the owner told the gardener. "Why should it be wasting the soil?"

But the gardener responded, "Sir, let it alone for one more year, until I dig around it and put manure on it. If it bears fruit next year, well and good; but if not, you can cut it down."

Jesus knew his listeners wouldn't miss the point. It is only when the tree's roots work downward into the water table that it can produce the fruit for which it was created. From Psalm 1, they knew that righteous people are "like trees planted by streams of water, which yield their fruit in season, and their leaves do not wither." When we exist on the surface of our lives, we may look like that lovely fig tree. It is only when we have sunk our roots deep into God's teaching, into the living water of Christ himself (John 4:10) that we can tap into God's word, which has waited in pools beneath us all along.

Discipleship is not about appearances but about fruitfulness. Shade is a fine beginning, but ultimately it is the fruit that counts.

Prayer: *Dear God, in a world where so many people thirst for you, guide me to deepen my roots in Christ, that we all might be nourished by your Word. This I humbly pray by your grace in Jesus. Amen.*

REFRESHMENT, RENEWAL, RE-CREATION

March 20-26, 1995   **Norval I. Brown**✤
Monday, March 20   Read Joshua 5:9-12.

We are approaching the Fourth Sunday in Lent, traditionally a day on which our attention focuses not on our sorrow for our sins but rather on the glory to be revealed in our Lord and Savior Jesus Christ. This theme is reflected in our readings for this week. Joshua and the children of Israel find themselves at Gilgal and renew the covenant of circumcision. We must remember that during their journey through the wilderness, circumcision was not practiced. God affirms that even the journey in the wilderness was a part of the enslavement in Egypt, and through the renewal of the covenant of circumcision that evil time is left behind (v. 9).

Following the act of circumcision, the children of Israel celebrated the Passover. On the plains of Gilgal, in sight of their enemies, this meal is shared by the community. Through the rite of circumcision and the celebration of the Passover, the children of Israel reaffirm their covenant as God's "treasured possession . . . priestly kingdom and a holy nation" (Exod. 19:5-6). The journey through the wilderness and the enslavement in Egypt are over, and the children of Israel are no longer a nomadic people; they have come home. God no longer provides manna; now the people eat the produce of the land provided by God. God reveals God's glory as the promised land becomes the delivered land.

Prayer: *Most gracious God, remind me that the sufferings of this present age cannot compare with the glory that is to be revealed. Amen.*

✤Pastor of Southlawn United Methodist Church; Chicago, Illinois.

Tuesday, March 21   Read Psalm 32:1-5.

"Confession is good for the soul" the old adage goes—and in this psalm we learn that it is also good for the body! It is obvious that the theme of this psalm is sin and its consequences and the renewal that comes from confession and forgiveness.

The psalmist has a keen awareness of sin; to wit, he uses four terms to denote its harshness—*transgression, sin, iniquity, deceit.* There is no sugarcoating of this very real evil, no mention of frailties or weaknesses or failures in judgment. The sting of these words hits to the very heart and soul of our lives. And the psalmist writes from personal experience! The preface of the psalm in verses 1-2 speaks of the blessedness of forgiveness, but there is a difficult road to travel to get there. Full of sin, the psalmist keeps silence before God, unaware that God already knows about the sin. Hiding the sin brings on a wasted body and a draining of strength. The psalmist (perhaps David) illustrates the connectedness of body and soul, for the troubled soul gave rise to physical symptoms. From where was renewal to come? It could only come by returning to God.

Confession—acknowledging our transgression of God's law—is the first step to renewal, to re-creation. What happened when confession was made, when sin was named as sin? The scripture says, "You forgave the guilt of my sin." What sin do you attempt to hide from God? Why not name your sin and seek renewal, re-creation, forgiveness?

Prayer: *Gracious God, today I name these sins: _____. I confess my transgressions in order to receive your forgiveness, that I might feel wholeness of soul and body. Amen.*

Wednesday, March 22   Read Psalm 32:6-11.

It has been said that "experience is the best teacher." Unfortunately, we rarely learn from the experience of another. But that is the purpose of these remaining verses of the psalm. Utterly convinced of God's forgiveness, the psalmist now turns to others, in essence saying, "This is what happened to me. Learn from it!" When you are overwhelmed by evil ("the rush of the mighty waters"), turn to God. God, as your hiding place, will be your protector from evil, regardless of the front from which it attacks you.

Verses 8-10 provide us two options for interpretation depending upon who we believe the speaker to be. Perhaps the speaker is God, pronouncing the responsibility of teaching and inviting the people to heed the law of Moses. Or the speaker may still be the psalmist, calling people to repentance, that they might encounter the joy that comes from God's forgiveness. Regardless of who we think is speaking, the bottom line is clear: Receive your instruction and walk in God's way as a human being who can recognize God's sovereignty rather than being like a horse or mule, having to be taught by discipline and punishment. To deny God is to condemn one's life to the pangs of the wicked. In forgiveness and instruction, we find refreshment, renewal, and re-creation.

If we trust in God and receive God's instruction, then God's steadfast love will surround us.

Prayer: *Lead me, O Lord, lead me in thy righteousness.*
Make thy way plain before my face.
For it is thou, Lord, thou Lord, only,
who makest me dwell in safety. * Amen.*

*Based on Psalms 5:8; 4:8.

Thursday, March 23   Read 2 Corinthians 5:16-21.

Each day the media bombards us with cosmetics; exercise equipment and programs; hair tints, straighteners, curlers, and growth formulas; and clothing to make us look younger, healthier, and more appealing. Makeovers are designed to mask who we really are and to make us feel good about ourselves. In today's reading, Paul outlines the only real makeover that should concern us: "So if anyone is in Christ, there is a new creation: everything old has passed away; see, everything has become new!"

Rather than hiding or masking blemishes, rather than changing our appearance to try to look like some ideal picture we have in our mind, we become a new creation by immersing ourselves in Christ. We then take on the image of Christ, the image of our creation. Our lives are not continuations of an old journey; rather, the newness signals the beginning of a new journey.

A part of the new journey involves us in a ministry of reconciliation—bringing others back to God so that they may be made new as well. As God's handiwork, we become living ambassadors for God, as God makes the appeal through us. As ambassadors, our citizenship is in heaven, but we labor in foreign lands. As ambassadors, we speak for our homeland, and our actions reflect upon our homeland. As ambassadors, we hold up the honor and glory of the One who called us and made us new but also who sends us out to do his bidding. Paul, as a new creation, bids the church at Corinth to be reconciled to God and be made new. He appeals also to us to be reconciled and made new, that we might be living examples of God's power to re-create.

Prayer: *Re-creating God, not face, not hands, not feet, not hair, not body, but give me a new heart that loves you, a new heart that knows the depths of forgiveness. Give me a new heart through which you might make your appeal to others. Amen.*

94

Friday, March 24   Read Luke 15:1-3.

It is odd how hierarchies develop among us. In today's lesson we find the scribes and Pharisees grumbling at Jesus' association with tax collectors and other sinners. In a rather strange turn of events, all they saw were the things that made them different. They missed the commonality of their experiences.

The scribes and Pharisees, the "tax collectors and sinners" were all Jews, reared with common teachings and traditions. But because certain types of labor were demeaned, people who performed those labors were deemed unfit, unclean. And because righteousness was judged by who most strictly adhered to the law, many people were deemed sinners. All these people lived under the oppression of a Roman government, yet because some had found favor with the Roman government, they felt empowered to look down upon those, their brothers and sisters, who did not enjoy such favor. Each of these people was created in God's image, yet the selective blindness of most of the scribes and Pharisees would not allow them to see that exalted creation in others.

Hearing their complaints, Jesus seizes this moment as an opportunity for teaching. Rather than bluntly exposing the self-instituted hierarchical system of his day, Jesus tells a story designed for self-reflection, self-conviction, and confession. He tells a parable.

Today we also are called to think of those we demean, those over whom we hold power, those to whom we deny the proper image of their creation.

Prayer: *God of all, help me to affirm the image in which you have created everyone, and let me not seek to deny the gospel of Jesus Christ to anyone. Amen.*

Saturday, March 25   Read Luke 15:11*b*-24.

Everyone wants independence, wants to affirm his or her identity. The affirmation of one's identity seems somehow to be an expression of one's independence. Today's reading introduces us to a young man who discovers that his identity and independence come only from a relationship with God.

This young man demands of his father the share of goods he would receive upon his father's death. Then, wanting to distance himself from the moral authority of his father, he travels to a distant land where he squanders his resources. Reduced to feeding swine (a despicable act to any Jew), the young man has an "aha!" experience: "He came to himself." So he returns to take a servant position, but is accepted back as a son that he is. It is a new position, because the father makes no mention of how or where the son spent his money. All is forgiven and forgotten.

The young man comes home—and there is great rejoicing because of the new birth. Note the language: "This son of mine was dead and is alive again." Only in the restoration of the relationship with the father does the son come fully to his identity and, thus, to his independence. Note that it is only the father who can bring about this renewal. Had the son had his way, he would have been a day-laborer in the household. The father brings re-creation through a robe, kept only for the most honored guest; a ring, a symbol of authority denoting that the prodigal was still son and heir; and sandals, for only slaves went barefoot. He brings renewal by naming this young man "my son"; and he brings refreshment by leading the party.

Prayer: *When I have traveled to a distant country, may I come to myself and remember the joy of your house, O God. And in remembering, may I have the presence of mind to arise and return to you. Amen.*

Sunday, March 26   Read Luke 15:25-32.

Sunday morning—the Lord's day. Many will gather in sanctuaries to worship and praise our God joyfully. Yet others gather out of a sense of grim obedience.

We conclude our journey through the theme of refreshment, renewal, re-creation by examining the older brother in this popular parable. He, like his younger brother, was searching for his identity and his independence, never realizing that they were already his. Once the property was divided between the two men, the elder son would become the principal landowner. The elder son, very much as the scribes and Pharisees who were the audience for this parable, could not see the commonality of experience he shared with his brother. Rather, he chose to elevate himself to a position of judging his younger brother. (Note the accusation: "This son of yours . . . has devoured your property with prostitutes.").

Sometimes our own renewal, our own re-creation comes at the renewal of another. While his brother's return should have been a source of rejuvenation for this man, he allowed it to cause an even greater schism between them.

On the Lord's day, bound together with one another, let us rejoice over the lost who have been found. Let those who have always been at home ask ourselves why we worship in church this Sunday. Do we do so out of grim, dutiful obedience or loving service?

Prayer: *Gracious God, sometimes I don't even need to leave home to be lost. Help me to come to myself, too, so that I might rejoice in the return of others. Amen.*

A NEW DIRECTION

March 27–April 2, 1995
Monday, March 27

Robert Corin Morris♣
Read Isaiah 43:16-21.

The God of new paths

God is a trailblazer inviting us to pioneer the future.

The Judean community in Babylonian exile is holding on for dear life to the ancestral past, hoping for the restoration of the old kingdom. The voice of this radical prophet interrupts their fearful nostalgia: stop relying on memories of God's way "in the sea" during the old Exodus. Prepare for the new Exodus of your own lifetimes: "I am about to do a new thing . . . I will make a way in the wilderness." We do not find the God of the Bible by keeping our noses stuck in a book but by writing the book's stories so deeply on our hearts that we, too, are able to see into the depths of the present moment.

The prophet challenges the exiles to get ready for a whole new world situation. A different kind of international society is dawning with the Persian Empire. With it comes the task of seeing and serving God in ways that will challenge the old tribal ways. Israel's concern is to be for the life of the world, not just for its own safety and prosperity.

The prophet summons a people caught between nostalgia for the past and the difficulty of coping with the Babylonian culture in which they are forced to live. A new trail can force our souls, like theirs were, to meet new challenges, evoking from within us new strengths previously dormant.

Prayer: *O God of unexpected twists and turns in the path, lend me a share of your own courage for the journey! Amen.*

♣Episcopal priest and spiritual director; Director of Interweave Center for Wholistic Living, Summit, New Jersey.

Tuesday, March 28   Read Psalm 126.

The tears of new life

Sometimes new directions begin with tears. We must leave something behind, make a sacrifice, or face an unanticipated difficulty.

Most of the exiled community in Babylon chose to protect themselves from being stirred by a "path in the wilderness." Called to shake off seventy years of habit, they declined to find inner resources to face resettling Judea. Returning to Zion involved tears they were unwilling to shed—and laughter they would never know. For those who did return, life was more difficult than the prophetic songs had led them to believe.

In this psalm, the returned exiles face a time of difficulty with tears, demands, and an affirmation: Those who sow in tears reap with shouts of joy.

The psalmist alludes to the ancient custom of ritual weeping during the sowing of the seed. The tears had originally been for the hidden divinity in the wheat, which must fall into the ground and die to make new life (see John 12:24). They were also a magical invitation for the rain to fall.

In this once-pagan custom the psalmist sees an affirmation of God's way with us: dealing with what is rather than what might have been is essential to honest spirituality. Rather than singing the prophet's songs to keep their spirits up, the people are called to "sow with tears."

Much spirituality involves pining for an idealized life rather than finding God in the hard edges and unexpected surprises of where—and who—we are. Our real responses to life are the stuff out of which strong souls can be grown.

Prayer: *God, let my tears be the seedbed of honest prayer. Amen.*

Wednesday, March 29   Read Philippians 3:4b-8.

Changing directions

Paul stands in the line of great biblical figures whose chosen path was crossed by a God headed in a different direction. As a result of his desire to "gain Christ" he has "suffered the loss of all things" and found a new basis and a new direction for his life.

The old basis had been self-justification, being "confident in the flesh." Here, *flesh* refers not to the physical body but to personal identity dominated by willfulness, pride, and self-interest.

Paul had used his considerable energies to make himself feel worthy through pride in his family pedigree and through blameless rule-keeping, ardently devoted to "righteousness under the Law." *Law* here carries the Greek sense of *nomos*, restraining regulations, rather than the Hebrew feel of *torah*, "illuminative teaching." Such a life of ethnic pride and conformity was at the heart of both Hellenistic and Hebrew societies: "I am my family and my accomplishments."

Paul has been knocked off that horse, and his feet are firmly planted on new ground. He characteristically calls himself Messiah's slave, meaning, "My usefulness to Messiah's purposes defines who I am." The new ground of Paul's labors is "knowing Christ Jesus my Lord."

Paul's Christ is not limited to the memory of the man Jesus. Messiah is "a life-giving spirit" (1 Cor. 15:45), the One in whom all things hold together (Col. 1:17). Knowing this Christ is, therefore, knowing God's creating and redeeming energies at work. Paul's identity is found not in his own ego-drama but in the small part he plays in Messiah's purposes for the world.

Prayer: *Baptize me anew into your desires for your world, O God. Amen.*

Thursday, March 30   Read Philippians 3:9-11.

Messiah's faithfulness

Paul wants "to know Christ and the power of his resurrection." This "knowing" (Greek *ginosko*) is much more than an intellectual knowing. It is an intimate connection with God's presence and is central to the promise of the New Covenant (Jer. 31:34). While Paul is ferocious in his rejection of the emerging power of gnosticism that claimed a secret mystical knowledge, he is equally firm in claiming a real *gnosis* for himself and for all whose lives are touched by the breath of Messiah's life (1 Cor. 2:6-16).

This Christian "knowing" is a deepening sensitivity to Messiah's desires for the creation rather than secret, esoteric revelations that separated its believers from responsibility for the created world.

Knowing Messiah this way, we find our security "in the faith of Christ." The meaning is two-sided in Greek. It is usually read as faith *in* Christ, but the Greek also means the faith *of* Christ, that is, *Messiah's* own faithfulness to us and to the world.

Messiah's faithful love itself becomes the basis of our pilgrimage, not our believing. Unless we grasp this, we stay centered on our own efforts to believe and know, not on Messiah's desires made known to us.

Focused on God's Christ, we are available for the "power of his resurrection," at work here and now in life. Our task as servants of Messiah's cause is to join the resurrection energies wherever we find them at work in God's world and to pray for their life-giving presence where death seems to reign. Christ's world-healing presence, not our spiritual careers, is central.

Prayer: *Living Christ, may your resurrection work through me. Amen.*

101

Friday, March 31   Read Philippians 3:10-14.

An athlete's effort

Paul has turned his ferocious efforts away from his own self-perfecting and toward Messiah's purposes: "I press on toward the goal." He evokes the image of the runner who is "straining forward to what lies ahead."

Sometimes Christian teaching loses touch with the biblical affirmation that human effort is an essential part of serving God. As the Hebrew Bible puts it, "The word is very near to you . . . for you to observe" (Deut. 30:14). Western theology since Augustine has been tortured by an exaggerated opposition between human effort and divine grace, "works" versus "faith" in God's grace.

But the real opposition in Paul is not between human effort and divine grace but between two different goals for human effort. Paul had used the works of the law in a self-serving attempt to justify himself before God. By his own admission, he had the power to keep the outward rules blamelessly, but he kept them toward a futile goal.

Now Paul's human efforts are offered to be part of Messiah's activity. The outward law is indeed to be obeyed, now for Messiah's sake. The motivation is loving service, not self-justification. Obeying the law as a way of loving God and serving the best interests of others is a far cry from keeping the rules to feel superior to others.

Prayer: *Loving Christ, you have made me your own. Let my goal be cooperation with your desires. Amen.*

Saturday, April 1   Read John 12:1-3.

Mary's discipleship

Mary of Bethany is a disciple who shows she knows Messiah's needs. The sister of Martha and Lazarus who "sat at Jesus' feet" (Luke 10:39) acts not only in thanksgiving for her brother's rescue from death, but also in anticipation of Jesus' own death. The "pound of costly perfume made of pure nard," an incredible extravagance, tells us about the depth of Mary's love and about Jesus' relationship to people.

Jesus was at home with people of every stratum of society. He had wealthy followers. Mary and Martha probably had some wealth, since they appear to have been householders.

Wealth, like effort or law, is meant to be used to serve Creator and creatures, not for self-justification. Not every disciple was told to sell everything. People like Zacchaeus, whose money came from ill-gotten gain, and the rich young ruler, whose attachment to money kept him from following his heart's truest goal, were commanded to give their wealth away.

Mary uses her considerable wealth in an act of love for the Master. It is a graceful response to what love requires in the moment. Following the Spirit's movement in her soul will bring her censure from the other disciples, who only know what is "right" according to the rules. She acts with shocking intimacy, wiping Jesus' feet with her unbound hair. Both ethnic propriety and societal/religious rules are being challenged by a woman whose only concern is to relate to Jesus' deeds and needs. She helps him face the death already weighing on his soul with comfort so intimate and lavish that he will carry the odor of it with him into hell itself (Eph. 4:9).

Prayer: *Living Christ, let my thanksgiving know no measure. Amen.*

Sunday, April 2   Read John 12:4-8.

Measures of love

As everyone reclines at the festive banquet, only Mary and Jesus are attuned to the dark valley into which God is leading them. The evangelist alerts us to these somber undercurrents by noting that this is "six days before the Passover" (12:1) and preceding the story with his account of the plot against Jesus' life by the authorities.

But while Mary, attuned to Jesus, responds sensitively to his needs, the other disciples have their eyes on the abstract horizon of their own impending triumph and their places in the new establishment.

In John, Judas is made the mouthpiece of an objection voiced by the disciples in Matthew. He argues from a "blameless under the law" position: the only right thing to do with wealth is to help the poor. He is so fixated on his own principles that he, like the others, is not sensitive to God's call in this moment.

Such principled righteousness limits genuine response to the real needs of people. It is not open to the readiness of the personal God to respond in a way unique to this moment. It serves law, not grace. And, as the evangelist reveals, such overt, judgmental righteousness is often a cover for covert wickedness.

Help the poor? "Of course," Jesus affirms, quoting Deuteronomy 15:11, where we are urged always to "open [our] hand toward the poor and needy" who will never cease from the land. That is our duty day in and day out. But what about right now? There may be someone right here who has need of a lavishness of love without measure which demands going far beyond the measured tithes of good stewardship.

Prayer: *Lord Christ, let your love be the measure of my giving. Amen.*

April 3-9, 1995   **Helen R. Neinast❖**
Monday, April 3   Read Philippians 2:5-11.

Our journey this week toward Jerusalem and Palm/Passion Sunday is a bumpy one. We start the week with great expectations, journey on with hope, run up against setbacks and disappointment, and find ourselves at the end of the week somewhere in a confused mix of joy and fear.

For persons of faith, the week ahead *is* a bumpy one. But today we revel in the ancient Christian hymn of today's lection. It begins not with the image of the suffering Christ, as we might expect from an imprisoned writer, but with the Christ who is equal to God—glorious, powerful, and magnificent. This Christ, Paul says, for the sake of others surrendered his divinity and became a vulnerable human being. He accepted his humanity even to the point of death; and then God raised him from the dead and made him Lord over all things.

This stirring hymn of faith is saying one thing to us very clearly: It challenges us to give ourselves—our status, our power, our mind and our heart—over to God. As we journey with Christ toward Jerusalem, we must empty ourselves so that we, too, may experience the bumpy road through death toward resurrection, renewed faith, and everlasting joy.

Suggestion for meditation: *Prayerfully reflect on what you need to "empty yourself" of in order to travel the road toward Jerusalem. What hurts, grievances, illusions, struggles, or aspirations do you need to release so that you may receive what God has for you?*

❖Clergy member, New Mexico Conference of The United Methodist Church. Chaplain and Director of Pastoral Services at Charter Hospital, Land O'Lakes, Florida.

Tuesday, April 4   Read Psalm 118:1-2, 19-29.

Sheer joy and thanksgiving—that's what this psalm is all about. The joy and celebration that come with entering God's house. The thanksgiving that comes when God grants salvation and sends someone in God's name to give light to the people.

Ancient Israel celebrated God's abiding love with this psalm of thanksgiving. The festive processional to the Temple gates, followed by dancing, singing, and praise to God, marked a time of great joy for the people of Jerusalem. Through their celebration, they gave witness to God's great deeds, to God's great mercy, and to God's enduring love.

Every phrase of Psalm 118 shouts with the joy of thanksgiving, and several are faith statements familiar to us from childhood: *Give thanks to the Lord, for God is good. This is the day that the Lord has made; let us rejoice and be glad in it. God's steadfast love endures forever.*

We can imagine Jesus, as a faithful Jew, recalling these same familiar phrases of thanksgiving from Psalm 118. Perhaps, on his way to Jerusalem, he spoke some of them in prayer to God. They might have been, for him, a reminder of the steadfastness of God's love in the midst of whatever awaited him as he approached Jerusalem.

This psalm is a call for each of us, too, to remember the strength and steadfastness of God's love. That remembrance is good preparation for the approach to Jerusalem.

Suggestion for meditation: *Keep the words of Psalm 118 before you in the day ahead. Write the words* "God's steadfast love endures forever" *on a piece of paper and carry it with you today. Or keep these words of thanksgiving in your heart, and repeat them to yourself throughout the hours of the day.*

106

Wednesday, April 5   Read Isaiah 50:4-9*a*.

This passage, from the third Servant Song in Isaiah, captures the frustration that sometimes comes to those who try to carry the message of God to others. Here, the prophet Isaiah cries aloud to God with the frustration of one who has tried to bring God's comfort to fellow Israelites but who has been treated despicably by those listeners. "I gave my back to those who struck me...I did not hide my face from insult and spitting."

Frustrated and hurting, Isaiah's Suffering Servant does not despair. Instead, the scripture says, the Servant sets his face like flint: "I know that I shall not be put to shame; [the one] who vindicates me is near." This is a statement of faith in the midst of trouble, pain, and misunderstanding.

It is a statement that Jesus might have need to call upon along the way toward Jerusalem. His message had, often enough in the past, been misunderstood, ignored, or ridiculed. There would be more of the same awaiting him in Jerusalem. Hoping to bring comfort and a message of hope, Jesus will be met with insults and blows. But, according to Isaiah 50, it is God who will have the last word. It is God who helps the Suffering Servant. Indeed, it is God who helps all those who seek to carry God's message to the people.

Isaiah's Suffering Servant can be for us, as it was for Jesus, a powerful encouragement to take heart, even if hard times are ahead. The road to Jerusalem is bumpy, but God travels that road with us.

Suggestion for prayer: *Pray for ways to carry the message of comfort and hope to those whom you meet today. When you encounter rejection or disappointment, recall the words of the Suffering Servant: "It is the Lord GOD who helps me."*

Thursday, April 6   Read Psalm 31:9-16.

Kathleen Farmer in *The Women's Bible Commentary* notes that the Book of Psalms is full of song after song in which doubt and assurance wash back and forth over the people of faith. She calls it the "ebb and flow" of assurance and comments that "the transition from anxiety to assurance in the psalms, as in human life, is not always neatly or permanently made."

That is most certainly true of Psalm 31. Its initial cry for help—"Be gracious to me, O LORD, for I am in distress"—gives way to the anxiety of doubt and fear. Verse after verse describes in detail the trials and terrors of the writer's present situation. Yet there is an abrupt and remarkable turnaround halfway through the psalm: "But I trust in you, O LORD; I say, 'You are my God.' My times are in your hand."

To trust in the midst of terror in some ways points to a central truth of the faith. In the midst of the bleakest situations we can face, we are called upon to trust in God—for our protection, for our security, sometimes for our very lives.

Jesus faced the challenge of the call to trust in the middle of terror. His journey to Jerusalem had its moments of terror—as do each of our own journeys. The faith statement of the psalmist, "My times are in your hand," is a moving reminder that God is trustworthy, powerful, and steadfast.

Suggestion for prayer: *Use the words of Psalm 31:14-15 as your companions through this day:*

> *But I trust in you, O LORD;*
> *I say, "You are my God."*
> *My times are in your hand.*

Friday, April 7   Read Luke 19:28-34.

Jesus' entry into Jerusalem as told in the Gospel of Luke is, in some very important ways, different from the other three Gospels' versions. When Jesus comes into the city, he is accompanied only by his disciples, his followers. There is no welcoming crowd gathered there (Matt. 21:9). The story as Luke tells it is more subdued and less crowded. It is an event for Jesus' disciples and followers, a more intimate scene. It is a scene set for those who are committed to the faith.

The most striking part of this portion of Luke's story about Jesus' entry into Jerusalem is the answer Jesus directs the disciples to give to anyone who asks why they are untying the colt that Jesus will ride into the city. If anyone asks, Jesus says to tell them, "The Lord needs it."

The Lord needs it. A simple, straightforward answer. An answer that, apparently, satisfied the questioners.

That simple answer becomes, for us, a straightforward call to discipleship. Why are you taking that colt? Because the Lord needs it. Why are you lending your presence to those who are following Jesus into Jerusalem? Because the Lord needs it. Why are you making a commitment of faith to this man from Nazareth? Because the Lord needs it.

The Lord *does* have need—of our commitment, of our faithfulness, of our discipleship. As we approach Palm/Passion Sunday, let us remember how much the Lord needs us and recommit ourselves to serving those needs.

Suggestion for meditation: *What gifts, graces, talents in you does the Lord have need of? What in your life can you give to Christ as he enters Jerusalem on the road to the cross?*

Saturday, April 8   Read Luke 19:35-40.

There are cloaks strewn along the road on Jesus' way into Jerusalem. These cloaks are the cloaks of the disciples. Luke says that as Jesus was approaching the path from the Mount of Olives, "the whole multitude of the disciples began to praise God joyfully with a loud voice for all the deeds of power that they had seen."

Their shouts of joy are met with objections by the Pharisees. We do not know why the Pharisees objected. Perhaps they were afraid that the disciples' calling Jesus a king would be misinterpreted by the Romans. Maybe the Pharisees were making known to Jesus their own disbelief. The Pharisees could have been concerned with Herod's reaction.

No matter what the reason, Jesus' response is clear: "I tell you, if these were silent, the stones would shout out."

The stones would shout out. The message of God is so powerful and so wonderful that, if people were silent in the face of it, creation itself would shout out in glad witness. It is an amazing image, one that sings of truth.

God's redemptive power in history cannot be stopped. It is a story as old as the stones of the earth themselves, and the voices of those stones, along with the voices of the faithful, will be raised in witness to Christ's resurrection from the dead. On the Saturday before Palm/Passion Sunday, that is an important truth to remember.

Suggestion for meditation: *At the end of her book* Stones for Ibarra, *Harriet Doerr writes of the old Mexican custom of piling up stones in places where people want to remember that something has happened. What stones of remembrance might you carry with you today as you recall Jesus' journey to Jerusalem?*

Sunday, April 9   Read Luke 23:1-49.

These verses of scripture retelling the final days of Jesus' life are painful ones to lay alongside the joy of Jesus' entry into Jerusalem. And yet that is where our journey to Jerusalem takes us—from joy to sorrow, from celebration to grief.

The tension between these two is almost unbearable, but Palm/Passion Sunday is rich with both. There is the headiness of Jesus' disciples and friends on the way into Jerusalem; there is the horror of those same friends and disciples on the way out of Jerusalem, toward Jesus' death.

Why must the faithful relive this emotional, bumpy journey on Palm/Passion Sunday? Why must the faithful witness Jesus' death? Luke knows, and he tells us in verse 49: witnessing Jesus' death is necessary in order that we may also be witnesses to his resurrection.

On this Palm/Passion Sunday, gather it all into your heart—the celebration and the pathos, the joy and the pain. Carry all that with you as you journey with Jesus today.

Suggestion for meditation: *Sit quietly and imagine for yourself the range of emotion Jesus' followers must have felt at this time in their faith journeys.*
        At what points in your own life have you felt some of those same feelings—either of joy or sorrow, celebration or grief? Give those feelings over to God during your prayer time today.

April 10-16, 1995 **J. Barrie Shepherd**✤
Monday, April 10 Read Isaiah 42:1-9;
John 12:1-11.

Deliverance—that's the watchword of this week—liberation from every dungeon of despair and from the ultimate dungeon, the tomb. So John begins his Holy Week narrative with this return visit by Jesus to his old, dear friends in Bethany. Over the years I have learned that everything John wrote has more than one level of meaning. His creative mind was never content merely to recount "facts"; his narratives overflow with interpretive possibilities. So this week that ends with Jesus' resurrection begins where Jesus has already tasted victory over death.

In our time, with "near-death experiences" and the everyday miracles of modern medicine, it would not be difficult to explain away Lazarus's recovery. But that would be to miss the point entirely. Jesus was not merely some magician who went around revivifying corpses. "In him was life" as John asserts at the outset, "and the life was the light of all people." And no matter how thick the darkness, it could not overcome the light (1:4-5).

In other words, the life of God among us in Jesus was so powerful, so permanent, that in its presence death and all its trappings were eliminated. And when Jesus descended from the cross to those dungeons and darknesses, which Isaiah and other biblical writers described, the prison bars were shattered, the massive gates torn from their hinges. And all of this begins today, as Jesus sits at table with his friends.

Prayer: *Deliver me, O God, this day from every form of death into the life that is now and forever. Amen.*

✤Pastor of The First Presbyterian Church in the City of New York.

112

Tuesday, April 11   Read Isaiah 49:1-7;
                                                      John 12:20-36.

I have never forgotten these words from John's Gospel carved into the solid oak of a pulpit in my native Scotland: *Sir, we would see Jesus.** Today's readings are about chosenness, what it means to be chosen by God. Isaiah makes clear that this is an election not to a position of privilege but to a task which without God's call would be overwhelming. It is the task of bringing "light to the nations . . . salvation to the end of the earth"; and the one who undertakes it can expect to be "deeply despised, abhorred." Thus, early in Holy Week we are reminded of both the promise and the portent of the call that has led Jesus from his mother's womb to this very moment.

There is another call involved; the call to those who, having felt the impact of the risen Christ's life upon their own, set out to walk with him. Their call—our call—also has to do with light; not to *be* the light but to bear it; to permit it to shine through; to become by grace a means by which the petition—"Sir, we would see Jesus"—of all peoples of this darkened world can be responded to in generous love and genuine humility.

For us, too, this is no "light" and easy task. If it seems that way, perhaps we should ask whose call we are responding to. Without seeking out suffering (there is no place for masochism in our faith), the light of Christ we are called to bear may well evoke at least an initial hostile reaction from those who have learned to love the darkness. But we will remember that Christ is with us always and in all circumstances.

Prayer: *Shine through my day, O Christ, and may it be lived to your glory. Amen.*

---

*KJV

113

Wednesday, April 12   Read Isaiah 50:4-9*a*;
                                                    John 13:21-32.

Isaiah talks of the servant of God as one who knows how to sustain the weary with a word. Yet the word of which we read in John is a word of betrayal and abandonment. There is little to sustain anyone in this, one of the bleakest scenes in all scripture. How could he have done it? How could Judas have sold out the Son of God for a paltry bag of change? This question has troubled believers ever since. Did he choose of his own free will to betray Christ, or was he acting out some preordained plan by which the scriptures had to be fulfilled? Both possibilities are suggested in the narratives. I suspect the full truth will remain a secret until the end of time.

What we can and must note is that betrayal of our Lord was not then—and still is not—confined to that one furtive, desperate moment at the table or in Gethsemane. For all the hideous nature of Judas's act there are moments in my life, events and actions in the daily news, that tear the body of Christ and spill his blood just as savagely as those misguided deeds done under cover of Jerusalem's darkness.

To all these, thank God, there is a word that sustains. We have been given by God's grace a word to hold on to in the teeth of every betrayal that soils and shames our times, our lives: "Father, forgive them; for they know not what they do."*

Of all Jesus' miracles, that miracle of forgiving love, spoken and then lived out in his life of service and death on Calvary, is the one that leads directly into the heart of the Divine. And in that grace, despite all our betrayals, we are still sustained.

Prayer: *Sustain me in your word, O God, the living Word. Amen.*

---

*Luke 23:34, KJV.

114

April 13 (Maundy Thursday)

Read 1 Corinthians 11:23-26;
John 13:1-17, 31*b*-35.

Two items, a remarkable insertion and what seems at first a glaring omission, mark John's narration of events in the upper room. Of the four evangelists, John alone records what we call "the footwashing." But then John's description of that fateful night makes no mention of what we call the Lord's Supper.

Certainly the washing of the disciples' feet presents a powerful portrayal of the servant role undertaken by our Lord and to be undertaken by all who follow him: "I have set you an example, that you also should do as I have done to you."

As Christ broke through the pride of his friends, taking upon himself the slave's task they refused to perform for one another, so he left a model of how, gently but insistently, to break down the walls of resentment and vanity that set us at each other's throats when we should be kneeling at each other's feet.

The absence of any record of Jesus' words and actions over bread and wine is more puzzling, especially when John's Gospel is permeated with the imagery and theology of this central sacrament of our faith. It is only in John that Jesus describes himself as "the bread of life" and "the true vine." Might the explanation be that John, writing after the other Gospel writers and seeing the institution of the sacrament so fully laid out in the earlier Gospels, decided to concentrate on an act of consecration to precede every celebration of the Lord's Supper?

As we gather at the Table this sad and holy night, let us remember our servant calling and rededicate ourselves to it.

Prayer: *Teach me to kneel, O Christ; then seat me at your Table. Amen.*

April 14 (Good Friday)

Read John 18:11–19:42.

What is to be said about Good Friday that has not already been said or sung or painted or carved about this day—shrouded in hopelessness and grief? Perhaps this poem I wrote some years ago can help unveil again for us the shocking mercy of the cross.

The Last Miracle

What did you, could you think
as they pounded through your open palms
forcing coarse, bloody iron nails
to sink deep into the splintered wood?
Did you feel the grasp of panic,
that sudden, stomach-wrenching sense
that this, at the very last, is it,
no further chance of changing, turning back?

Were you, perhaps, bewildered,
having hoped, despite defiant words,
for at least one late and minor miracle
on your own behalf, considering all the rest?

Did flooding fear compound with rage and hate
at the sheer blind brutality of soldiers,
fellow sons of God, treating you
like meat to be hung raw in a butcher's window?

Or dare we yet believe what was written,
that your concern was, even at the end, to shield,
to plead the cause of all who wield the whips
and crushing hammers of this crucifying world?

Prayer: *Lead me to the cross, Lord; then point me to the skies. Amen.*

April 15 (Holy Saturday)

Read John 19:38-42.

Everything hangs in the balance today—Holy Saturday. The powers of death have done their worst, powers that can seem all too familiar when I look at my own life, when I look at this modern world I inhabit.

The powers of life and of goodness, even in the face of all the cruelty of the cross, have also been evident in a series of gestures, marginal and minimal at best, yet there just the same. There is, after all, the penitent thief; the astonished centurion; the faithful, weeping witness of the three Marys by the cross and of John; the cautious, conservative, yet continuing discipleship of Joseph of Arimathea and Nicodemus, who seek to care for the Lord's broken body with a tender and generous reverence.

Now the world, the entire cosmos—angels to atoms—pauses, waits, and wonders, holding its collective breath. Will this be the final straw, the ultimate offense that breaks the back of even the Divine compassion and mercy? Will the Creator tell this world to literally "Go to hell" and abandon it for some other place, some other time?

We already know the answer, of course. We have heard the tale before and can anticipate the resolution of the plot. Or can we? Is there not a sense in which, in every moment, the universe itself exists solely by the grace and mercy, the forbearance of a God whose compassion is beyond all human comprehension, whose enduring love is the miracle by which and within which everything exists? Is there not a sense in which, even today, we should be holding our breath . . . and waiting?

Prayer: *Wait with me, Lord Christ; and in my waiting turn me toward the dawn. Amen.*

117

April 16 (Easter)

Read John 20:1-18.

There is a shocking quality to Easter which, if we sacrifice, we do so at peril. Twenty centuries of tradition, the telling and retelling of the narratives, their depiction in every form of art from catacomb painting to docudrama, and the natural impulse to smooth ragged edges—all have conspired to neutralize the enormity of what took place. It may be impossible today fully to know the scandal of the cross, the absurdity of the empty tomb, the sheer unlikelihood of all this being a revelation of the Divine.

Yet revelation is the core—the revelation of the grace-tendering, universally powerful and finally invincible Love that God is. Revelation takes place in every event of this week—the ironic Palm Sunday parade, the cleansing of commerce from the Temple, debates about authority with the authorities, the elegiac moments of the Last Supper, Gethsemane and the trials, Golgotha's holy terror, and the glorious garden tomb. In everything that happens, Jesus is opening a window into the Almighty and disclosing a heart that seeks to gather in all humankind to one reconciled and reconciling family.

As we have moved through the scenes of Holy Week, it is my prayer that, beneath the wonder of tradition and rich memory, we have experienced the shattering, yet mending reality that is God's passionate love for us, love that was formed around donkeys and debates; around betrayal, bread and wine; around wood and nails; around tears and anguish and final, utter astonishment, so that we, too, might be pierced, wounded, and made whole forever.

Prayer: *Astonish me, Lord, with the reality of an empty grave, a stone rolled away, a world that is reborn into eternity. Amen.*

GOD IS OUR PRIORITY

April 17-23, 1995   **William R. Cannon**✤
Monday, April 17   Read Acts 5:27-29.

God should be without a competitor in the life of a Christian. The Divine Being has prior claim to everybody and everything for those who believe and trust in God and accept Jesus Christ as their Lord and Savior.

The apostles demonstrated the truth of God's priority in their lives when they were brought before the council. The high priest demanded of them why they had filled Jerusalem with their doctrines about Jesus against the high priest's orders not to teach in Jesus' name. Their answer, spoken by Peter, was, "We must obey God rather than any human authority."

How strange that this human authority alluded to by Peter was the Temple and its priesthood. Even today, and more often than we would like to think, organized religion, institutionalized Christianity, precludes obedience to God, whom it is designed to serve, and stymies God's voice in the mouths of those called to proclaim it.

The priests said, "You are determined to bring this man's blood on us." Even now we, like them, are often concerned more for our reputation than for truth. Only when we give God priority in everything can we live satisfying and victorious lives in God's world and serve God's people.

Prayer: *God, displace our control over our life with thine own. Amen.*

✤A bishop of The United Methodist Church, retired; lecturer in Methodist theology and history, Candler School of Theology, Emory University, Atlanta, Georgia.

119

Tuesday, April 18   Read Acts 5:30-32.

We are schocked by those in religious authority who claim the things of the Spirit but contradict what they profess by their behavior. So it was with the religious leaders of Jesus' day. The apostles responded in indignation to the high priest: "The God of our ancestors raised up Jesus, whom you had killed by hanging him on a tree."

We, too, must cry out in righteous indignation when religious leaders fail to live up to the high standard of God's call. Over the past few years several very public religious leaders have fallen short of the high moral standard required of them. There are, unfortunately, other unpublicized incidents. I remember once when I was on the faculty at Emory, as I was dictating a letter to a district superintendent, the student taking my dictation broke into tears. I asked him what upset him. He said, "That man was my district superintendent. When I was away, he would come to my parsonage and commit adultery with my wife. I could not do anything about it without ruining my wife, and I still love her."

Jesus alone can bring us to repentance and forgive us our sins, thus renewing us for whatever calling God has for us; the One whom his own people condemned to death as a criminal proved their only hope for salvation.

An apostle was a person who had shared with Jesus his mission on earth and who was a witness to our Lord's resurrection (Acts 1:22). We have by God's grace inherited that mission. The glory of Christian living is to witness to the Resurrection, being examples of Christ's life, attitudes, compassion, and deeds. By doing so, we demonstrate that Christ is alive in us and that we share in the work of the Holy Spirit.

Prayer: *O God, help us to love others as you love us. Amen.*

Wednesday, April 19   Read Psalm 150.

This is the last psalm in the Hebrew psalter. Many if not most of the psalms are petitions, beseeching God for help in trouble, asking deliverance from enemies, crying out for mercy, and praying for victory over sin and death. But there is not a single petition in this psalm. The psalmist does not ask God for anything. From beginning to end this is a paean of praise.

The Hebrew scriptures divide the Book of Psalms into five parts. The first three end with "Amen and Amen," the fourth with "Amen, Hallelujah," and the last with only "Hallelujah." The last six psalms are hymns of praise, this one being the climax of the lot and the glorious closing note of the psalmody of Israel. This psalm has only six short verses, and "Praise the Lord" occurs in them thirteen times.

We are to give praise for God's surpassing greatness. We worship God, who is great and good enough to satisfy all our needs.

This praise begins in the sanctuary. The instruments mentioned in this psalm are instruments usually played in the Temple by the Levites. So it was for them a description of their calling to praise God. God's praise starts in churches. It is the privilege of Christians to declare their thankfulness. The church exists to glorify God, whose majesty is revealed in the firmament and all the created order. What the church declares all nature echoes.

How are we to praise God? That the psalm lists all the musical instruments of Israel means we are to praise God in every way we know how. And this is the obligation and privilege not just of religious leaders but of everybody everywhere. "Let everything that breathes praise the LORD!"

Prayer: *Praise belongs to thee, O God. Amen.*

Thursday, April 20   Read Psalm 150.

In school we learned the answer to the first question of the catechism: Our chief end in life is "to glorify God and enjoy him forever." This is the assumption on which worship rests. God expects our worship.

Those who call themselves Deists ask the question, "Why should God expect our worship?" God is, after all, perfect and needs nothing from the outside. To demand that we bow down, laud and praise God's name, and do everything we can think of to please God would be the height of selfishness and conceit on God's part. And it would distract us from doing more constructive things. While we are wasting time in church, we could be out in society serving people in need and doing all in our power to assure equal opportunity and happiness to all God's people. So goes the thinking of the Deist, one who adheres to the philosophy that God creates us and then leaves us to fend for ourselves. Our duty, they believe, is not to praise God but to promote the common good.

But how can we promote the common good unless we know what the common good is? Certainly it ought to include more than full stomachs, well-clothed bodies, and existence surfeited with pleasure and self-indulgence. Are there not reaches of the mind and depths of the heart and a restless spirit that cannot find solace apart from God?

Out of an attitude of worship we learn to listen to God, so that we may come to discern the common good and receive the power to achieve it.

Prayer: *O God, only in loving thee can we love others. Amen.*

Friday, April 21   Read Revelation 1:4-8.

This passage of scripture forms the introduction to the apostle John's Letters to the Seven Churches of Asia. He writes a letter, distinct and different, to each church, both commending and criticizing it, pointing out its virtues and its faults. The introduction is applicable equally to all, for it is an apostolic benediction. The Book of the Revelation opens and ends with a benediction.

John refers to God as One "who is and who was and who is to come." He speaks of God in the present before the past, emphasizing thereby that we must honor God through our own experience before we can appreciate what we have been taught about him out of the past. Likewise, it is our life with him now that makes us anticipate life with him in the future.

He speaks of the seven spirits, implying one spirit for each of the seven churches. By this we know that the Spirit of God adjusts to each community and each person according to his/her unique nature and special needs.

Jesus Christ is declared to be "the faithful witness, the firstborn of the dead, and the ruler of the kings of the earth." His love for us is so great that he has freed us from our sins by his blood and made us royal priests of God through our loyal service.

This benediction (vv. 4-6) reflects the work of Christ, who redeems us by God's undeserved mercy (grace) and grants us peace through confidence in the good works God enables us daily to perform in behalf of others.

Prayer: *O God, we adore thee for who thou art and for what thou hast done for us. Amen.*

Saturday, April 22   Read John 20:19-23.

Jesus had already appeared to several people individually on the day of his resurrection: to Mary Magdalene, to Peter and John, and to two of his followers on their way to Emmaus. But this is the first time he appears to the disciples as a group, the nucleus of the emerging church. The church would rise out of the disciples' unified witness to Christ's resurrection.

Immediately we are faced with a dichotomy. Jesus enters the room in spite of locked doors. He surprises the group by standing in their midst. His body is no longer a hindrance to him. Nothing can exclude from the disciples the presence of their risen Lord. And yet the ugly wounds of his death are apparent. They see his nail-pierced hands and the gash in his side. Here, within Jesus' presence, is the reality of his humanity and the reality of his divine, spiritual nature—death and resurrection abiding simultaneously in his being. Both realities are visible—and available—to the disciples, even in the midst of their surprise and astonishment.

Jesus in this nocturnal meeting gives his disciples their commission. As the Father sent him to them, so he sends them to carry on his mission in the world. He breathes on them, and his breath is the Holy Spirit entering their lives. He assigns them their mission and with it the power of its fulfillment.

What Jesus did then for his original disciples he still does now. He gives us our work to do and the power through the Holy Spirit for its accomplishment.

Prayer: *Come, Holy Spirit, make us thine that we may win others to Christ! Amen.*

Sunday, April 23   Read John 20:24-31.

Thomas was not present when the risen Lord appeared to the other disciples on the night of Easter, so he did not have proof as the others did of Jesus' resurrection. The only thing that would convince him would be to put his finger in Jesus' nail-pierced hands and to thrust his own hand into the open wound in his side. He demanded proof of his Master's resurrection.

One week later Jesus gave him that proof. As a result of what he saw, Thomas exclaimed in awe and wonder those words which constitute one of the earliest, most beautiful, and most enduring confessions of Christianity. Thomas's disbelief was shattered, and he cried out in affirmation, "My Lord and my God!"

All of us are in the same situation as Thomas prior to his personal encounter with Jesus after the resurrection. We are dependent upon the disciples' reports, now nearly two thousand years old, that they had seen and talked with the risen Jesus. But there is this radical difference between Thomas and us: Thomas was able personally to verify the reports, while we are not. Jesus anticipated our situation when he said, "Have you believed me because you have seen me? Blessed are those who have not seen and yet have come to believe."

Proof for us lies in what happens to us when we do believe. We do not see and talk with the risen Christ in the same way Thomas and the other disciples did. Our companionship with him is even more immediate, for he lives with us daily and makes his dwelling in our hearts. We feel the intensity of his love and receive the guidance of his spirit.

Prayer: *Lord Jesus, come and live with us here that we may live with thee hereafter forever. Amen.*

NOW THAT EASTER IS OVER

April 24-30, 1995 **Linda Johnson**✤
Monday, April 24 Read Acts 9:1-15.

Once the fiercest of enemies of Christianity, Paul becomes one of its mightiest evangelists. Once responsible for the murder of Christians, now he is being called to help give birth to the church. Encounter with the risen Christ resulted in a drastic change in Paul. He turned completely around and went in a new direction.

Most people resist change. We don't usually change in any significant way until we are forced to do so. Strangely, that's true even when the change would be for the good. How hard it is to go on a diet, stop smoking, begin an exercise program, do disciplined Bible study or daily devotions, get involved in work with the poor, tithe, or whatever it is we're always planning to start doing but can't seem to get around to at the moment.

Did Easter happen for you this year? Sometimes Easter happens in a dramatic way, and we feel the Resurrection power as it makes a real difference in our life. And sometimes Easter doesn't happen for us. Sometimes we're just glad it's over and we can get back to life as usual. But Easter is not "over 'til it's over"! As the risen Christ appeared again after the Resurrection, so the risen Christ works among us still. Our turnaround might not be as dramatic as Paul's We might turn more gradually.

What is important in this season of Easter is that we remain open to God's life-changing power.

Prayer: *God of power and might, call me by name and give me the faith to hear and respond, even if it means I will be changed. Amen.*

✤United Methodist clergy currently on leave of absence; member of the Tennessee Annual Conference; mother of two daughters; Nashville, Tennessee.

Tuesday, April 25   Read Acts 9:15-20.

Where did we ever get the idea that discipleship would be easy? Maybe from those pictures we were shown in Sunday school as children. The ones of the "typical" United States family on their way to church. There was a mother and father, a son and daughter, all clean and nicely dressed, looking healthy and happy. The truth is, that is not now, and maybe never was, a "typical" picture of Christianity. Somehow the idea has been promoted that Christian faith results in prosperity and success. Christianity has been co-opted to fit in with the American dream.

We certainly did not get the idea from Paul. In the account of his conversion and call we read that he will suffer for Jesus' sake. And later we even read details of his sufferings.

For some people the cost of discipleship may mean giving up a comfortable living and going to seminary when they are middle-aged. For others it may mean the willingness to sit in church next to a person whose clothes and hair are unkempt and whose odor is offensive. For some it may mean moving to a strange place and an unknown way of life. For others it may mean spending the night in a shelter for people who are homeless or serving food in a soup kitchen. For some it may mean continuous care for a seriously ill or handicapped family member. For others it may mean giving up one's own dreams to follow a Christ-led future.

Easter Sunday may indeed be a lovely day of flowers and hymns and celebration. But the response to Easter may not be so pretty. Responding to Easter means service in the name of the Risen One, and that service most surely will challenge our comfort.

Prayer: *God of resurrection power, make me equal to the task you set before me. Amen.*

Wednesday, April 26   Read Psalm 30.

A person may not appreciate a friendship until the friend moves away. A parent may fail to realize the importance of children until he or she loses them through neglect. Parents suddenly realize they were too busy to really enjoy their children's childhood, and now they've left home. We think we will never stop appreciating the breathtaking beauty of the first green of summer, but by August we are taking it for granted. Being able to drive a car means little, until they say you're too old to do it safely anymore. Simple things like walking and reading are easily taken for granted until they are lost due to illness.

The psalmist here tells us something about what God is like and something about what we are like. Today let's consider the lesson about ourselves. The writer is singing a song of praise and thanksgiving to God for healing from an infirmity. Before becoming ill, however, the psalmist, secure in health and prosperity, felt no need for God: "I said in my prosperity, 'I shall never be moved.'"

When things are going our way we tend to think they always will. And perhaps we think life is good because, we reason, in some way we have earned or deserve the good life. We do like to take the credit for our success. We are reluctant to acknowledge our dependency on God or to acknowledge that people are necessarily interdependent. We in the United States especially have inherited an attitude of rugged individualism.

But, implies the psalmist, don't take God for granted as I did. Don't wait until illness or loss strike to realize what is really important.

Suggestion for meditation: *What is really important to you? Do you give priority to the things you consider most important? Does your life reflect what you value most?*

128

Thursday, April 27   Read Psalm 30.

In its poetry, this psalm speaks of human suffering, healing, thanksgiving, and praise. In the process the psalmist tells us something of what God is like.

Someone has suffered from a very serious illness. To describe the misery, the psalmist likens it to being in Sheol or the Pit, meaning, in the realm of the dead.

There are many experiences in life that feel like being in the realm of the dead. There are times when we seem to be moving more towards death than towards life. The power of death is anything that blocks our growth and development. It is being stuck, held down, having our breath knocked out of us. Or, as one of my favorite people used to say, "It's like getting stuck in Good Friday and never moving on to Easter morning."

The psalmist gives thanks to God for rescue and deliverance from the realm of the dead, for restoration to life. In praise, the psalmist tells us what God chooses for us—life. God's anger is brief; God's favor forever. Weeping is part of life, but joy comes in God's morning. God's will for us is not mourning and sorrow. God would clothe us in garments of joy and rejoicing. God invites us to take off that sackcloth and move onto the dance floor.

God is with us when we feel like we are living in the realm of death. God is with us even in death. Yet God is still the God of life. The psalmist tells us and the Resurrection shows us that God prefers life.

Suggestion for prayer: *Pray for those you know who are living in the realm of death—whether through illness, sorrow, addiction, unemployment, grief, disappointment, fear, or hopelessness. Pray for their mourning to be turned into dancing.*

Friday, April 28   Read John 21:1-14.

Now what? the disciples must be asking themselves. Perhaps bewildered by all that had happened to them since they had first been called to follow this man Jesus, some of the disciples have gathered by the Sea of Tiberias. Peter decides to go fishing.

Is he going back to his former profession? Back to life as it was before? Is he doing something ordinary and familiar to stabilize against the chaos of extraordinary happenings? When life gets too overwhelming to handle, hanging a sign on the door, saying, "Gone Fishin'" is not a bad way to revitalize one's coping equipment. But back to life as it was? No way! Not after knowing Jesus. Not after a crucifixion and a resurrection.

How have the disciples responded to Jesus' resurrection? From the little we're told in scripture, they have not shown signs of responding at all beyond amazement. And joy. When Peter realizes the man on the beach is Jesus, he jumps into the sea and splashes to the shore.

And what happens in this post-resurrection appearance? Jesus cooks and serves breakfast. Almost as amazing as the Resurrection itself is this picture of Jesus, the Messiah, the Son of God, recently crucified and newly raised from the dead, cooking and serving up breakfast. He feeds and nurtures his weary disciples.

What should we be doing in this post-Easter season? Later Jesus will tell us, but now he shows us.

Prayer: *God of resurrection power, I give you thanks that in simple acts of kindness and nurture I am imitating our risen Lord. Amen.*

Saturday, April 29   Read John 21:15-19.

What I like about Peter is that he made mistakes, big ones, but he kept on trying to get it right. In this passage, Jesus is giving him yet another chance.

Three times Jesus asks Peter if he loves him. Peter quickly assures Jesus that, of course, he loves him. How could Jesus doubt it? The scripture says that Peter felt hurt after Jesus asked him the same question for the third time. Has Peter already forgotten how he denied even knowing Jesus three times? In asking his question three times, is Jesus somehow trying to cancel the denials and restore Peter back to rock status?

After each of Peter's responses Jesus says: "Feed my lambs"; "Tend my Sheep"; "Feed my sheep." If you love me, Peter, show it this time. Show it in what you do, where you go, how you act, how you live your life. If you love me, act like it. Follow me. Feed others as I just fed you. Serve others as I have served. If you want to know whom to feed, think about the people I tended tenderly. If you wonder how people should be treated, remember how I treated them. If you love me, feed and tend the people I love, the people I came to serve and to save.

What should we be doing after Easter, after the strains of the "Hallelujah Chorus" are beginning to fade and the new clothes don't seem so new anymore? We may not understand the full theological implications of the resurrection, but at the end of John's account of it, Jesus makes our response to it painfully clear. If we love him. . . .

Prayer: *Merciful God, give me the vision to see how I can follow Jesus. Give me the courage to serve him faithfully, for I do love him. Amen.*

Sunday, April 30
Read Revelation 5:11-14.
(Revelation 4 for context.)

What splendor and majesty are portrayed in this first vision recorded by John. It is a feast to the eyes with precious jewels and golden crowns, and to the ears with rumbling thunder and a mighty chorus singing. All of creation joins the choir.

I have experienced moments of worship that offered, perhaps, a glimpse of such divine worship. To the sounds of a pipe organ I have sung with a large congregation, giving themselves fully to "The Hallelujah Chorus." What a thrilling experience!

My first powerful experiences of Easter worship occurred in a small rural church where I (a youth unable to carry a tune) was allowed to sing in the choir. They just put me by Ivanell, who covered up my mistakes, her magnificent voice lifting my weak one. Easter meant standing outside the church, waiting to process down the aisle with a lily in my hymnal. It was a feast to my eyes: the signs of new life at early spring, the loving faces of my church community. It was a feast to my ears as we sang the songs of Resurrection. The power of Easter became real for me in being given a place within a loving community.

John's vision contains elaborate riches as a way of symbolizing the honor and glory given to Christ. But we must not be blinded by these riches and miss the central symbol of the slaughtered lamb. The Lamb of God, rejected, betrayed, and cruelly crucified, is now victorious; love has conquered sin and death.

The setting and structure for worship are not important. What is important is that we worship in a community where God's love is celebrated and made real.

Suggestion for meditation and prayer: *Consider your weekly worship experience. Where are there signs of loving community? Pray that you may be a witness to that community for someone in its midst.*

PEOPLE OF THE LAMB

May 1-7, 1995   **William H. Willimon**♣
Monday, May 1   Read Acts 9:36-43;
Revelation 7:17.

At Joppa there is a woman, Tabitha (Dorcas)—the only woman in the entire New Testament to merit the feminine form of the word *disciple*. Her discipleship is in her "good works and acts of charity." Tabitha becomes ill and dies. When Peter arrives, he is greeted by the weeping widows who show him the clothing that Tabitha has made for them. With no one now to see to their needs, what will happen to them? Tabitha, their protector, is dead; now these widows are as good as dead.

Surprise! Death will not have the final word. Peter's, "Tabitha, get up" reminds us of Jairus's daughter (Luke 8:49-56) and also of the way Jesus called dead Lazarus from the tomb (John 11:43-44). Jesus' disciples have the same power over death which Jesus had. Into regions of death where people grieve, a word of life is spoken. If you thought Easter happened only once, think again. The Easter commotion continues.

Where in your life are things fixed, closed, settled, and dead? Take heed! When life-giving gospel words are spoken, the dead rise, the future is open, and everything makes way for Easter.

In the Revelation, John dreams of that day when the Lamb, the once crucified but now risen Savior, will lead all those once hungry, thirsting people to "springs of the water of life." Here, as Tabitha rises to life, we see that the Lamb's day has come. Death, in whatever forms it presents itself, is defeated.

Prayer: *Lord, call me this day from defeat and death to life. Amen.*

♣United Methodist clergy; Dean of the Chapel, Duke University, Durham, North Carolina.

133

Tuesday, May 2   Read Revelation 7:9-17.

"A great multitude"

There were fewer in church last Sunday than a few Sundays ago. We had a crowd on Easter; we had to bring in extra chairs. But that was Easter, and this is four Sundays after Easter, and the crowd dwindles. The weather is warm, so there are trips to the lake, to the mountains, to places other than church; and the Easter throng gradually diminishes to the faithful few.

My denomination has lost nearly two million members in the past thirty years. Being Christian no longer appears to be the accepted, typically North American thing to do. Other loyalties claim allegiance, and the 1950s' multitudes become the 1990s' minority.

Imagine how it felt at Patmos for John, a member of a still-small movement in a great empire. At Patmos, John is given a vision. The curtain is raised upon the future; the last act of the play is revealed. Imagine his astonishment to see that, in the end, when the story is finally told and Christ's work is done, "there was a great multitude that no one could count, from every nation, from all tribes and peoples and languages, standing before the throne and before the Lamb."

My congregation, be they few or many this past Sunday, is not the whole church. More is going on in God's kingdom than that which takes place in the late twentieth-century U.S.A. Take heart. We are not the only hope for the ultimate triumph of the Lamb. You and I march in a grand processional with the saints of all times and places, all tribes and cultures, toward the throne.

Take heart. We do not walk the path of discipleship alone. The people of the Lamb, a great multitude, walk with us.

Prayer: *O Lamb of God, encourage us in our struggles to be faithful to your way. Amen.*

Wednesday, May 3 Read Revelation 7:9-12.

"Salvation belongs to the Lamb"

Peering at me through the bars of his prison cell, a frightened young man greeted me with "Hey, preacher! What's the good news?"

What *is* the good news for a young man at nineteen, condemned to death for taking the life of another? Here in this dark place of death and despair, what is the good news?

For the child dying of cancer in the hospital, the couple facing the end of their marriage, the man now two years out of work, the teenager on Death Row, what is the good news? What dare we say in the face of such omnivorous death?

Read Revelation 7:9-17. In the end, says this grand vision of heaven, in the end, the Lamb, the Lamb who knows what it's like to suffer, to be condemned to death, to be slain and humiliated, the Lamb once crucified, now sits upon the throne. The Lamb, once pushed aside by the ways of a cruel world, that Lamb now rules from the very center of heaven. All "blessing and glory and wisdom and . . . honor and power and might" belong to the Lamb.

Therefore, we do have good news. We can say to those who suffer, to those who find themselves in the grip of death, "Salvation belongs to our God . . . and to the Lamb." All honor, glory, power—everything that God has—the Lamb has, the Lamb who knows what it is like to suffer because he has been there, the Lamb who knows what it is like to die because he has been there. This Lamb now rules in power.

That's the good news.

Prayer: *O Lord, Lamb of God, help us to show forth your life-giving power over heaven and earth in all that we do and say this day. Amen.*

Thursday, May 4   Read Revelation 7:13-14.

"Who are these?"

I spent this time last year on a medical mission team in Honduras, the second most impoverished country in the Western Hemisphere. I think of those whom we met there. Christians in Honduras are working against great odds to alleviate some of the suffering of people. There is not enough food, little medical care, and much pain, but also much good work among the poor.

Why is there so much suffering? Hunger and thirst, brief, temporary experiences for me, are the stuff of everyday life for countless millions.

"When I see suffering like this, particularly among the children," said one of our mission team members, "I become angry with God." Why, if God is good, is there such heartache and pain?

The vision given to John in Revelation is not the answer to such an awesome question. Yet it is an answer. When the curtain is lifted in heaven and the end toward which all creation is moving is revealed and the Lamb begins to reign in power and glory, note toward whom the Lamb moves. Not toward the self-satisfied, the well-heeled, and the well-fed. The Lamb declares that those who have been hungry, who had little but tears to drink, shall hunger and thirst no more. No longer offered the false comfort of the broken promises of the rich or the cheap consolations of the superficially pious, now "God will wipe away every tear from their eyes."

Who are these before the throne, these singled out for special care by the Lamb?

Prayer: *Lamb of God, who takest away the sin of the world, forgive us our sins of indifference to the plight of the poor. Amen.*

Friday, May 5   Read Revelation 7:17.

"The Lamb will be . . . their shepherd"

Something occurs toward the end of this week's passage from Revelation, something which, according to our teachers of writing, ought never to occur. A metaphor is mixed; an image is confused. Revelation has spoken of the Lamb, the once-bloodied, slain Lamb who now rules upon heaven's throne. The Lamb who once suffered so terribly is now the One who reigns mightily. All those who have suffered in behalf of the Lamb now stand before the throne of the Lamb and receive the Lamb's royal blessing.

But then Revelation says, "The Lamb at the center of the throne will be their shepherd, and he will guide them to springs of the water of life . . . will wipe away every tear from their eyes." See the curious mix of metaphor? How can the Lamb also be the shepherd who guides the sheep? Sometimes a good metaphor must step aside and give way to good tidings.

The Lamb, the Lamb who knows what it is like to suffer, the Lamb who hung helplessly upon the cross, the victim of horrible evil, has now been wondrously transformed into the wise shepherd who guides the sheep. Who better to guide suffering sheep than one who knows what it is like to suffer?

The shepherd who leads us toward "springs of the water of life" is no aloof, uncaring, inexperienced master. The shepherd has stood beside us, lived, suffered, and died with us so that he might now lead us.

"All I can do these long nights," my parishioner said in her misery, "is pray to Jesus. Just pray to Jesus. At least he knows what I'm going through. He's the only one who can lead me out."

Prayer: *Lamb of God, be our shepherd. Guide us this day toward that place to which only you know the way. Amen.*

137

Saturday, May 6   Read Psalm 23.

"The LORD is my shepherd"

It's Saturday, a good day to go to my local "do-it-yourself" hardware store and buy needed materials for fixing up this and that around the house. Doing it the "American" way—by myself. We like to describe ourselves as self-made men and women. We take pride in what we've achieved for ourselves.

Many of us approach the Lord in the same way. The Lord is the one who gives us the encouragement or the insight or whatever we need to "do it ourselves," spiritually speaking. We are basically competent, able, powerful people who have responsibility for ourselves. Please, Lord, I would rather do it myself.

Which makes all the more amazing that our favorite psalm is this one, Psalm 23. Here, there is no self-help, pull-yourself-up-by-your-bootstraps theology. Here, the Shepherd, the loving Shepherd, does it all. The verbs all point to loving actions by the Shepherd. The Shepherd makes, leads, restores, prepares, anoints, follows. We are the passive sheep, dependent upon the initiative and the care of the active Shepherd.

Psalm 23 is, therefore, the one we remember from our childhood. In the days of our childhood, when the world was confusing and we felt small and vulnerable, we learned this psalm by heart. As a pastor I've noted that when a person's life is drawing to a close, Psalm 23 is the last scripture most can remember, the gentle Shepherd leading us through even the darkest valley.

In this psalm, even we allegedly strong, assertive, self-confident ones learn to pray a better prayer:

Prayer: *Please, Lord, do for me what I can't do for myself. Amen.*

Sunday, May 7   Read John 10:22-30.

"My sheep hear my voice"

It's Sunday, the day for church, for worship.

Sometimes as a pastor, when I'm looking out over a congregation, I have been known to ask myself, *Why are they here? What has brought them here to church?*

I can think of reasons why they might not be here. May mornings are warm, and the beach or the lake or even the backyard are tempting places to spend a Sunday.

Why are they here? Some come out of a deeply felt awareness of need; others come out of an only dimly sensed awareness. There have been disappointments, failures, setbacks. They come to church seeking comfort or a reassuring word.

Yet the local golf course offers fellowship, and a walk in the woods may be more therapeutic. Aches and pains, heartaches and woes are assuaged in a myriad of ways other than in church. Who says that church will make them feel better? Sometimes, after going to church and being confronted by a different perspective, an unsought bit of honesty, I go home feeling worse!

Why are they here? The most basic answer, when one has rummaged about in all of the possible reasons for being or not being here, is this—*we have been called.* Each of us, in our own way, has heard our name, has been summoned forth to worship God.

Again I must be reminded as pastor, as a shepherd of the Shepherd's sheep, that they are here because they have been called. All true church begins in this: "My sheep hear my voice," says Jesus. "I know them, and they follow me."

Prayer: *This day in worship, Lord, help us to listen for your claim upon our lives and, in hearing, help us to follow. Amen.*

LIVING WITH GOD IN LARGER BOUNDARIES

May 8-14, 1995   **Ron Mills**✤
Monday, May 8   Read Acts 11:1-3.

Jewish Christians resisted the first wave of Gentile Christians surging into the early church. Covenant people struggled to interpret this new attitude toward persons with whom they were formerly forbidden to associate. The new folks ate differently, dressed differently, acted differently. Unexpected guests were spoiling Jerusalem's salvation party.

Why do we so often feel threatened by those who do not share the same experiences, traditions, or stories that shape our lives? The awareness that God welcomes those who are "not like us" calls into question what makes us *us*. We grow accustomed to thinking of ourselves, our fellowship, our spiritual journey in a certain way. Newcomers trouble us.

Perhaps our desire for certainty in our relationship with God causes our suspicion toward new arrivals in the church family. The spirit of God, however, dismantles our misbegotten attempts to secure a faith by fencing in ourselves and our faith community. God continually reveals the larger boundaries of grace. The divine spirit perpetually falls on a vast diversity of human lives, even as they approach the borders of life with God within a faith community. To welcome them leads us toward greater understanding of God's will for all humanity.

Prayer: *Save us, O Lord, from a salvation too small, a fellowship too exclusive, a grace enjoyed but not offered. Amen.*

✤Lives and writes in Patrick Springs, Virginia, and takes part as pastor in the ministry of the congregation of Providence United Methodist Church.

Tuesday, May 9   Read Acts 11:4-18.

"The Holy Spirit fell upon them just as it had upon us at the beginning," Peter says to those who stood behind self-erected, exclusive religious barriers. His accusers are skeptical that God has acted in the lives of new Gentile Christians. Peter describes his vision and his experience in Caesarea. It becomes evident to his hearers that God stands behind this venture. Peter challenges his accusers to use their own experience of God to validate the Gentiles' experience. He thrusts his questioners upon the bedrock of their salvation claims: salvation comes as a gift received through faith in Jesus of Nazareth. Distinctions collapse among those who have received new life in the Spirit as a gift from God.

We are part of a countless multitude of persons whose life with God has been justified by grace and received through faith. Being recipients of divine grace creates in our hearts a hospitality that welcomes others, even strangers.

In fact, one of the New Testament Greek words translated *hospitality* literally means "love of stranger." The spirit of God reminds us that we were once strangers and aliens loved by God in Christ. Because of who Jesus is, "strangers" are invited to come into the welcome of God's grace-based love. Peter's insight into a life with God that opens out to all persons helps us, like the reticent Jewish Christians, to enlarge the boundaries of our life with God and make room for others, even as God made room for us.

Prayer: *O Lord, give us such a keen sense of your unmerited favor toward us that we disassemble the barriers we have erected and so welcome others into our life with you. Amen.*

Wednesday, May 10   Read John 13:31-33.

Judas put into motion the instruments of Jesus' death. Jesus understands his betrayer's action to be part of the procession of glory. Knowing the end imminent, Jesus lifts his head saying, "Now the Son of Man has been glorified." *Now*—not when he changed the water into wine or fed the thousands by the sea. Not when he restored sight to the blind or gave the lame new strength. Not when he walked on water or cast out demons. But *now*, in the moment when death moves toward him—a moment which carries more of the notion of defeat than the aura of victory—Jesus pries loose this self-descriptive word *glory* from his heart.

Again we encounter the familiar tension of an expression of glory in the shadow of the cross. Jesus gazes toward the approaching darkness with utter confidence that his presence and his mission will continue. Resurrection! He sees the same divine activity that characterizes his life moving beyond the boundaries of his physical existence. After all actions have been taken and all other futures dismantled, God works in a new way. Glory!

In our believing, we continue to come to the end of ourselves and the beginning of God's new work. As we take up the way of Jesus, our lives merge into our Lord's movement from agony to glory, from death to resurrection. A difficult, cross-shadowed trust gives way to empty-tombed confidence in God to bring to completion what God has started in our lives.

Prayer: *Lord, help us to see glory beyond the dark boundaries that cover tomorrow, confident that when we can go no further, you continue to work. Amen.*

Thursday, May 11   Read John 13:34-35.

The disciples did not fully recognize God's glory moving in their midst in the person of Jesus of Nazareth. We human beings rarely recognize such moments. Instead, we are left with traces of the divine presence, earthly residues of glory to ponder in our hearts. Jesus gives his disciples such a trace when he speaks to them of a new commandment. "The world will know about me through the presence of my love in your lives" (AP).

In a society whose commerce thrives on the aggressive marketing of ego to an insatiable appetite for self-pleasure, the presence of a group of people who live quietly against the grain of selfishness makes an impact. Anyone can dress themselves in Sunday clothes and frequent a church. The world peers cynically, though, at religious faith easily worn and talked. Selfless actions on behalf of others, however, wield potent testimony to the resurrection of Jesus. Love, as Jesus speaks it, involves actions, actions that create the possibility that someone will experience more of life and its goodness because of our concern. The possibility of this kind of love becoming real in all disciples' lives lies not so much in the commandment of Jesus to love as it does in the reality that we have been loved by him in precisely that way.

Persons who find their lives bogged down in the debris of self-centeredness may grow interested in the movements of an unselfish people who live and act so that others may experience life at its best. In hopeful curiosity, some persons may ask, "What must I do to be saved?"

Prayer: *Jesus, may all who watch my daily movements read in them the presence of your love in my life. Amen.*

Friday, May 12   Read Revelation 21:1-2.

God's church has made room for Gentiles. Early congregations expand in number. The disciples of Jesus manage to love one another in world-changing ways. The integrity of Christian professions of faith attract attention. Unfortunately, not all attention benefits the early church. As John writes his letter, God's people strain their ears from the threatening arena of persecution to hear a word of hope.

Sometimes the suffering in our lives grows so intense and so painful that uncertainty about tomorrow threatens our trust in God. John's vision orients suffering Christians toward the larger boundaries of the kingdom of God. For God's people in every age, experiences of the harshness of evil and the terror of death discourage hope-filled faith. An alternative to despair does exist, however. God offers the faithful a glimpse of a new reality: a new heaven, a new earth, a new location for living with God. Through John's vision, we are invited to look beyond what we are experiencing presently and to glimpse the outcome of faithfulness. This vision has the power to redefine suffering places and to sustain hope.

In Genesis we read of God's powerful word, present in the chaos, speaking a world into being. Now, that same powerful, creative word speaks our lives beyond cruel circumstances and senseless sufferings into a trustworthy future. John's vision allows us to embrace joy and pain, supported in the daily movements of faithfulness by a confident vision of the vast boundaries of God's presence.

Prayer: *I lift up my eyes to look for you, O God. Fill me with the confidence that your reign includes tomorrow. Amen.*

Saturday, May 13   Read Revelation 21:3-6.

This passage is read at many funeral services because of the hopefulness it offers to those engulfed in sorrow. The grave utters its painful end to valued relationships. Sometimes the gray tone of mourning shatters any sense of God's trustworthiness to sustain a future for us. Suffering and death become yet another boundary, shrinking our movements in hopefulness and limiting us to a confining existence of fear.

Situations of suffering and death will continue to inhabit the same realm as joy and life. The persecutions of early Christians under Roman despots did not change as a result of John's vision in Revelation. Instead, the word of God uttered there enabled suffering ones to encounter the presence of God even with tears in their eyes. The promise of God rightly heard creates optimism even in dire circumstances. Christians are persons who, no matter what circumstances they are in, can still live, sustained by the power of the promise of God's nearness.

Some situations we face wield a power that can impede, or even halt, the daily steps of our spiritual journey. Which one of us—when in terrible pain, in anguish over the illness of a loved one, in grief for the death of a good friend, in sorrow over a lost job —has not wished to run away. The words of this passage do not invite us to embrace an escapist attitude toward the genuinely painful places in our lives. No, in the words of John, we discover that when pain and suffering restrict our vision and dismantle our hope, God still works on our behalf. God's promise to us moves beyond pain, beyond darkness. Our lives move toward a God-held future.

Prayer: *Lord, give me courage to embrace this moment of my life, for it is God-held. Remind me that because of your presence I have a future. Amen.*

Sunday, May 14   Read Psalm 148.

God "has raised up a horn for his people." An uplifted horn, the symbol of power and strength, burst from the psalmist's lips when considering the place of God's people in creation. The image calls to mind the proud stance of a wild mountain ram, head raised high, strong neck and massive horns displaying raw, unmastered power. The psalmist hears praise to God from every realm of existence. Angels and hosts of beings in unseen places praise God. The sun, moon, shining stars, and misty clouds acclaim the Creator. The sea, with its treasure chest of creatures, declares the Creator's touch. The storehouses of the elements— fire and hail, snow, rain, and wind—echo the Almighty's glory. The terrain of the earth and the rich variety of plant and animal life proclaim doxology to the Author of life. Humanity in its vast array of flesh—young and old, rich and poor, powerful rulers and humble servants—daily join the chorus, singing praise to the name that is the ground of all existence.

God, over all and in all, chooses to be involved in the life of a people. We are that people. The Almighty One, confined by no boundaries, gives strength to those who bring their lives near to the divine presence. When we move beyond the confining boundaries of our lives into the landscape of trust, our voices join in this unending song of praise to our merciful Creator. We sing—not because of our own efforts but because the One who knows no boundaries chooses to share power and life with us. Praise the Lord!

Prayer: *Strengthen me this day, O Lord. Let me pick up creation's tune and join in the chorus of praise. Amen.*

REAL PEACE

May 15-21, 1995   Everline C. Ricks✤
Monday, May 15   Read Psalm 67.

Our visions are often filtered or interpreted in light of recent experiences. Thus we gain many different insights and lessons from the same passage of scripture as each of us studies it from the perspective of our current situation. In a season of disappointment, we may find hope; in a season of loss, consolation; and in harvest, we may find blessings, expectation, fulfillment, and joy.

At harvest festivals—thanksgiving, Pentecost, or the Feast of Tabernacles—thanks may often be expressed for physical needs having been met. When considered in a context with Advent and Pentecost, a greater (our greater) blessing may be envisioned—a vision of joy, peace, and the Spirit.

In Psalm 67, the psalmist prays for God's blessing, favor, and, in the vein of Numbers 6:25-26, God's peace. God blesses us with the harvest of Advent, the joy of Christ's redemption for eternity, and the revelation of real peace. Pentecost reminds us of the harvest of directions from the Holy Spirit. Our challenge is to harvest these spiritual blessings and share them with others through pronouncement and example so that "all the ends [people] of the earth revere Him."

Prayer: *"The LORD bless you and keep you; the LORD make his face to shine upon you, and be gracious to you; the LORD lift up his countenance upon you, and give you peace."* * *Amen.*

✤Director of Christian Education, Asbury United Methodist Church, Washington, D.C.
* Numbers 6:24-26.

Tuesday, May 16   Read John 14:22-24.

Our mentor and leader revealed his pending departure to his disciples. Where will they find consolation? From where will come direction; who will explain the life experiences and mysteries?

We approach a season of commencements. Young persons leave school and commence their trek into independent life. June is the traditional month for marriages when many leave the direction of parents to commence a different trek into life. In each case, what have we been taught about the new life? How shall these teachings be put into practice? What have we taught from those lessons we have learned? Through the church and home, have we taught the prime importance of relationships— with God, self, others—filled with love? To be a good teacher, one must have a vision. What will the new life be like or hold for us? We cannot know.

We *can* know that those who practice the principal of love, as taught by Christ, will be loved by God. As with Job, we must strive to be steadfast in God's love, even though we do not know or understand all the factors and futures of the relationships.

We will sometimes part from our earthly mentors, leaders, or loved ones, but we need never part from the love of God and God's teachings. If we love God, we will be obedient to God's teachings, we will yield our will to God's will, and we will do God's work here on earth. We must show love, as Christ did, by actions outside as well as inside the religious community and its places of worship.

Prayer: *Lord, make me an instrument of your peace. Fill me with your vision for my life that I might grow in your service, as your instrument. Amen.*

Wednesday, May 17   Read John 14:25-29.

We often think of peace as economic security, political and social tranquility, and the absence of physical or emotional pain. We often think of peace as being "without a problem in the world," but this is an unrealistic expectation and is not the peace that Christ promised. Even Jesus himself was not spared problems or suffering. Problems will always be with us. Christ's peace gives us comfort and strength to endure in the midst of our problems.

This promise of peace recorded by John is not a peace limited to the aftermath of Jesus' pending departure and the disciples' anxieties and feelings of loss. This peace is much greater. It relates to the sense of well-being that comes from knowing that one is connected to and guided by God and so is a promise of peace to those of us far removed from the events of that time. No matter what the disappointment or loss, we will find consolation in the harvest of God's blessing of peace.

Jesus could make this promise of peace because he knew he would not have to leave his disciples alone to try to spread his teachings in a hostile world. God would send an Advocate, the Holy Spirit, to teach and guide the disciples. So may it be when the reasons or outcome are not as familiar to us, but they are to God. We can have the peace that Christ promises when we entrust all of these situations, the familiar and the unfamiliar, to God's wisdom when we follow obediently his teachings as best we can.

Suggestion for meditation: *Why am I anxious about circumstances around me when God's peace is available?*

Thursday, May 18　　　　　　　Read Acts 16:9-15.

The story of Lydia reminds me of some situations in early U.S. history where the householder brought or invited all members of the household to religious service, whether they were children, servants, or slaves. Lydia also invited other women as well as Paul and Silas to prayer sessions, some possibly at her home.

Jesus' followers were from diverse backgrounds. Certainly, not all were male, as we see with Lydia. Lydia apparently was a wealthy woman whom Paul met in Philippi. She dealt in cloth used for royal (purple) garments. She played an important role in the early church not because of her wealth but because of her vision of the life with Christ. Her vision and her devotion to the good news, and her commitment to tell others the good news helped Christ's church survive and grow.

Lydia's role in the growth of the early church is perhaps a precursor to the role women have historically played in the spread of the gospel. Consider the typical congregation today. What fraction of the adults are women? What gender supports and carries out most of God's works and ministries? Do these devotees cross economic lines as well as intellectual lines? The gift of nurturing, while not by any means limited to women, is certainly a gift that women since Lydia have brought to their congregations.

Suggestion for meditation: *What roles do women play in my congregation? How can we give more respect and recognition to the contribution of women in the life of our congregations?*

Friday, May 19   Read Revelation 21:10, 22-27.

Two important symbols in the Hebrew scriptures and in the Gospels were the Holy City and the Temple. Darkness and light are symbols that were and are used—darkness implying lostness, sin, fear; light or day implying illumination, insight, seeing the way, being able to follow a right path. The writer envisioned a place or condition in which God's light is eternal, God is the temple, and nothing unclean (in thought or deed) is allowed to be present.

Christ has described the presence of the Holy Spirit within us as the light and that we may consider ourselves to be the "temple" of God. If we surrender our will to God's will and follow God's directions, then God will live in us and be our light, and God's light will shine through us to the world.

Thus, the blessings of God are to be found more within us than around us. True blessings are eternal and everlasting. They are not that which we may see or possess, for these are only temporary and can be taken away or lost in an instant.

Prayer: *Thank you, God, for your blessings of peace. Let your light shine through me, that others may see the way to peace and eternal life with you. Amen.*

Saturday, May 20   Read Revelation 22:1-5.

What would be a description of the most beautiful place you might imagine? Would it be a place appealing to the eye? to one's sense of smell? to the hearing? to all of the senses? Would it be a place of beauty because of the condition or state of mind it brought forth? One might wonder how sensitive the spirit would be to the physical surroundings.

What could be a better description than John's of an almost unimaginably beautiful place? This place is made even more beautiful by God's presence in the very midst of the people. Perhaps the beauty of the new heaven and new earth is not so much in any extravagant display of jewels or lavish furnishings or even breath-taking elements of nature. The true beauty we see in these verses is the vision, the dream, the hope that God will, indeed, actually come to live among God's people. The beauty here is the anticipation of what it will feel like to have God himself physically and spiritually comfort his people in their grief and pain—yes, comfort *us* in our grief and pain.

Many times each of us has wished for a new start, a new beginning. Here, John writes of "the one seated on the throne" as being in the process of "making all things new." Hallalujah! With newness comes hope and with hope comes the vision to move forward in joy and celebration. And that is surely a great deal of what the kingdom of God is all about!

Prayer: *God, thank you for being always available in our lives. We look forward to the day when we can be even closer to you and all of your people. Keep us looking ahead with hope, carried forward by the vision of the new heaven and new earth you have planned. Amen.*

Sunday, May 21   Read John 5:1-9.

The Gospels contain many accounts of Jesus' miracles. The more remembered ones may be those that dealt with physical conditions, such as today's text. His life and ministry, however, were not focused on the physical condition, but rather the spiritual condition.

One need not wonder if those who were cured encounter any further problems in their lives. While they were thankful for the physical healing, did they gain spiritual healing and peace? To have knowledge of Christ and even to have met Him, does not necessarily mean that one will surrender to Him and follow His teachings. Most students know their teachers; children know their parents; however, students and children often fail to follow their instructions.

Christ's healing and other ministries often address the physical and other immediate needs of persons. He met them at the point of their need and sought to move them further in spiritual growth. He healed the sick, fed the hungry, while also teaching life's lessons—lessons of even greater value tnan temporal needs.

As we follow Christ's examples and seek to bring people to God, we must remember to approach them at the point of their need and on their level of spiritual maturity. We each must be nurtured wholly—physically, economically, educationally, and emotionally, as well as spiritually.

Prayer: *Gracious God, continue to help us to be your servants, that we may nurture others in the faith and guide them to your peace. Amen.*

FROM BONDAGE TO UNITY

May 22-28, 1995   **Raymond Fenn**✤
Monday, May 22   Read Acts 16:16-24.

Release from bondage

A week of scripture readings is always a source of both interest and speculation—the first because each passage opens up a window on what we believe; the second because we are dealing with people of an age completely different from our own. Although we struggle to understand the reading from their point of view, at the same time we see it with our own eyes, from our own perspective in time.

There is nothing in our culture to which we can compare the event in today's passage. We would either ignore an interruption of this kind as we were on our way to church, rapidly hurrying away from such a persistent and bothersome young woman, or we would phone the police to deal with it.

So what is there here that speaks to us? Her owners are using the slave girl for profit and their persistence irritates Paul. In exorcising the "spirit of divination" in her, Paul is motivated by irritation rather than compassion. The effect is to restore her to sanity.

Perhaps we can assume that we are sane and do not need to be restored. This slave girl had discerned the truth about Paul's mission: to be a servant of the most high God, proclaiming the way of salvation. We should always be on the lookout for truth to come from unexpected people in unexpected encounters. God is never limited. Be watchful!

Prayer: *Loving God, help me always to be alert to unexpected revelations and truth. Amen.*

✤Anglican priest of the Diocese of Kootenay, Canada; honorary associate priest, St. George's, West Bank, British Columbia.

154

Tuesday, May 23   Read Acts 16:25-34.

Release from captivity

The story in today's reading is about captivity in a broader sense than the physical. Paul and Silas were imprisoned. By prayer and praise they demonstrated their lack of fear. The story is written so as to highlight the wonder of God's intervention.

The essential in this account is release from spiritual bondage for the jailer. He was bound by fear of losing his job and perhaps his life because he would be held responsible for any prisoners who escaped. When Paul called out that everyone was present, the jailer asked with emphasis, "What must I do to be saved?" At that point his was a survival question rather than a religious one. He was overawed by two obviously powerful "magicians," Paul and Silas. He believed that they were responsible for the earth tremor.

Paul used the jailer's question for his statement about the power of belief in Jesus Christ. We can be sure that the two Christian leaders would not have proceeded with the baptism until convinced that superstitious fear had been transformed into genuine faith. The whole household would have been included because they had shared in the same experience. It may well be that the meal to which the apostles were invited turned into a thanksgiving for the blessings that had come out of the calamity.

The underlying theme here is that the gospel sets us free from all inner bondage. It begins to do so when an inquirer asks, "What must I do to be saved from fear and bondage?" Like the jailer, we ask that question when we recognize in someone a quality of faith that is different in every respect from anything we have experienced before.

Prayer: *Enable me, Lord, to ask like the jailer the question that will change me. Turn me away from fear onto the path of the light and love revealed through your son, Jesus Christ. Amen.*

Wednesday, May 24   Read Psalm 97:1-5.

Release into recognition

The word *kingdom* suggests to us an area of economic or political concern over which one person has supreme power. In a sense, this is an outmoded term but still one that most people understand.

This particular psalm quite possibly was used at the enthronement of a new king. In the Septuagint, the most influential of the Greek translations of the Hebrew scriptures, the heading for this psalm is "David, when his land was restored." It could be that the translator believed this to be an ancient song, used to mark the restoration of Israel from the Babylonian exile.

The first part describes the majesty and might of God. One scholar describes the writer as "a masterly hymn-writer" but not an original poet. The first verse proclaims the reign of God; the whole earth even to the remotest parts is urged to share in the recognition of this supreme event. Then we the readers are urged to relate this to the beginnings of the worship of the Lord. Undergirding this is the recognition that righteousness and justice are the foundation of all God stands for.

This psalm speaks of the cleansing power of God—through fire, through lightning, through earthquake and volcano. The depiction is of both a physical and a spiritual event. When this takes place within us, we are cleansed, released from bondage, so that we recognize that God is Lord of all the earth. Religion which leaves us unimpressed, unchallenged—or even apathetic—has lost its purpose. Catching even a glimpse of God is the beginning of recognizing that God is Lord of all.

Prayer: *Teach me, Lord, to look at everything with your eyes. Enable me, because I cannot do it on my own, to recognize that you are my Lord, and let me experience release from everything that holds me away from you. Amen.*

156

Thursday, May 25   Read Psalm 97.

To set us on the way

Throughout the Hebrew scriptures and the New Testament are many word pictures of the battle between good and evil; between the true God and false gods; between truth and falsehood. In our sophistication we think that this sort of distinction belongs to the past with certain notorious exceptions. However, it is interesting to note that when I begin to write down modern examples of evil—Saddam Hussein, Hitler, Stalin—I find that there are many more than I realized.

This is an ongoing battle. We are never free from some form of evil—that which hinders us from following the true way. The distinctions are perhaps more difficult for us to discern than for the psalmist. The mountains, the psalmist tells us, in comparison with the stability of the Lord are like melting wax. The most powerful evidence that the natural world is unbending and unchangeable is as nothing compared with God's strength and power. Today we view the wonders of the world as a challenge to human ingenuity to overcome; we think of "other gods" as an expression belonging to the past. Yet are we not adept at creating useless gods?

In contrast, we are set on the way of adventuring into God's realm when we recognize that the whole created world points us to God; when we realize that the gods we have created are worthless, that life-giving, sustaining, loving power belongs to God alone. This psalm ranges from the natural world, which reveals the majesty and wonder of God, to the response of the soul to God's righteousness.

Prayer: *Lord, I am your creature. You have put the imprint of your nature within me. Assist me to walk in your way and enjoy the beauty of your holiness. Amen.*

Friday, May 26   Read Revelation 22:12-14, 16-17, 20-21.

To give hope

It is tempting to take each phrase of today's lection and explain it in detail, but for me it is more effective to look for an underlying theme. Revelation is a book opening up on a different world than ours. It is quite unlike any other part of the New Testament. Some, such as Martin Luther, would have denied it a place in the canon. But we need to be reminded that Revelation is representative of a type of literature, called apocalyptic, that was common in the period between the testaments. The apocalyptic passages or books dealt mainly with events of the last times. In general, such passages are not easily understood.

In today's reading there are three main themes: the claim of Christ; the great invitation; and last words. The first theme informs us that the risen Christ will return very soon. Everyone will be rewarded by his or her quality of witnessing. Christ is both beginning and end. This dichotomy of *Alpha* and *Omega* (the first and last letters of the Greek alphabet) holds the idea of completeness. There is also the idea of eternity: the risen Christ includes in himself all time, from first to last, beginning to end.

The second theme (vv. 16-17) is held firmly in place by the great invitation: "Let anyone who wishes take the water of life as a gift." Everything needed by a Christian for spiritual nourishment is available without charge. Thirdly, amidst the agonizing persecution of this time, John longs for the speedy return of Christ. It did not happen in the way in which he envisioned, but Christians today believe in Christ's constant presence. How fitting that the final word of the Bible is *grace*. Every hope and blessing is in that word.

Prayer: *Lord, may I never lose faith that everything in the world is in your keeping, and all is under your grace. Amen.*

Saturday, May 27   Read John 17:20-23.

Recognition of true unity

From early on the church has been split by disunity. Yet, the Gospel reading for this week puts great emphasis on the inherent unity between God, the Father, and Jesus, the Son. Their unity finds expression through the church. Obviously, we do not accept all the implications that unity has for our life together, or perhaps, more accurately, we pretend to a unity that we do not actually experience.

The lection reading today could be entitled "Prayer for the Future Church." John's Gospel was written some years after the events described in it, probably toward the end of the first century. The author is concerned with bringing the reader to the point of decision; that is, to belief that Jesus is the son of God and that real life will be experienced through him.

The church's future depends on belief transmitted through the friends of Jesus. Unity among Christians is necessary—not a unity which requires everyone to agree on every doctrine but a unity out of which all work together for one purpose, proclaiming God's kingdom that the world may believe. When the Christian community is divided about its purpose, then its message is always weakened and perhaps meaningless.

John is making the point that witness to the united life of the church is not only a confirmation of God's revelation in Jesus but also a sign that the objective of that revelation is being achieved. The question for each of us in relation to this is: Do we really care about working with others for true unity? If so, are we sufficiently concerned to make it a priority of our witness?

Prayer: *Lord, the greatest gift from you to me would be to show me my brother and sister in Christ so that I see them as part of the unity that belongs to your realm. Amen.*

159

Sunday, May 28   Read John 17:24-26.

Achieving all-inclusive love

Today's verses sum up this week we have spent together. We have looked at aspects of the Christian faith as these influence us day by day. One commentary's headline for this section is "Final Appeal." Jesus, in addressing God the Father, says, "I desire"—a more emphatic expression than a wish that the intimate group of his friends will share in the resurrection glory. Jesus claims that the disciples are in on everything that God has planned. The strong underlying motivation is "that the love with which you have loved me may be in them." Our Lord's use of the phrase *and I in them* is the link with the new commandment (13:34): "Just as I have loved you, you also should love one another." This is the trademark of discipleship, which is concerned with both leading and being led.

So we have traveled from release from bondage to the recognition of true unity. The way we have come together comes within the realm of the possible only as we, who are the present-day disciples, struggle to accept nothing less than the all-inclusive love of Jesus. No aspect of life is perfect. We are living beings; therefore, we can only aim for the highest. And this requires our always being aware of the divine discontent urging us on. We are each included in the friendship of Jesus.

Prayer: *Lord, we thank you that we are more than your servants. Yet we believe that it is through this love which you share with us that we can become as those who serve others for whom Christ died. Thank you, Lord. Amen.*

May 29–June 4, 1995   **Larry R. Kalajainen❖**
Monday, May 29   Read Psalm 104: 24-35*b*.

For people of faith, the beauties of nature testify to the presence of our Creator. Psalm 104 is an extended hymn to God as Creator. It is a recital of both the glorious and mundane aspects of the created order. God is praised for everything from setting the boundaries of the seas to causing grass to grow so that livestock and people may have food.

In the concluding section of the psalm, the psalmist acknowledges the dependence of every living creature upon God not only for daily food but for the very breath of life itself. The Hebrew word for *spirit* and *breath* is the same. In the creation story (Gen. 1:2) the word is translated as "wind."

The life in each of us, in every living creature, is this divine wind, the divine breath, the divine spirit that is blowing ceaselessly over the face of the earth. We are animated by the very life of God the Creator. Small wonder that the psalmist feels the need to celebrate the work of God's spirit in creation. This hymn of praise ends with a plea that the original harmony of creation be restored, that wickedness and sin (in good Hebrew fashion, the psalmist personalizes these into "sinners" and "the wicked"), the destroyers of life, be themselves destroyed.

Suggestion for meditation: *If, indeed, it is God's spirit which created and inspires every living creature, what are the implications for the way we live in the creation?*

❖Senior Pastor of The American Church in Paris; author; clergy member, Southern New Jersey Annual Conference, The United Methodist Church.

Tuesday, May 30   Read Acts 2:1-21.

Luke's narrative of the Day of Pentecost reads like a straightforward piece of historical reporting. In fact, however, it is a sophisticated piece of storytelling in which events and theological meaning are skillfully blended. The form of Luke's narrative was inspired by one or both of two earlier narratives, one a biblical story and the other a rabbinic interpretation of a biblical story. The biblical story if the narrative of the Tower of Babel (Gen. 11:1-9). At Babel, in response to human arrogance, God allowed the human community to become fragmented by the confusion of language. At Pentecost, Luke appears to be saying that the spirit of God provided the basis for a new human community by "unbabbling" Babel.

The rabbinic interpretation of the giving of the law to Moses on Mount Sinai (Exod. 20:1-21) is the second source behind Luke's Pentecost story. The rabbis taught that God gave the law simultaneously to all the known nations of the earth in their own languages but that only Israel accepted the covenant with God which the law expressed. Luke appears to be saying that once again, through the community of the risen Jesus' disciples, God is entering into covenant with the whole world. He cites the prophecy of Joel to support his case: "I will pour out my spirit on all flesh," says the Lord (Joel 2:28); and the evidence is in the extraordinary manifestation of that spirit in the lives and proclamation of the disciples at Pentecost.

Salvation for the whole world is God's design, revealed in Jesus Christ and carried out by the Spirit's activity in and through the community of Christ's disciples.

Suggestion for meditation: *Does the community around your church know from the spirit-filled nature of your faith community that God is offering them salvation?*

Wednesday, May 31   Read Acts 2:1-11.

Luke conveys several very important truths. First, it is God who promises and delivers on the promise to send the Holy Spirit upon the community of disciples. The Holy Spirit is not a force that we can control or manipulate: "The wind blows where it chooses" (John 3:8). We cannot be filled with the Spirit by our own initiative; we can be filled with the Spirit only at God's initiative.

Second, our part in receiving the Spirit is to be obedient to Christ and open to what God chooses to do in our lives and in our community of faith. The disciples were told to stay in the city and wait. Waiting is hard for most of us, but it is necessary if we are to receive God's promises. Third, the Spirit came upon individuals-in-community. The Holy Spirit is a gift from God given to the community of the risen Christ's disciples. The Spirit is not a private gift for one's own comfort or empowerment. Individuals receive it, but only in the context of the community of the risen Lord.

Finally, Luke reminds us that the Spirit is given to empower the community to become witnesses to God's saving work in and through Jesus Christ. When the Spirit came upon the community in Jerusalem, they began to proclaim "God's deeds of power." The purpose of this proclamation was so that "everyone who calls upon the name of the Lord shall be saved" (2:21). If we had only these few verses of Luke to help us, we could define the church as a community of people empowered by the Spirit to proclaim God's saving work to the whole world. Not a bad definition, wouldn't you say?

Suggestion for meditation: *Are you filled with the Spirit? Are you part of a community where that can happen? How can you be more open to God's Spirit? How can you help your community be more open also?*

Thursday, June 1   Read Romans 8:14-17.

Paul uses the term *spirit* no fewer than twenty times in the eighth chapter of his letter to the Romans. It would be hard to overlook the importance of both the term and the role the Spirit plays in Paul's understanding of the Christian life.

It is the power of the "Spirit of life in Christ Jesus" that sets the believer free from the domination of the powers of sin and death (8:2). Those who have been thus liberated now live "according to the Spirit" and "set their minds on the things of the Spirit" (8:5), a course of action that brings life and peace. To be "in the Spirit" is not to be "in the flesh" (8:9). When Paul uses the phrase *in (the Spirit, Christ, the flesh)*, he uses it in a spatial sense. One lives at this address. Either one lives in the domain where law, sin, flesh, and death rule as lord, or one lives in the domain where Christ and the Spirit are the ruling power.

Moving from the context into the specific passage we are considering, we can see that regardless of whether Paul is speaking about the believer's location in the Spirit or in Christ, or the Spirit's (or Christ's) presence within the believer, he is simply using different metaphors for the same reality—the transformed identity and life of the believer. In this passage, he extends his metaphorical reach farther to pick up the image of adoption. The work of the Spirit is, first of all, to effect our transfer into a new family, the family of God. In the second place, the Spirit "[bears] witness with our spirit that we are children of God." The soul's awareness of this new relationship allows it to cry, "Abba, Father!" (or "Daddy"). To be able to do so is the birthright of every Christian.

Suggestion for meditation: *Do you have that inner witness that you are a child of God? That God accepts you completely? If not, what is preventing you from claiming your birthright?*

Friday, June 2   Read Romans 8:14-17.

The evidence that a person is indeed living at a new address as a member of a new family—God's family—is the evidence of a transformed way of living. Paul's understanding of salvation was that being claimed and adopted into God's family by grace resulted in a transformation at the deepest centers of motivation and will. Thus, salvation is not simply an inner, spiritual experience; salvation manifests itself in ethics—in the way one behaves in relation to others. If the manner in which we make decisions and act in relationship to others shows that the central motivating and guiding force in our lives is the Holy Spirit, then each of us testifies to the knowledge of being a child of God.

What is the behavioral evidence of the Spirit's leading that testifies to our new family relationship? Paul gives us the clue when he says, "For you did not receive a spirit of slavery to fall back into fear, but you have received a spirit of adoption." More and more, we are learning how much our fears can determine our behavior. These fears may manifest themselves in a variety of ways: competitiveness, feelings of guilt that aren't attached to any specific act, disproportionate anger, compulsiveness, depression, and low self-esteem, to name only a few. Behavior that manifests these traits often testifies that at our deepest center of motivation and decision-making, our fears influence us more than we would wish. Set over against behavior influenced by fear is the security and freedom that are the hallmarks of a life grounded in the Spirit's leading. And the more we open ourselves to the Spirit's leading, the freer we become.

Suggestion for meditation: *Do you feel led more by the Spirit or by inner fears? Ask God to help you overcome the fears that drive you. Be open to ways God may be prodding you to face your fears.*

Saturday, June 3   Read John 14:8-17.

If Paul prefers to speak of the Christian (individual-in-community) as being "in the spirit," John favors the image of the Spirit's presence within the believer and the believing community. Both Paul and John are concerned with the new social reality, the community of disciples. Both understand the Spirit to be the means by which the risen Christ remains with the community of his followers. Paul's imagery tends to focus on the ethics of the new community which results from the new freedom from the powers of sin and death, while John's imagery tends to emphasize the interpersonal intimacy between Christ and the community and among the members of the community.

In this passage, John contrasts the inability of the world to either see or know the Spirit with the community's intimate and personal knowledge of the Spirit. Knowledge comes in two varieties: there is the knowledge that one gains through study that we can call acquired knowledge. A person can acquire a great deal of knowledge about, say, the life of Gandhi. One can read his speeches, watch old newsreels, read a biography, and through such study come to "know" Gandhi. But those who were actually with Gandhi, who lived with him, struggled with him, and worked with him, would have an entirely different kind of knowledge. It would not be knowledge *about* but knowledge *of* Gandhi, the knowledge gained through personal experience and intimate relationship.

That is the knowledge of the Spirit that John is talking about in verse 17. This kind of knowledge comes only through intimate personal relationship, and such a relationship is only possible for those who love Christ and keep his commandments.

Suggestion for meditation: *Do you know the abiding Spirit in your community of disciples?*

166

Sunday, June 4   Read John 14:25-27.

In this passage, Jesus says that God will send the Holy Spirit "in my name." The Holy Spirit is a representative of Jesus, much as an ambassador is a representative of the president or prime minister. The Holy Spirit is not the main focus. The purpose of the sending of the Spirit is to extend the presence and ministry of Jesus to the community of his followers. (The *you's* in this passage are all plural; it is the community of believers, rather than individuals, which is in focus.)

How will the Holy Spirit represent Jesus? The Spirit "will teach you everything, and remind you of all that I have said to you." The Spirit teaches the community of Jesus' followers all that Jesus himself would teach if he were still present in the flesh. The word which is translated "remind" is an important word. It does not mean *remind* in the sense of reminding someone to stop at the store on the way home. It is more like, "I was going in for the job interview, and I was really nervous, but suddenly I heard my mother's voice in my mind telling me what she always told me, 'Believe in yourself, and you can be whatever you want to be.' Then I wasn't scared anymore." The Holy Spirit is that voice of Jesus within the community of the church and within our hearts, speaking to us in our present circumstances, so that we will know how to live and act as Jesus would want us to.

The result of the Spirit's work is peace and freedom from fear. When we have been "reminded" of Jesus' words and presence, we can face the present with confidence.

Suggestion for meditation: *What is the Spirit calling to your remembrance? What is Jesus, through the Spirit, saying to you or to your church?*

GOD'S WORKING WITH US

June 5-11, 1995   **Susan W. N. Ruach**✣
Monday, June 5   Read Psalm 8.

Who hasn't looked at a starry night sky and, along with the psalmist, felt small and insignificant. Why does God care about us anyway? The psalm doesn't tell us. It only affirms that God does in fact care.

But here are my guesses to that age-old question of why God loves us. God wanted conscious company, a different order of consciousness from beings that had previously been created. I believe God created us so God could love us, and God created us with the hope that we would love God and would also love what God has made and is making, including and especially each other. Those are pretty big hopes to pin on us small and insignificant creatures as we stand and look at a starry sky.

As you move through this day, I want to invite you to consider two things. *1)* Look for what it is that God loves about you. *2)* If you want a special challenge for the day, look for what it is God loves about a person or persons with whom you have difficulty. (If you read this at night, do this exercise tomorrow.)

Prayer: *Thank you, God, that you love me. Help my love for you to grow, and help me to see the lovableness of each person I meet. May my life be filled with your spirit today. Amen.*

✣Minister; Associate Council Director, South Indiana Conference of The United Methodist Church; Bloomington, Indiana.

Tuesday, June 6   Read Romans 5:1-5.

I am struck by the phrase "this grace in which we stand." Think about standing in a pool of water. As you look down, you may not even be able to see your feet if the water is murky. In any event, your feet will not look the same even if you can see them. Do you suppose that grace changes our vision, too?

In this text, we certainly have an impressive list from Paul of things which turn into other things. But suffering does not always produce endurance; sometimes suffering just beats a person down. And endurance doesn't always produce character; sometimes endurance builds fatigue, giving up, and resignation. Character doesn't always produce hope because sometimes the character that is produced out of our life experiences is a pessimistic character. Then it can produce despair or sarcasm.

Yet Paul is right. Sometimes suffering does produce endurance and endurance does produce character and character does produce hope. Two things determine what we become, what suffering produces in us. First, we are standing in this pool of God's grace. Second, that somehow changes our vision. We see the suffering differently, and it does produce endurance. And the grace somehow feeds the endurance so that it does, in fact, build strong positive Christian character. The character that is firmly based in the grace of God produces hope. And the hope does not disappoint us because it lies in our Lord Jesus Christ and in the Holy Spirit, who pour God's love into our hearts.

Suggestion for meditation: *Meditate on what it is like to stand in God's grace all day today.*

Wednesday, June 7   Read John 16:12-15.

This passage talks about the tasks of the Holy Spirit, the Spirit of truth. The first of these tasks is to guide us into truth. The act of guiding means to show or to lead. I think of a guide on a fishing trip in an area that you don't know or someone who takes you through a historic building or a park and points out things that you might miss otherwise, who gives you history and background and helps you understand more clearly both meaning and relevance. This task of the Holy Spirit is to show us the way, to point out things along the way that we might miss otherwise, and to help us understand more clearly the meaning and relevance of things.

The second task of the Holy Spirit is to speak what comes from Christ—love, care, compassion. This message from Christ will express the desire for good for all persons.

The third task of the Holy Spirit is to tell us what is coming in the sense of Old Testament prophecy. The prophets didn't foretell the future, but they did say that if you continue doing what you're going, these things will happen. And if the ways we pursue are loving, kind, and just, the results will be something else.

If the course we pursue is unjust or blind or even simply coming out of a vision that is too narrow, then another set of consequences will result. So telling us what is coming has to do with teaching us about the consequences of actions and attitudes. I suspect these lessons are some of the hardest lessons most of us have to learn in our lives.

Prayer: *Holy Spirit, today help me hear your guidance and learn from you, that I may understand the consequences of my actions and attitudes. Amen.*

Thursday, June 8   Read Romans 5:1-5.

In these verses we see another role of the Holy Spirit, to pour God's love into our hearts. While I was camping recently, it started to rain off and on during the night. By mid-morning the rain had settled in for the day. There were several things I had to do that day, including carrying things to the car from the tent and eventually taking down the tent to fold it up. Even though I had rain gear on, I got wetter and wetter as the day went on. Today I want to invite you to imagine (all day) that it is raining—not drops of water but drops of God's love, even indoors. This imagining will be a way to symbolize that the Holy Spirit is pouring God's love into your heart. (If you are reading this at night, do this exercise tomorrow.)

However, before you start to imagine the gentle waters of God's love, examine your heart to see if it is shrouded. If so, is the covering one that might keep out God's love? If you find that your heart is covered, picture yourself either taking off that outer covering, or at least opening it, so that God's love can enter more fully. Think about God's love washing over your being like fresh spring water and finally reaching your heart. Think about God's love all day, flowing into your heart, hopefully to the point that your heart will be so full of God's love it will begin to overflow and spread to those around you.

Prayer: *Thank you, God, for your wonderful love. Help me open my heart so that your Holy Spirit can pour love into it. Amen.*

171

Friday, June 9   Read John 16:12-15.

The promise offered in this passage is that there is much more to learn than we have learned so far. The warning here is that in order for us to learn certain things, we need to be ready.

This promise we have from Christ assures us that as we grow and progress in the world, as we learn more about the structure of life and persons on the earth and all creation, we are guided in our new understandings toward truth by the Holy Spirit. We are also guided into attitudes which are loving and compassionate, attitudes which follow after the mind of Christ through the Holy Spirit; thus, we are not stuck in some past time.

The warning that we cannot go on to learn new things until we are ready is, in certain ways, also important. We cannot learn to read without knowing the letters. Sometimes we cannot understand another person until we have grown in *self-*understanding. For instance, until we are in touch with our own grief, it is hard for us to understand the grief of another. Sometimes the readiness to learn may be toward seeing a larger picture. When I was a child, I understood things one way; when I became a parent the world looked entirely different.

People must read and know scripture passages before they can draw strength, comfort, encouragement, or guidance from the the sayings, parables, history, and stories found in the Bible. As we are growing in our skill at prayer, we have to learn to begin the conversation before we can, on a consistent basis, really hear what God is saying to us.

Suggestion for meditation: *Meditate on your own faith journey. What is it that you need to learn now?*

Saturday, June 10   Read Proverbs 8:1-4, 22-31.

In this passage, we see the wisdom of God in different locations summoning us to come and learn from her. Then we see wisdom working beside God "like a master worker" in the creation of the world. This passage also says that wisdom was God's delight and that wisdom found delight in what was created.

The invitation to learn from wisdom raises the question of what wisdom teaches. Surely, wisdom would teach how to work beside God to help bring God's vision to fruition. Surely, wisdom would teach us to be master workers "for the common good" (1 Cor. 12:7), using the gifts God has given each of us. And, presumably, we would learn how both to delight in God's creation and to be a delight to God.

Have you ever thought about whether or not God sees you as co-creating what God is doing now each day in the world? Have you ever thought of yourself in that way? What are the moments when you delight God?

Prayer: *O God, today may I work wisely in your will and on your path. May I be a delight to you and rejoice before you always. Amen.*

Sunday, June 11   Read Proverbs 8:1-4, 22-31.

Metaphors we choose can and often do heavily influence how we think about something or someone.

As in other scripture passages, Proverbs 8* offers us several metaphors for various characteristics of God. Thus, this passage invites us to enlarge our understanding of God by presenting a metaphor that offers a particular characteristic of God—that of the wisdom and understanding of God. Wisdom has to do with living life well, as God created life to be. Wisdom has about it calmness, peace, and gentleness, yet, at the same time, strength of purpose.

From the passage, we see other characteristics. Wisdom is ancient (the first of God's acts), companionable (present when God created), skilled (like a master worker) and co-creating with God (beside God). It is clear also from verses 30 and 31 that wisdom delights in God's creation, especially in the human race, and rejoices. I see this wisdom of God as the wise, teaching characteristic of God that is both gentle and rigorous, caring and skilled.

Suggestion for meditation: *What would it mean for you to live out of this wisdom of God? What would it be like for this wisdom to flow more freely through you?*

---

*The Book of Proverbs is part of the group of biblical writings known as "wisdom literature," which includes Job and Psalms, among others.

SIN AND GRACE

June 12-18, 1995   David Maldonado, Jr.✿
Monday, June 12   Read 1 Kings 21:1-21*a*.

As ruler of the Northern Kingdom, Ahab possessed more than all of the people surrounding him. In fact, he could have almost anything he desired. However, even for a king there is a limit. There are parameters—a sense of right and wrong—which govern our actions. For Ahab, it was the word of God made known through the prophets and through Hebraic tradition. But Ahab's desires were in tension with the word of God and tradition. The things he enjoyed were not enough. He wanted more. He wanted Naboth's vineyard; and to satisfy his greed, Jezebel, Ahab's wife, had Naboth stoned to death.

To be caught between our desires and the word of God is not unique to kings or to those in other powerful positions. Discerning what we are to do is a daily struggle for all of us. However, taking advantage of the less powerful in the pursuit of our desires can be tempting. Regardless of how powerful or justified we think we are, there is a cost to our actions. In Ahab's case, his and Jezebel's actions provoked God's anger.

Jesus taught that God wills us to love God and neighbor. To step beyond the bounds of God's will is to distance ourselves from God and neighbor. To sin against neighbor is to sin against God, and sin against God and neighbor leads to death. It is in Christ and his commandment to love that we find life.

Prayer: *God, we confess that we have sinned against you and against our neighbor. Grant us your grace that we may truly learn to love you and neighbor. Amen.*

✿Professor of Church and Society; Perkins School of Theology, Southern Methodist University, Dallas, Texas.

Tuesday, June 13   Read Psalm 5:1-8.

To begin the day in God's presence and in worship is something we all wish we could do. What a blessing and joy that would be! Blessed is the person who starts the day in prayer and praise. However, this psalm reminds us that not all who start the day in prayer and praise feel blessed. In fact, this psalm suggests that the worshiper is beginning the day in a most distraught way. The psalmist feels surrounded by enemies who say and do evil things. What a way to begin the day!

Naboth could very much identify with this psalm. His enemies had falsely charged him in order to obtain his vineyard (1 Kings 21:1-10). He had been set up by those in power. He was a powerless man against the rulers of the land. What was his word against the word of those in power? Naboth was no match, and he was stoned to death. At first, it would seem that those in power can do as they will—that the powerless are totally in the hands of the powerful. It would seem that God does not hear the sound of their cries.

The full reading of the text, however, reminds us that indeed God does hear the cry of the marginal and powerless. "The LORD abhors the bloodthirsty and deceitful." Justice will be done. Ahab was condemned for his greed and sin against the powerless Naboth (1 Kings 21:17-24). Our God is the God who listens to the pleas of the poor and who acts on behalf of the oppressed.

Prayer: *God, we confess that we have taken advantage of others and that we have not sought justice for the poor. Teach us to hear the cry of the powerless, that we may become instruments of your will. Amen.*

Wednesday, June 14   Read Luke 7:36-39.

This story provides at least two insights to understanding God's will. First it concerns Jesus' acceptance of an invitation from a Pharisee to eat at his home. To accept such an invitation could be interpreted to suggest that Jesus approved of the Pharisee and thus provided him credibility. It also could be that Jesus was a friend and thus shared much with the Pharisee. Such action was certainly open to speculation and suspicion. But could not this act by Jesus be another reminder, indeed, revelation, that God's grace and word are available to all? Jesus associated directly and openly with those who were despised and marginalized in society, but Jesus also presented the gospel to those whom society seemed to favor. Those who were wealthy and powerful were given the opportunity to respond tc the different values Jesus offered.

The second observation concerns Jesus' allowing a woman openly known to be a sinner to get close to him, to bathe his feet and anoint him with ointment. How could Jesus, known by many to be a teacher and a prophet and by some to be the Son of God, allow such a person to touch him and to serve him? Again, Jesus shows us that God's grace was available and indeed was meant for all regardless of social position or status.

Jesus reached out to the outcasts, the despised, and to the people from below. He touched their lives and brought them God's grace. Jesus' actions also taught us to watch for times when the marginal and despised do indeed reach out. The Pharisee invited Jesus into his home; the woman came to him and washed his feet. God's grace is accessible to all, poor *and* rich, in spite of our prejudices.

Prayer: *God, have mercy upon us and grant that we may be channels of your love and not barriers for those despised in this world. Amen.*

Thursday, June 15   Read Luke 7:40-50.

There was Jesus in the home of the Pharisee having his feet washed by a woman with a bad reputation. Was Jesus being too permissive—too kind with those who were openly sinners? Why was he spending his precious time with these kinds of people?

Jesus understood the discomfort and confusion, and he could sense the questioning of his actions. Why was he allowing such a woman to touch him and to clean his feet? His words to Simon tell a story of the forgiveness of debts. Those who owe much and have their debts canceled have much to appreciate; those for whom little is forgiven have little for which to be thankful. What is often overlooked is the fact that both debtors—one with a small debt and one with a large debt—are in need of forgiveness. Jesus came that we *all* might know God's grace, not just those who lead faithful lives.

It is interesting to note that the woman who washed Jesus' feet did not ask for forgiveness (vv. 37-38). She did not present a litany of her sins and petitions for forgiveness. Instead, she sought to be near Jesus and to serve him. She did not have to say it; Jesus could see it in her action, and he provided God's grace. Had she done it in order to be forgiven? Jesus did not suggest that. On the other hand, God's grace was freely given.

We are no different from the woman. We have all sinned. Certainly, we have not all sinned in the same way, but all of us are in need of God's grace. Our task is not to compare our sins with the sins of others but to love and serve God with all our hearts and to love our neighbor. The rest is left to God's grace.

Prayer: *God, you know our hearts. You know our sins. Grant us your grace, that we might be graceful to others. Amen.*

Friday, June 16   Read Luke 8:1-3.

As Jesus went about through the villages preaching his new and unconventional message, he was accompanied by a strange and interesting array of followers. It must have been quite a sight to see this unusual combination of persons. By looking at this group, it would have been difficult to think that it could be a group selected by anyone to establish the kingdom of God.

However, as Jesus fulfilled his ministry, he reached out to many kinds of people. He went to the homes of Pharisees, asked water from a stranger, and had his feet washed by a woman with a bad reputation. He crossed ethnic and economic barriers. He reached out to fisherfolk, tax collectors, and men and women from all walks of life. It would seem that to establish the kingdom of God, Jesus should have been more selective. Instead, he chose ordinary men and women—educated and uneducated, poor and wealthy, respected and despised.

The church of Jesus Christ is an inclusive community not because we choose to make it so or because we feel social pressure to make it so but because it is at the root of the kingdom as initiated by Jesus himself. Jesus brought together persons who were divided by ethnicity, wealth, gender, religion, and social position. He showed by example that all of us have a place and role to play in his church and kingdom. The church is to be not an exclusive, self-selected body but a community brought together by the love and call of Christ and held together by the power of God's spirit.

Prayer: *God, grant that our minds and hearts may be open to others who are different than we are. May we see our need for each other even as we seek your will. Amen.*

Saturday, June 17 Read Galatians 2:15-16.

As a Jew, Paul was mindful of the factors that had formed him. His cultural and religious heritage had shaped his world view and basic understanding of what is right and just. He had been taught that to do right was to do according to the law that had come down through his Hebraic cultural and religious tradition. However, once he knew Christ, Paul became keenly aware of the inadequacy of the law and tradition which had shaped him up to that point. To do according to the law was not sufficient before the eyes of God. It was only through faith in Christ that Paul could see himself acceptable before God.

All of us have been shaped by our cultural and religious traditions. No one is free from these human realities. To be human is to be part of a social reality which includes culture, social position, and world views. These have provided us with rules for social life and foundations for self-understanding. Most of us take pride and joy in our cultures. In fact, we think that ours is probably better than most other cultures. And most of us would also like to believe that *our* religious tradition is the best and that our system of belief provides the best understanding of the Christian life. Unfortunately, most of us also measure ourselves according to these realities, whether cultural or religious.

Paul reminds us that although we are products of our cultural and religious traditions, we are acceptable to God regardless of our cultural righteousness or correct religious tradition. It is not a matter of the right religion or the right culture but a matter of our faith in Christ.

Prayer: *God, help us to place our trust not in those things which we have created but in Christ. Amen.*

Sunday, June 18   Read Galatians 2:17-21.

As a Pharisee, Paul knew the law and the power it held over those seeking obedience to God. He understood how it provided many with the belief that they were justified before God. But Paul also understood human nature and the inability to be fully justified under the law. It was not until he knew Christ that Paul was able to fully experience God's grace. It was the Christ experience which provided Paul with the breakthrough in understanding God's grace: it is freely given through Christ. God's grace is not earned or deserved but experienced as we know Christ.

Unfortunately, many of us assume that we are justified and in the right because we are obedient according to our laws and traditions. When tradition or the status quo protects our self-interest, social position, power, or wealth, we find a special sense of justification and assurance, even when our neighbor is poor, marginalized, or victimized. We attribute our privilege to God's blessing rather than to our personal self-interest and social sinfulness.

Paul says that he has been crucified with Christ, that he no longer lives but Christ lives in him. To be crucified with Christ means to deny oneself of the self-centeredness of sin and to reject the privileges of our social positions. It means to be in partnership with Christ and to participate in his task in this world. Thus, we become not the end but the means of God's grace for others.

Prayer: *God, we confess that we have sought our self-interest and not the well-being of those for whom Christ came to this world. Grant that we may die to our sinfulness and be born to your grace. In Christ we pray. Amen.*

June 19-25, 1995   **Marcia Mary Ball**✤
Monday, June 19   Read 1 Kings 19:1-10.

Our readings for the week tell us about people who were in great trouble. Elijah, the psalm writer, the early Christians, and the demoniac—all needed help and found it. Let us learn from them to dwell in safety.

Elijah had just had the most exciting spiritual event of his life. He had successfully defeated the priests of Baal. But in doing so he had incurred the implacable anger of Jezebel. He feared for his life.

Notice how the Lord led him "back on track." First, Elijah needed rest; he was exhausted. Also he needed good food; he was hungrier than he knew. Then he needed time to think, so he withdrew to Mount Horeb. There, with rest, food, and time Elijah gained a new vision and restored faith. God was there.

We, too, are eligible for God's guidance in hard times. For many June is a month of endings and beginnings. Some are finishing school and others are ending projects. A change of pace can get us back on track as we rest, eat, and think out our future with God's safety net around us and a renewed faith to claim in God's eternal care.

Prayer: *As we come to a time of change of pace, Lord, guide us in rest, refreshment, and thought. Amen.*

✤Retired missionary to Zimbabwe; minister, Trinity United Methodist Church, Pomona, California.

Tuesday, June 20   Read 1 Kings 19:11-15*a*.

As Elijah began to recover, he was filled with self-pity. So he thought to himself: *Why me? I have tried but they won't listen. They have turned away and deserted me—even my life is in danger. No one comes to my help! Look at all I have done! What good has it been? I'm better off dead!* (AP)

God did not say, "Nonsense, pull yourself together, man!" God did not say, "You poor soul, I feel sorry for you." No. God knew Elijah needed new inspiration. God caught Elijah's attention in a big way, first with a mighty wind, then with the quaking of the earth; next followed fire, and then—a long silence. All these rather shattering natural events certainly helped Elijah get his mind off himself and the current problems in his life! Once God had Elijah's attention, God gave him a new job—go to Damascus and *return to living!*

Self-pity is hard to shake. It often takes calamity for others to pull us out of our self-pity, calamity such as earthquakes, floods, hurricanes, or tornadoes. Disasters like these can lead us away from ourselves to help others in worse situations.

Go out today expecting God to be present to you in unexpected ways and unexpected places. Find God's glory again in nature and friends, and realize the sun will rise again tomorrow—all is not lost. God is ever ready with new inspiration. We need only to look for it.

Prayer: *Lord, save us from the trap of self-pity. Lift our discouragement and give us new visions of your glory. As we become aware of your presence in unexpected ways and places, help us to share our experience of your presence with those around us. Amen.*

Wednesday, June 21   Read Psalm 42.

The Reverend John Jijita pastored a rural church in northeastern Zimbabwe. Converted to Christ as a high school student, he was a simple man of great faith. He was sixty years old when civil war broke out in Zimbabwe.

The war was a reaction of Africans against white colonialism, paternalism, and unofficial apartheid. Bands of young fighters roamed the countryside lashing out against the ideas of white people. In some cases Christianity was a victim of their wrath.

One afternoon a group of fighters stopped Mr. Jijita on a path, taunting him, "Where is your God? You have been deceived by the white man. Stop your preaching! Return to the tribal beliefs of our ancestors. We are watching to see what you will do."

Mr. Jijita answered their taunts and threats, "No, I cannot stop preaching. I know my God and trust him to be with me always. God is my safety in trouble."

The following Sunday he preached onthea faithfulness of God to sustain him even in danger. On Wednesday he started out on a pastoral call. He was ambushed and killed, his body thrown into a nearby pool. His wife found his clothes on the path, and the fighters came threatening her. When the war ended in 1980, Christians gave Mr. Jijita a proper burial. His life and his death attested to his faith that true safety could be found only in God.

Suggestion for meditation: *Where are the places in your life, the places in your heart, that you feel most afraid? Where are the places that you feel most assured of God's presence?*

In thinking about Mr. Jijita, do you believe that he was given God's safety in time of trouble? What does "God's safety" mean to you?

Prayer: *Why are you cast down, O my soul . . . ?*
                     Hope in God [and] praise him,
                         my help and my God. Amen.

184

Thursday, June 22   Read Psalm 43.

"O, send out your light and your truth; let them lead me." One of our most loved and respected missionaries, the Reverend K. Eriksson, went blind at middle age. Some thought he would have to resign as seminary principal. But no, although his detached retinas could not be operated on, he took a year's leave; went to a school for the blind; and learned how to walk, eat, dress, and live in a darkened world.

Although his world was dark, a light still shone in his spirit. He returned to his work and with a secretary kept up with his job. He also taught church history. Some of us read the textbooks into tapes so he could review his lectures each day. He gave tests which he graded with his secretary's help.

He preached regularly and always stressed that though his sight was gone, his soul could see better than ever before. He had a good singing voice and often added a hymn to his sermon—usually "How Great Thou Art."

Mr. Erikson developed a phenomenal memory. He could remember the steps and turns from his home to his office chapel and classroom. He traveled on buses, trains, and airplanes with ease. He was called on for many conference committees and gave wise counsel.

One of his greatest contributions was in his help to young visually impaired students. After retirement he served on the faculty of a school for the blind in Norway. His light and truth led all he knew into the greater light and glory of God, in whom he trusted for his safety in all situations.

Prayer: *May the light which shines from the soul of all believers lead us to your holy hill, O God. Amen.*

Friday, June 23   Read Galatians 3:23-29.

"There is no longer slave or free." One modern definition of a slave is one who loses control and freedom of action. This hidden slavery has nothing to do with physical slavery, and it manifests itself in numerous ways. For example, the persons who have a rampaging temper or constantly nag or demand their own way or let their fear of people who are different from them dictate their thoughts and actions or have always been indulged are some of today's slaves.

The advertising industry aids and abets our thirst for material gratification by telling us we need certain products for happiness. When we let advertising do this, we become its slaves.

But our Bible shows the way to freedom—by being clothed with Christ. Through our faith we are restored to those attitudes that bring true happiness. Rather than being a physical condition, freedom is a spiritual condition which is measured by what we allow Christ to do with our lives. As we grow spiritually, our freedom grows; for the power of those things that bind us is lessened. Our fears, jealousies, prejudices, greed, need for security—whatever has been utmost in our life—recede as we acknowledge Jesus Christ and his teachings as our primary loyalty. Jesus said that we cannot serve two masters (Matt. 6:24). The one offers slavery; the other offers freedom.

Prayer: *Help us to examine ourselves honestly, Lord, to see where we remain slaves. Show us how to break old habits by remembering that we belong to you and that our safe dwelling place is in Christ. Amen.*

Saturday, June 24   Read Luke 8:26-39.

We know his name only as "the demoniac," "the man who had demons for a long time," or the self-given name of "Legion." This name, along with the wrenching, powerful force inside that causes his extreme behavior, shows the magnitude of the mental illness from which he suffers.

He cannot live in a house; he lives among the tombs. He is unable to keep from hurting himself. He will not be restrained, for his or others' safety. He endures being driven into the desert (the abode of Satan and the demons).

How terribly, utterly lonely this man's existence must have been! God created people to live in community. Yet, this man lived an alienated existence apart from the community—not due to banishment but as the the result of his condition. Perhaps he lived among the tombs because, in more lucid moments, he was painfully aware of how different he was from others.

Jesus shows no fear as he approaches the man. No doubt, Jesus saw far beyond behavior and appearance into a place inside the man's being that cried out to be made well, to be restored to life and the full possibilities of his God-created self.

As Jesus casts out the demons of illness, he grants the man *life*. Jesus also gives him *a new way of living* that begins with the desire and privilege of sitting as a disciple at the Master's feet. The man begs to go with Jesus. Instead, Jesus sends him into his own community to "proclaim" (preach) there what God, through Jesus, has done for him—to be *a living witness* to God's power.

Prayer: *Lord, grant us healing from whatever keeps us alienated from you and from our community. Grant us compassion for those who are distressed, sorrowing, or torn apart by illness or by life's circumstances. Then give us what we need so we can reach out and bring them to the places and people—and the God—who can heal. Amen.*

187

Sunday, June 25   Read Psalm 23.

"I will fear no evil: for thou art with me" (KJV). How often I have stood beside an open grave and either conducted the service or stood with grieving relatives! A warmth always steals into my heart when I read or hear Psalm 23.

There was the father who traveled 2,000 miles to kneel at the grave of a son who had died of venereal disease. There were the parents of two boys of great promise. One was killed in a two-car accident, the other at a train crossing. There was the son of a beloved church member who had died of leukemia. There was the mother of a reckless daughter who ran a red light. There was a grandchild whose grandfather died of cancer.

In all of these cases I stood by to share their grief. All of the mourners were Christians. Through tears and sorrow they found comfort and a triumph of spirit as they recalled these ageless words of promise. The way they handled their loss was a witness to me of the presence of a loving God in whose hands this world and the next rest.

So we learn again the lesson of Elijah—God is in the silence. Or the lesson of the Reverend Jijita—"I will trust in him." Or the lesson of the Reverend Eriksson—"Now my soul can see." Or the lesson of freedom from misplaced priorities. Or the lesson of saneness, harmony and balance. In all these things and more we can "walk through the valley" (KJV) and "fear no evil," for we are a people who dwell in the safety of God's steadfast love.

Prayer: *Thank you, Lord, for witnesses all about us and for other Christians who triumph through Christ. Amen.*

THE WAY OF DISCIPLESHIP

June 26–July 2, 1995   **Sister Barbara Jean, S.H.N.✤**
Monday, June 26   Read 2 Kings 2:1-2, 6-13.

The story in today's reading is of the giant among prophets— Elijah, whose name means "Yahweh is my God." It is also the story of his principal disciple, Elisha, whose name means, "God is salvation." It is the story of the end of one ministry and the beginning of another.

Elisha's request to inherit a double portion of his master's spirit is not an impertinence. Rather, it is a desire to be recognized as the chief heir of Elijah. Elisha wants the portion that would go to the firstborn son.

Unlike so many of us who desire our inherited position to bring us fame, wealth, and easy living, Elisha's entreaty shows us his earnest desire to succeed his mentor in the profound responsibility of the prophetic ministry. The primary obligation of such a ministry was to stand in proclamation that Yahweh is the only true God. Elisha had studied under his mentor and learned all the tricks of the trade, but he had also become imbued with a deep sense of loyalty and commitment to the life of sacrifice which necessarily accompanies the office of prophet. Even so, Elijah cannot make an independent choice concerning who will succeed him. Ultimately, everything is in the Lord's hands, and that is the most important truth Elisha must accept if he is to be the Lord's prophet.

Prayer: *Lord, help us to accept the place you have made specifically for us in life. Amen.*

✤Member of the Episcopal order of the Sisterhood of the Holy Nativity; works at St. Mary's Retreat House, Santa Barbara, California.

189

Tuesday, June 27   Read 2 Kings 2:13-14.

Dietrich Bonhoeffer left the world a legacy of immense proportions in his beautifully written book *The Cost of Discipleship*. In it he addresses the necessity of understanding the fact that there is no such thing as "cheap grace." If we make the decision to follow Christ, we must accept the fact that the road will be demanding and the consequences unyielding. The Lord will lavish us with the indwelling Spirit's grace, but that does not mean that we will be able to coast through life without effort, energy, and determination.

In taking up the mantle of Elijah, Elisha accepted not only all the rights and privileges of being recognized as the leading prophet in Israel but also accepted all the responsibilities, the harsh treatment, and the dangerous assignments that went with the job. More than all of this, however, Elisha accepted his role as "man of God—exemplar."

What must it be like to be "God's man" or "God's woman"? What must it be like to have no other concern or desire than to do the Lord's will? It must be both thrilling and frightening— thrilling to experience the privilege of God's power working through you and frightening to realize just what extraordinary things might be demanded of you. Perhaps astronauts, sitting atop thousands of gallons of rocket fuel and waiting to be hurled into space, come closest to experiencing this mixture of delight and apprehension. But the opportunity to become an astronaut is open to only a select few; whereas, the opportunity to become a "chosen one of God" is open to anyone whose desire for God's will outweighs all other desires. Yet, just as with the astronaut, we, too, must count the cost of our commitment.

Prayer: *Lord, give me more of a desire for you. Amen.*

Wednesday, June 28   Read Psalm 77:1.

A true disciple is one who takes the relationship between the soul and God very seriously and very personally. Psalm 77:1 puts emphasis on this personal aspect and represents to us the sure hope of a faithful soul in the promises of God. Most notably this can be seen in the stress on the word *my*. "I will cry unto God with *my* voice" (KJV). I will not leave that to someone else. My relationship with God is my own responsibility, and I must take care of it myself. I believe that I must pray with the articulate, intelligent voice of a human being, not with the inarticulate sounds of a beast.

In the monastery, the recitation of the Divine Office (set prayers at designated times of the day and night) is the primary work of those called to live that chosen way of life. Within the Divine Office are the psalms, used from ancient times to express the needs and desires of our human condition. These are the prayers of another, and it is so easy only to say the words and not to pray the prayers. Each monk must not only be present for the offering of the Divine Office but he must be fully engaged. Those prayers must become his own. The cry to God must be heard as coming from every voice, however strong or feeble, however melodious or off-key. The offering of such communal prayer is diminished if each person is not taking personal responsibility to meet God there.

We must each cry to God with our own voice, for with our mouths do we confess and profess our place in God's saving action.

Suggestion for meditation: *Read Psalm 77:11-20 aloud. Read it aloud a second time, as though the words were your own words. Then pray this psalm, letting these words become your words to God.*

Thursday, June 29 Read Psalm 77:2, 11-20.

The day of trouble, in which we desperately need the guidance of the Lord, is our whole earthly life. The great saints of the church, instead of wasting their lives in vain complaints or frustrated murmurings over the difficult conditions in which they often found themselves, turned always and immediately to God. Turning to God was second nature, not something they did only when all else failed.

Growth in holiness comes through diligent effort, through reaching forth, stretching, straining after God. Picture Michelangelo's image of God reaching out to touch Adam. God's arm is taut with the effort of reaching down to him. In Adam, on the other hand, we see an almost lazy response. His hand is limp, as if the touch of God meant nothing to him. But we know that the touch of God means everything. It gives life; it moves us beyond all difficulties and all discouragements. The touch of God, especially in the dark places of our lives, gives us the strength and encouragement we need in order to go boldly through our earthbound pilgrimage.

Our impetus to seek earnestly for God comes from a memory, a recalling to mind God's many deeds in the history of the chosen people. This impetus comes even more vividly when we recall all the times God has intervened in our own personal histories. To meditate upon the works of the Lord is an awesome experience. It will not take long before we are swept into amazement, hope, and trust that the Lord will surely be with us in the time of trouble.

Suggestion for meditation: *Put yourself in a quiet place where you will not be disturbed. Let your mind wander back to the first time you ever recognized the Lord's intervention in your life. Rest there and recall the wonder of the Lord's presence with you.*

Friday, June 30   Read Galatians 5:16-23.

Discipleship involves a concentrated effort to turn away from our human inclinations, which are often marred by sin, and toward the divine. Paul does not refer simply to the body when he writes about not gratifying the desires of the flesh. Rather, he uses the term *flesh* to mean all that is fallen into alienation from its heavenly purpose. In other words, Paul recognized that the raw physical stuff of human life does not lead us to God. Instead, we are to be crucified with Christ and reborn, refitted, for the life which God originally intended. That can be accomplished only through the power of the Holy Spirit.

As Paul enumerated the nine virtues of spiritual living, he had a keen sense that those virtues could not be cultivated by an act of self-will. They are the by-products of living with one's whole being turned toward Christ. They are an outflow of Christ's living in us. Life in the Spirit means a life of virtue. It is important to remember that living such a life requires continuous application, a constant determination to live in Christ's presence. As we focus on living in Christ, those virtues can do nothing else but grow.

We can often draw parallels between our lives and things in the natural world. If a fruit-bearing plant is planted in rich, life-giving soil, the plant will receive the necessary nutrients and will be healthy. Anything less than such an environment will leave the plant weak and in poor condition. It will be not able to produce the good fruits it was created to produce. It is only as we become grounded in Christ that we become the beings God created us to be.

Prayer: *Come to me, O blessed Jesus. Pour out your spirit upon me, that I may be nourished by your life and grow in virtue and in holiness. Amen.*

193

Saturday, July 1   Read Galatians 5:1, 13-16.

One of the strange paradoxes of the Christian life shows up here. If we yoke ourselves to Christ in the power of the Holy Spirit, we are truly free. To remain yoked to the ways of the world, that is, going where we will, doing what we want, living by our own standard, is slavery. It is bondage which leads to moral disintegration. Being yoked to Christ, by contrast, sets us on a path of true freedom. We are able to become all that we were created to be. Freedom in Christ sets up for us the opportunity to reach our potential, to realize that truly we were created only a little lower than the angels.

The freedom that the Spirit gives, enables the process of discipleship to become fully mature in us. When we put on the liberty of Christ, we become keenly aware that our mission and ministry is one of service motivated by love. Our adoption into the fellowship of faith becomes for us the principle of all our Christian activity. It is no idle inheritance. Christian freedom means we are called to continue to follow Christ and his commandment, "You shall love your neighbor as yourself."

We cannot understand the full implication of Christian freedom until we first accept and understand the all-encompassing nature of sin. Sin is separation, and the ultimate separation from God is reflected in our continual separation and alienation among the children of God. The full implication of Christian freedom also demands that we accept and understand the nature of reconciliation. Christ paid the full price to win our freedom, and he graciously allows us to be partakers in his victory over the destructive forces of sin.

Prayer: *Lord, lift the yoke of bondage to this world's riches and yoke me to you, in whose service is perfect freedom. Amen.*

Sunday, July 2   Read Luke 9:51-62.

As recorded here in the Gospel of Luke, Jesus set his face unswervingly toward Jerusalem. He knew what time it was, and he was ready. Many of the accounts in the Gospels depict Jesus as aware of his ultimate goal, his destiny. Even as a child, left behind in the Temple, he told his parents that he must be about his Father's business. Did Jesus know all along that his human pilgrimage would take him to and through the most difficult aspects of human existence? Certainly his actions showed him facing his mission without reservation, especially that part of his mission that would take him through the Passion and Crucifixion.

What awaited Jesus in Jerusalem were the throngs who proclaimed him Messiah and those who yelled, "Crucify him!" The teachings, the miracles, the humiliations and condemnations—all worked together for one bold plan. Nothing could be left out. Thankfully, we know that ultimately the road to Jerusalem not only led to Golgotha but also to the empty tomb and to the Mount of Ascension.

But, what about us? What or where is our Jerusalem? For each pilgrim there comes a point at which one must set his/her face toward Jerusalem, to live up to the responsibility and cost of discipleship.

The way of discipleship is the way of adventure, both thrilling and frightening, exhilarating and frustrating. It is a matter of abundant living and, at the same time, of painful sacrifice. The way may not be clearly marked, but mentors and the grace of the Holy Spirit help us on our way.

Prayer: *Lord, strengthen me as I discover* my *Jerusalem. Grant me the grace to set my face firmly to meet what awaits me there. Amen.*

GIVE THANKS BY *DOING* GOD'S WORD

July 3-9, 1995   M. Garlinda Burton✣
Monday, July 3   Read 2 Kings 5:1-14.

Give some people an inch and they want a mile! Naaman, the
mighty warrior of the king of Aram, suffered with leprosy. A
concerned servant girl of Israel tells him of a prophet blessed by
God with curative powers. Naaman's king gives him permission
to seek healing in Israel and even sends a letter of introduction
and gifts to the king of Israel on Naaman's behalf.

Yet, even after the king of Israel receives him warmly, even
after Elisha agrees to heal him, Naaman is not grateful. Rather,
he is insulted that Elisha does not give him a *personal* audience
but instead sends a messenger who tells Naaman to bathe in the
Jordan to be healed. The rivers in his own land are superior,
Naaman says indignantly. Wouldn't they work just as well or
better? Just as Naaman is about to leave in a huff, though, his
servants challenge his troublesome pride. Coming to his senses,
Naaman follows Elisha's instructions: he dips himself seven
times in the Jordan and is cleansed.

How many times has pride kept us from God's blessings?
been too stubborn to apologize after an argument with a friend?
too concerned with appearances to laugh out loud or to say,
"Hallelujah!" when God overwhelms us with love? Gratefulness
for God's gifts challenges us to put aside the pride that threatens
to separate us from God.

Prayer: *Gentle, selfless God, as I celebrate the me you've allowed me
to be, help me to live gratefully, humbly, and joyfully. Amen.*

✣Layperson; journalist on staff, United Methodist News Service;
member, Patterson Memorial United Methodist Church, Nashville,
Tennessee.

Tuesday, July 4   Read Psalm 30:1-4.

Often, when I grow impatient with someone, I'm apt to mutter, "You'd better be glad *I'm* not God!" As hard as I try, impatience remains my private demon. But I have developed a trick that helps me curb my exasperation. I have learned to create pictures in my mind, replays of incidents when someone has been patient with me. Sometimes I remember my grandmother sitting night after night at my bedside during childhood summers when I was deathly sick with allergies and asthma.

Other times, I say a silent prayer of thanks for my Uncle Paul, who sent me $1,000, no questions asked, when I was going hungry while in graduate school. Most times, I think about my mom, who has suffered with me through everything from ruining her new lipstick while playing dress-up to calling home to hear a sympathetic voice after a silly argument with my husband.

With loving arms, God embraces, comforts, and inspires us, even when we are at our worst, at our most unlovable and unworthy. No matter how many times we stumble, God, like a patient, selfless mother, smiles and says, "Bless you my child."

So, if I can catch myself before I blow up at someone, and if I can remind myself of all the patient and loving people in my life, I often can conquer terrible impatience.

A substantial part of gratitude to God is being patient with our brothers and sisters who are also "moving on to perfection." When you're tempted to fuss, remember a time when someone graciously and kindly showed you patience.

Prayer: *Dear God, even the forbearance of a loving grandmother or mother or uncle cannot match your boundless love. As you challenged Job and taught him patience, teach me how to be patient with those around me, so that they can experience your love through me. Amen.*

Wednesday, July 5   Read Psalm 30:6-12.

A preacher once exclaimed in a sermon, "I've never seen such fearful, nervous Christians worship such a *bold* God!"

I am an almost obsessive worrier. When my faith is strong and sure, I know that God's hand guides and protects me. I have never suffered any adversity that my Loving Friend has not brought me through.

Still, when I cannot make our household income meet expenses, when illness and death affect my immediate and extended family, when I am challenged by the strife of my sisters and brothers around the world, it is hard not to worry.

But, as the psalmist declares, God has always "turned my mourning into dancing." As sure as I wear the sackcloth of sadness, disappointment, and occasional despair, somehow—in time—the God of love "clothe[s] me with joy."

I find assurance in the knowledge that, no matter how fearful we are as less-than-perfect creatures, our Creator is bold and benevolent enough to make all things right in time.

Suggestion for meditation: *Name in your heart persons in your life who need to know God's assurance. Pray God's comfort for each.*

Prayer: *Lord of the dance, you are as sure as the day you have created. Teach me to pray; teach me to trust; teach me to obey.*

> *You have turned my mourning*
> *into dancing;*
> *. . . . .*
> *so that my soul may praise you*
> *and not be silent.*
> *O LORD my God, I will give thanks*
> *to you forever. Amen.*

Thursday, July 6   Read Galatians 6:1-6.

My high school music teacher was a second mother to me until her death two years ago. An independent, youthful 80, she spent her last five years in a nursing home due to a stroke.

One Christmas Eve, I entered her room carrying an old cassette tape. Before her illness, she had conducted an annual community-wide singing of Handel's *Messiah* at Christmas. This year, she could neither stand alone nor talk. I wanted to bring back some of the magic from those Christmases when other alumni and I would come home for the holidays just to sing in Browne's choir.

I slipped my cassette into her tape player. Suddenly, she sat bolt upright in bed as she recognized the opening strains of Handel's "And the Glory of the Lord."

Despite her restrictions and loss of speech, she hummed along in perfect soprano, as I sang along in rusty alto. As the music grew louder (she kept motioning for me to increase the volume), a nurse's aide came in. She stared at Browne in surprise and exclaimed, "She's singing!" For the next hour or so, Browne and I sang while she conducted us with her one functioning hand.

"Those who are taught the word must share in all good things with their teacher," reads Galatians 6:6. I can never repay all those teachers, church-school leaders, and surrogate parents who have guided me during my life's journey. God grant that I can do justice to what they have taught me about being a disciple of Christ in the world.

Prayer: *God of melody and of movement, thank you for the opportunity to serve you in creative, vibrant ministries of presence. With your help, may I continually use my talents of heart and hands for the building up of your people and your realm. Amen.*

Friday, July 7   Read Galatians 6:7-16.

I remember from my rebellious teen years distinct feelings of irritation while listening to older people in my church singing about how wonderful life would be when we died and went to heaven. I had one Sunday school teacher who ended every prayer with, "Lord, we look forward to the day when you welcome us and say, 'Well done, good and faithful servant. Well done.' "

I didn't get it. At age 15, barring extraordinary illness or accident, I was years away from death. I remember thinking, *If all God can do for me is offer me happiness after I die—and if all I can do as a Christian is sit and wait and "be good"—I want no part of it.* After all, the world needed so much from God right then. So did I, for that matter.

As I have matured, I have come to realize that one key to faith-filled living is to remember that to belong to God is to be called to love and work in the context of being God's own. This doesn't mean that I close my eyes to the challenges and calling of earthly discipleship. Far from it. Through knowledge of belonging to God and having a place in eternity, I understand that I am required to live and work and be steadfast, so that when I do reach my heavenly home, I will have made a difference among the family of God.

Thus, even in the face of life's daily disappointments, I am able to keep my eyes on the heavenly prize, for I fully expect to "reap a harvest" (v. 9, NIV)—not only a resting place in the hereafter, but daily knowledge that I am being of use to the Creator who has given me life, love, and work.

Prayer: *Because of your love and faithfulness, Spirit of Love, I feel like going on. May every good work I accomplish be of use and service. In Christ's name. Amen.*

Saturday, July 8   Read Luke 10:1-12.

Imagine yourself sent away from the safety of your home into a new city. Imagine yourself entering that strange city with no money and no luggage. You walk up to a stranger's door, knock, and tell the person at the door, "I bring you peace." Imagine expecting that stranger to welcome you, feed and clothe you, and listen to your views on religion. Talk about being "like lambs among wolves"!

But the 72 were called to live by Jesus' example, to share the word of God by stepping out in faith. They were called to make themselves vulnerable in the world in order to demonstrate the heady, healing power of God.

Our challenges as Christians are no less rigorous today. Our lives as people of God are dependent on how we live out God's teachings in a sometimes hostile world. I know of two women who attend the same church, neither of whom have spoken favorably to or about the other for some 20 years. Finally, one walked up to the other after service one Sunday and took her enemy's hand. "I don't know why we are enemies," she said to the astonished woman, "but if I have done anything to offend you or to hurt you, I beg you to forgive me in the name of our Savior, Jesus Christ."

I have seen and experienced many encounters between people, but that was one of the bravest acts I have witnessed. As brothers and sisters forgiven by God's grace, we should do no less than strive to live in harmony with one another, sharing the gospel story as we go.

Prayer: *O Supreme Giver of the peace that passes all understanding, order our hearts and minds so that in seeking justice and wholeness for all people—enemies and friends—we and all your children may find peace. Amen.*

Sunday, July 9   Read Luke 10:16-20.

In his ministry on earth, Jesus was deeply committed to humility before God. When the 70 returned boasting about the miracles performed in his name, Jesus did not join the brag-fest. Instead, he reminded them that the power was not given to glorify them or even Jesus. Rather, he said, by doing God's will, they should rejoice that their "names are written in heaven."

Power, whether measured by God or by humanity, is clearly most effective when used for good and not just for self-aggrandizement. My favorite biblical character, Lydia (Acts 16:12-15, 40), is an example of power used for godly purposes. A wealthy, independent businesswoman, Lydia graciously opened her home to Paul and Silas as they traveled and worked—even after they were released from prison.

Instead of showing off her power and money by ordering about her servants and acting the part of the pampered elite among the townspeople, Lydia led her employees and the women in her city to accept Christ. Her evangelistic works emphasized crossing barriers of class as a tangible sign that in God all are sisters and brothers.

What do you count among your blessings? Money, position? Good health, home, family? Musical or artistic talent? Business acumen? Are there ways you can share those blessings with the poor in your community; with neighbors, friends, family members?

Prayer: *For all you have given us, loving God, we give you thanks. We are especially thankful for the ultimate gift, the constant presence of Christ in our lives. Help us now to share what we have and what talents we have been given and, in so doing, show our gratitude in ways that make a difference to the lives of your children and your realm. Amen.*

July 10-16, 1995   **Bill Mauldin✤**
Monday, July 10   Read Psalm 82.

A few years ago, while exploring a cave in the Ozarks, I experienced something of the power of darkness. Having reached the last of a series of "rooms" in the cavern, my friend and I turned off our flashlights. We sat in silence in complete and utter darkness. After a while, I began to see movements that were not occurring, to imagine things that were not happening. I was astonished and I was afraid.

The psalmist wrestles with spiritual darkness, the origin of evil and injustice. The writer offers a then current belief of the ancient Near East—the idea that one god has given to lesser gods control over various aspects of human life. The malfeasance of these gods causes the injustice that exists in the world.

The despair over evil and injustice is not unfamiliar to us, though this portrait of the council of the gods is alien. There is something worthy of note though in the words of this ancient psalmist who was surrounded by the darkness of injustice toward the destitute, the weak, and the needy. The psalmist declares that there is a supreme God and that this God has power over all that is, thereby pointing the direction out of the complete and utter darkness into the edge of God's light.

Suggestion for meditation: *Close your eyes and concentrate first on physical darkness, then spiritual darkness. Now think about where you feel spiritual darkness. Concentrate on where the light of God's presence and hope is in the midst of this spiritual darkness.*

✤Associate pastor, First United Methodist Church, Columbus, Mississippi.

Tuesday, July 11   Read Colossians 1:1-14.

When I turned my flashlight on again, the light in the cave was overpowering. My eyes drank light like water. As I made my way from "room" to "room" in the cave, my eyes gradually adjusted, and the light feast I had experienced settled down. Another surprise came as I rounded the last corner and viewed the mouth of the cave in the distance. The walls of that last long cavern danced with light. As I approached the opening to the outside world, the most beautiful lush green color imaginable revealed itself.

The writer of the Letter to the Colossians had a good idea of what it meant to journey in spiritual light. From greeting to thanksgiving to intercession, this scripture emanates light. In a reminder to the Colossians to give thanks to the Father, we find the imagery of light and darkness. The readers are reminded to give thanks because God has made it possible for them to "share in the inheritance of the saints in the light." God has saved us from "the power of darkness and transferred us into the kingdom of his beloved Son." In the Son, we receive forgiveness of our sins because of an inheritance that we have done nothing to deserve. The grace of the gospel bears fruit in the faith, hope, and love for which the Colossians are well known. The whole passage is a summary of what it means to live and to travel in spiritual light—the grace of unmerited forgiveness bearing the fruit of faith, hope, and love.

Traveling from the dominion of darkness into the "inheritance of the saints in the light" was a dazzling change for the Colossians—like leaving the depths of a cave for the brightness, the texture, the color of a spring day.

Suggestion for meditation: *Reflect on God's spiritual gifts to you as though they were brightness in the darkened world.*

Wednesday, July 12   Read Luke 10:25-28.

Those who seek the light come in a variety of forms. The seeker in today's passage was a scholar of the Law. He had given his life to understanding and following the law of Moses because it was there that the light of Yahweh was to be found. Thus, when Jesus turned the question back upon the questioner, it was to be expected that the answer would come from the Law. The requirement of loving God with all one's being came from the *Shema* (Deut. 6:4-5). The requirement of placing this statement on doorposts, hands, and foreheads was to insure that it never left the consciousness of a devout Hebrew. Moreover, the lawyer knew that the only proof of love for God is to be found in our relationships with others. Thus, he links the first precept to the requirement of loving neighbor as self (Lev. 19:18).

The light shines forth: "You have given the right answer; do this, and you will live." This is where the difficulty arises. The concept of loving God with all one's being and loving one's neighbors as oneself is clearly one thing; the doing, the loving itself, is another. We are called to journey in the light of love. We struggle with what it means to translate precept into practice until we are reminded that we find our model in the life of Jesus. We find him alone with God in prayer again and again. We see him in attendance at times of worship and praise. We come upon him on the road showing love to others through his teaching, healing, and serving.

For us, too, light for the journey is found not in the abstract precept. Rather, it overtakes us as we pour ourselves into loving God and neighbor along the way.

Suggestion for meditation: *How am I being called into a deeper relationship of love with God and neighbor?*

Thursday, July 13   Read Luke 10:29-37.

How much is enough? Where can I draw the line? How far do I have to go with this matter of loving my neighbor? These are questions that the lawyer was asking Jesus. He had answered rightly about the Law. Now he wanted to justify himself. Now he wanted to know if he had done enough to inherit eternal life. The parable that Jesus told pushed the questioner beyond his limits.

What does it mean in practice to love God with all of one's being? In first-century Palestine, the dominant view was that ritual purity was the way to love God fully. To be pure was to be in God's light. The problem was that the rituals had become a limitation on loving one's neighbor. Since touching a dead body rendered one unclean, the priest and the Levite in the parable could not risk responding to the man on the side of the road. Defilement would have necessitated a time-consuming purification process.

Jesus' refusal to let his compassion be limited by the requirements of purity caused a great deal of consternation among the Pharisees. He was chastised for doing the "work" of healing on the Sabbath; allowing the hungry disciples to pick a bit of grain on the Sabbath; and associating with tax collectors, sinners, and others who were considered unclean. The parable of the Good Samaritan attacks head on the code of purity. Surely, mercy—surely, compassion—is more important to God than is ritual purity. This truth even the scholar of the Law grudgingly admits.

Suggestion for meditation: *What is there in my life and in the life of my church that limits the sharing of God's love?*

206

Friday, July 14   Read Amos 7:7-17.

Amos was probably doing fine, no doubt, as a shepherd and dresser of sycamore trees in the village of Tekoa in Judah. Then God said, "Go, prophesy to my people Israel," and Amos went. To many observers, things were going well in the northern kingdom of Israel, too, as Jeroboam II restored the glory of the good old days.

The problem was that Jeroboam and the rich were trampling underfoot the poor and needy. The religious services were beautiful, but injustice was rampant. Receiving God's light, Amos left his sheep and traveled northward about twenty miles to the royal sanctuary at Bethel. There he brought an unpopular message.

Doubtless, he would have preferred the ease of his regular life, yet he responded to the light and spoke God's truth in a place of injustice. Had Israel only listened, Amos, by speaking God's word, could have brought Israel out of the sin of their ways and into the light of living lives faithful to their covenant with God.

God has given each of us light along the journey. Through friends, family, and spiritual guides, we have been able to see the work of love, justice, or mercy that needs to be done. In the clarity of the light, we have discerned God's purpose for us.

Suggestion for meditation: *Where is God's light shining for you today? Reflect on the times that you have received light to guide you toward the good. Give thanks for your response to the light. Confess the times you have ignored the light. Be open to the light yet to be.*

Saturday, July 15   Read Colossians 1:9-12.

His plate was empty. His mouth was full. He was three years old and did not know the word for what he was eating. So he blurted out, "Give me some more of what I've got in my mouth!" This was a little boy who knew when something was good.

I believe that the Colossians knew that they were onto a good thing. From time to time, they probably prayed for more of what they had received. But just in case they had not asked lately, the writer of Colossians intercedes for them: "We have not ceased praying for you." The first prayer is for eyes to see the light, that is, for discernment: "that you may be filled with the knowledge of God's will in all spiritual wisdom and understanding." From this kind of discernment come lives filled with the fruit of good works. The second prayer is for strength: "May you be made strong with all the strength that comes from his glorious power." It is this kind of strength that brings patience and endurance.

What better gifts could be ours as we continue along on our journey of faith than to have the discernment to see God's will and to have some of God's "glorious power" in following the pathway? With these gifts we are able to walk in the same light the saints before us walked in. And what better could we seek each day than to grow more into the likeness of Christ? To have these gifts is truly to have more of what we already have in our mouths!

Suggestion for meditation: *Pray directly for more of the light of discernment. Pray for the particular places in your life where you need some of the "glorious power" to be faithful to the vision of God's reign.*

Sunday, July 16   Read Psalm 82:1, 8.

"All the nations belong to you!" Since the light of God's love for and empowerment of us began to issue from this verse earlier in the week, it has shone in many wonderful places on our journey of faith. God gives us an inheritance of forgiveness that we did not have to earn. God gives us the opportunity to live our lives in the light of faith, hope, and love. Having the clarity of vision that God gives us when we earnestly try to discern God's will, we are called by God to be ambassadors of the Kingdom.

When we respond, God commissions us, instructs us, empowers us, and sends us forth. We go into the world to serve, to heal, and to bless. We travel with a love that continually leads us into new territory. God gives us the discernment and the strength to move on. When we return, God receives us lovingly in spite of our failures or our pride. In this marvelous journey, the light of God's love for us is with us each step of the way.

The journey begins in the light of God's love and it ends in the light of God's love. Truly, the Holy One lives; and truly, the Holy One has ultimate control over all that is. God blesses us and calls us to live our lives journeying in the light.

Where we go from here depends on how much we long for more of the light. Each of us journeys with a question which draws us on: How fully will I allow God to bring me into "the inheritance of the saints of the light"? (Col. 1:12)

Suggestion for meditation: *Reflect on the grace, the love, and the empowerment that God has given you for the journey, and offer thanks to God. Reflect on the path upon which journeying in the light is taking you for the days ahead.*

July 17-23, 1995
Barry Stater-West✤

Monday, July 17
Read Amos 8:1-8.

Speaking over a formless void, God called creation into being. So, too, God speaks over the void within human hearts—hearts designed by God to be living temples but desecrated by sin's insidious power. Still, God remains passionately concerned with the "matters of the heart"—a passion clearly visible in this week's readings.

As a nation, Amos testifies, God's chosen people appear like ripened fruit—outwardly beautiful yet silently rotting within. Proclaiming God's judgment, Amos cuts through the veneer of Israel's prosperity and strips away the illusion of God's blessing. While the disease of injustice runs rampant throughout the land, its presence is symptomatic of a deeper malady—a contagion silently eroding a nation's soul. It is an idolatry rooted in the human heart.

Amos's words of judgment bear eternal significance. By carelessly inviting lesser gods to occupy the sanctuaries of our hearts, we rob God's word of the power in our own lives to transform our darkness into light and our cries of sorrow into songs of joy.

There is no such thing as cheap grace in the economy of God's kingdom. If salvation were not costly, it would not have been necessary for God's only Son to give up his life for it.

Prayer: *Loving God, help me not to settle for cheap grace. Grant me the courage to encounter your word of judgment in my life, so that before your throne, my heart may be pure. Amen.*

✤Freelance writer and ordained minister; Donor Relations Coordinator, Planned Giving, Holt International Children's Services, Eugene, Oregon.

Tuesday, July 18   Read Amos 8:9-12.

While injustice may be corrected through political change, the cause of a nation's idolatry can be reformed only through repentance. God yearns for hearts of stone to be transformed into hearts of flesh. In today's reading, Amos reminds the reader that only the spirit of repentance can recalibrate the heart to the life-giving presence of God's indwelling spirit.

So desolate will the soul become without the spirit of God to sustain it, says the prophet Amos, that the old cisterns that once quenched the soul's thirst will run dry. Religious feasts, once a source of joy and hope to the spirit, will become dry and lifeless. The famine of a nation's heart will bring mourning—the kind of mourning experienced in grieving the death of an only son. In the face of this famine, the most sought-after nourishment will not be for the body but for the human spirit. The hunger will be for life-giving words, words that sustain the heart with hope and the spirit with renewed strength.

Have you allowed God's life-giving word to penetrate your heart and permeate your spirit? Have you stood within the refiner's fire and invited God to purify you, stripping away your own heart's secret worship of lesser gods—those worldly idols whose power stands impotent before the One whose truth burns like fire and whose mercy is everlasting?

Before you a world staggers to and fro, dying of thirst for a word of life. Is your heart ready to receive God's word?

Prayer: *Lord God, you alone can quicken in my heart a true spirit of repentance. Transform my heart of stone into a heart of flesh, and recalibrate my spirit to your indwelling presence in my life. Amen.*

Wednesday, July 19   Read Psalm 52:1-9.

Words have the capacity to transform creation. Like a powerful weapon, the tongue can render blessings or curses upon all whom its words reach. In today's reading, the psalmist confronts the painful truth that when conceived in a spirit of deceit, words have the power to destroy. Like the psalmist, there are times when we become the victim of barbed words—words fashioned in a manner meant to "hook" us in our weak places. Today we ask the questions: What sustained the psalmist in the battle with injustice and evil? Can it sustain us as well?

Through the strength of his conviction that God's love is unfailing, the psalmist's heart is opened. Having felt the searing light of God's truth expose his self-righteousness and vengeful heart, the psalmist recognizes how little lasting justice human judgment can exact. In the face of an enemy whose boasting commands the world's attention and respect, the psalmist heard a sustaining word of hope—God will bring to ruin those whose lives are sustained by lies and deceit.

Does bitterness and wrath threaten to consume you? Do your adversary's words cut deeper than a razor, leaving invisible scars upon your spirit? If so, you are not alone. The lesson for today is this: the most powerful witness in the world to God's truth may come not in words of bitterness and retaliation but in the way we bear God's truth in the silence of our hearts.

Prayer: *Almighty God, only the presence of your Holy Spirit dwelling deep within me can save me from myself. Without you, O Lord, I am quick to judge and ever eager to condemn others. Teach me, Lord, in the silence of my heart, to wait upon you alone. Amen.*

Thursday, July 20   Read Psalm 52:6-9.

In yesterday's reading we discovered how God's spirit of truth carved out within the psalmist's heart a mighty fortress, shielding him from his adversaries' assaults. The psalmist finds solace in the eternal assurance of the truth that God's abiding justice is greater than evil.

For those whose hearts have been transformed by God, a new perspective and power begin to infuse life. "The righteous," says the psalmist, "will see and fear; they will laugh at him, saying, 'Here now is the man who did not make God his stronghold.'" By nurturing God's spirit dwelling within the heart, God's power births a wisdom that penetrates the folly of a darkened world.

Confronted by the onslaught of his adversary's deceit and boasting in wealth and worldly power, the psalmist reaffirms the source of strength—"trust in God's unfailing love for ever and ever" (NIV). And the psalmist renews that trust by filling his heart with praise and remembering God's saving acts throughout history.

Like the psalmist, we can take counsel from this reading when our souls are filled with bitterness or our spirits are reeling with resentment. Today turn your thoughts from replaying scenes from the past or entertaining fantasies of future revenge. Instead, focus your mind on praising God for being present in your life. Then let the name of Jesus be whispered softly upon your lips, as you surround yourself in the presence of the saints who have gone before you. Make God the source of your hope, and God will make you a repository of divine power.

Prayer: *You alone, most merciful God, can heal my shattered memories and restore peace to my troubled soul. Lord, reveal yourself to me today as the living source of my hope, that I might walk expectantly before you all the days of my life. Amen.*

Friday, July 21   Read Luke 10:38-42.

As believers, many of us periodically eagerly wish to force our hearts open to allow God's transforming spirit to burst forth in our lives. While the desire for intimacy with God is admirable, our ambitions are too often motivated by the wrong reasons.

Like Martha, our spiritual life may be characterized by our busying ourselves with the duties pressing around us, and so we neglect to offer Jesus a hospitable place to be adored within ourselves. In today's passage, Jesus reminds Martha that his entry into her home is not contingent upon a demonstration of her worth. No amount of accomplishment and success will ever cloud from the Lord's penetrating vision the nature of the human heart lying open before him.

Often we allow our own struggles around living holy lives to reveal to us our need of his transforming grace. If we are preoccupied with demonstrating our worthiness, we will miss his arrival, not understanding that he wants nothing more than our hearts to be filled with humble adoration at his desire to make a home within our hearts. Today, the Lord stands gently knocking at the door of our hearts. He does not ask for a litany of our achievements. He asks only that we make room for him to bless us with the glory of his love.

Today, take a lesson from Mary and learn that only one thing is needed. While the world may rob us of our accolades, God will never take away from us the portion of love promised us in the cross.

Prayer: *Lord Jesus, in a world driven by accomplishment and success, teach me "the better way" of drawing near to you. Holy Spirit, come, and make my heart a dwelling place for you. Amen.*

Saturday, July 22   Read Colossians 1:15-20.

In our world where power can be purchased and authority is subject to the changing laws of the land, Paul's revelation of Christ's supremacy over creation challenges human understanding. Yet through the power of the Holy Spirit, God gifts our hearts with wisdom as we ponder the mysteries of Christ's authority over creation.

God did not choose to remain distant and abstract but chose instead to give visible form to the divine invisible nature through Jesus Christ. Withholding nothing, "God was pleased to have all his fullness dwell in him" (NIV), a fullness that came and dwelt among us.

Pause today, and ponder the One you call Savior and Lord. Imagine his soul stretched out between the glory of the heavens above and the earth below. So woven into the fabric of his soul was the Father's plan for creation that even death itself—the most insurmountable obstacle facing every living soul, was defeated by his obedience to the One who called creation into being.

How feeble we are when we dismiss Christ's power as a thing of the past and claim the supremacy of our own reason over the mysteries of faith! Carefully we keep our fear hidden from sight—fear that in a blinding flash of his glory and power our lives might vaporize into insignificance.

Come before his cross today, on bended knee. To worship him in majesty, you must first humble your heart before him. Behold, he who presents you blameless before the throne is making intercession even now on your behalf.

Prayer: *Grant me today, O Lord, the wisdom to find your presence woven throughout the tapestry of creation. Amen.*

Sunday, July 23   Read Colossians 1:15-20.

Today Paul reminds us that Christ crucified overcomes our alienation from God's gracious love. Nevertheless, the atoning power of the cross requires us continually to turn our hearts toward the hope held before us in the gospel. The greatest mystery the world has ever known, says Paul, is the mystery of "Christ in you, the hope of glory" (NIV). You, once tarnished by despair, are now God's living expression of a promise awaiting all people.

Pause before the weight of this mystery of "Christ in you, the hope of glory." Can you, like Paul and the countless saints who have followed in his footsteps, recognize Christ's glory shining deep within you? Can you hear his eternal word of hope in the face of life's difficulties?

While you may feel discounted by the world, there is a resounding voice of truth whispering within your heart. You have been given the One whose name "is above every name" (Phil. 2:9, NIV)—and his name is written into the fabric of your soul. It is a name before which all creatures on heaven and earth shall bow, and it dwells deep within you, waiting to bring power and purpose to your life.

Today, begin your day by giving Christ the honor due his name. Grasp the hope within your heart, no matter how small or withered that hope may seem, and see if God will not fill you to overflowing with the only glory worth hoping for.

Prayer: *Jesus, quicken in me, through the power of your Holy Spirit, an ever-deepening awareness of the power of your name. Teach me to recognize your presence in my heart, that together with the angels and saints I might be bold to proclaim, "Christ in me, the hope of glory." Amen.*

GOD'S PROMISE OF RESTORATION

July 24-30, 1995   **Rosemarie Scotti Hughes**✤
Monday, July 24   Read Hosea 1:2-9.

Living examples

Hosea's career as a prophet does not seem to be getting off to a good start. His first action is to marry a wanton woman, and his children are walking billboards for God's displeasure with Israel's ways. Hosea's family and friends must have wondered what was going on with him—is this marriage doomed? And how can Hosea be an authentic prophet if he conducts himself in this manner?

People around Hosea did not understand that he and his family were, for a time, a living, breathing demonstration of God's word among them. Hosea's prophecy was not in saying as much as it was in being. We can learn from Hosea's obedience.

We do not learn to discern the voice of God instantaneously. Following our calling is a result of a love relationship with God, of recognizing the Divine Lover's voice, of being able to discern the call. When life is not "going well," in our terms, we must rely on that love for our own restoration to a sense of well-being grounded in trust in God's ultimate will for our lives.

Prayer: *Divine Lover, keep me close so that I may learn to know your voice. Strengthen my faith so that when you call, I will respond and know that it is you. Amen.*

✤Associate Dean, School of Counseling and Human Services, Regent University, Virginia Beach, Virginia.

Tuesday, July 25   Read Hosea 1:10.

Limitless restoration

The promise God relays to Hosea of descendants being as numerous as the stars in the sky and the grains of sand on the shore was also given to Abraham (Gen. 22:17) and Jeremiah (Jer. 33:22). This is a surprising verse, for it comes directly after a seemingly negative series of commands from God. But God always completes and restores; and so this verse is, in fact, what one would expect of a loving Creator.

The promise at the end of this first chapter is a preview of the ending of the Book of Hosea. Israel is disobedient and suffers God's displeasure, but, upon repentance, there will be forgiveness and restoration. The history of Hosea's family is a parallel to Israel's relationship with God. Gomer will have respect and love as an honorable wife, and the children will have new names of love and acceptance. Israel is to become a large nation, and the inheritance promised to the chosen people is to be expanded so that even the Gentiles (Rom. 9:25), indeed, all humanity, can experience being beloved of God.

For me, the seashore is a place of meditation and restoration. I am aware of being on the edge of land, and from here my potential in Christ seems as limitless as the vast ocean before me. I can come back to the beach for spiritual restoration an infinite number of times; like Israel, I can come back to God for restoration without limit.

Prayer: *Loving God, although I may have differing needs daily and come to you in changing ways, I rely upon your constant love. There, I can always find forgiveness and healing. Amen.*

Wednesday, July 26   Read Psalm 85.

Loving our children

Psalm 85 is a prayer that God will restore favor to the land and to the people. It begins with a recollection of the Lord's past favors, perhaps recalling the events of the Babylonian captivity. Next, the psalmist poses three questions to God: Are you going to be angry forever? Will your anger extend to our children's children? Will you help us so that we can again rejoice in you?

When children have been disobedient, they may in some form ask these same questions of their parents. The questions may be spoken aloud, or they may be in the children's thoughts. When punished or scolded, they want reassurance that no matter what they have done, their parents still love them.

In verses 8-13 the psalmist points to attributes of God—love, fidelity, justice, peace, mercy, truth, righteousness, kindness, faithfulness, goodness, and lovingkindness (compiled from many translations). All of these attributes are finally fulfilled in Christ's coming to us as human.

Those of us who are parents are called to be the living examples of these holy attributes to our children. Our example is not perfect, but as we find mercy and love in Jesus, so then are we obligated to convey those attributes to our children, and we are empowered to live them more fully. Whether parents or not, we all are called to present the same model to those who are a part of our lives.

Prayer: *Faithful God, help me to recognize when I am selfish with your gifts and do not extend them to others. Remind me of your past faithfulness to me. Just as you do not hold your anger against me, so help me not hold my anger toward my family and others around me. Grant me the peace to offer restoration and reconciliation among us. Amen.*

Thursday, July 27   Read Colossians 2:6-15.

Soul satisfaction

As you read this passage, underline each phrase that begins, "with him" (or "with Christ") or "in him." Then reread each phrase you have underlined. As you do, focus on the gifts that are yours as a result of living the Christian life. Once a person accepts Christ, not just from head knowledge but from heart and spirit knowledge, a lifelong process of spiritual growth and fulfillment follows.

Paul uses metaphors in verses 6 and 7 that people then and now can comprehend. He presents the corporate or legal image of union, the agricultural one of being rooted, and the architectural image of being built up. As we join ourselves to Christ we become rooted. When the roots are sunk deep, they anchor us, and our spiritual life blossoms. We are constantly being added to, just as buildings are added to, brick by brick. Living in and with Christ is an experience available to all, for it transcends all barriers of age, gender, race, economic class, and nationality.

The world's offerings, no matter what they may be, have never been able to satisfy the human heart as does Christ's forgiveness and welcome. Our own striving and effort can never bring us victory over our sinfulness. Only through Jesus' death and resurrection can we find triumph and joy.

Prayer: *Gracious Father, forgive me when I neglect to give thanks for my inheritance in your kingdom through Jesus. As you have so generously given of your mercy to me, may I extend those same gifts to others. Amen.*

Friday, July 28　　　　　　　　Read Colossians 2:16-19.

Joyful living

Have you ever gone on a diet? How easy it is to become self-righteous when we have decided to change our eating habits! We judge others in terms of the amounts of cholesterol, fat, sodium, or sugar that they are eating, while holding ourselves up as a paragon of virtuous nutrition. The same is true of other changes we might make, such as beginning a program of exercise or time management or pledging more consistent church attendance. In any of our new endeavors it is our human nature to judge others who are not similarly inclined.

Verse 16 calls to mind the legalism that creeps into our churches, cloaking itself in the name of Jesus. Living by Christian principles is, of course, desirable. But some people decide that they are the arbiters of what is lawful and what is not and, in doing so, distract us from the victories of life in Christ that we read about yesterday. Legalism shrinks spirits. It is joyless, conforming, and limiting. A legalistic faith is shallow; faithful living in Christ is fulfilling and freeing.

The call of Christ on an individual's life does not give one the right to impose that call on others. Jesus was harsh toward the Pharisees because of their legalism, not because they kept the laws but because in their overemphasis on jots and tittles they were blind to the purposes of the kingdom (Matt. 23:23-24).

Fasting or feasting, all is acceptable as we hold fast to Christ and the Spirit's call on our lives.

Prayer: *All-loving Father, keep my eyes focused on you so that I do not have to focus on what my sisters and brothers are or are not doing. Keep ever before me the joy of my salvation, and grant me peace in heeding the Spirit's call. Amen.*

Saturday, July 29   Read Luke 11:1-4.

The model prayer

Jesus had been praying, perhaps in Bethany or on the Mount of Olives, when one of the disciples spoke a prayer to him, "Lord, teach us to pray." In his answer, Jesus gave both a prayer and a model for prayer. Prayer is not a new concept in the Bible, but this model of prayer *was* new.

This prayer was to the One God, who can be approached as Father. We all have this one Father, reminding us that we go to God in community. We are to pray with confidence, not with arrogance but as a child approaching a loving Daddy (which is closest to the meaning of the Aramaic word *Abba* that Jesus used for Father). We are also to come to God in reverence, with recognition and respect for God's holiness. We must surrender ourselves to God's reign in our own hearts and recognize God's plan for others.

We are dependent upon God for our daily provision, as the servant needed the daily ration of food from the master for sufficient energy to perform the day's tasks.

Penitence is crucial in our prayer life, for we can only be forgiven by God as we forgive others. If we cannot forgive others' sins against us, how can we expect to be forgiven for our sins, so much greater in nature, against God.

Finally, we must have a desire to walk in God's ways so that we are delivered from evil temptations.

Prayer: *Ever-caring Father, give me the spirit of willingness to pray as your Spirit calls me. I can only approach your throne through Jesus' atonement; never let me forget to be thankful for the opportunity. As I seek to deepen my prayer life, lead and guide me so that I am following your leading and not my own. Amen.*

Sunday, July 30   Read Luke 11:5-13

Persistence in prayer

At first, these verses seem paradoxical. Is this demanding, assertive, persistent person a model for a Christian? But the lesson is not one of personality characteristics but of our relationship to God in prayer. The cultural setting of this parable helps us understand its significance. In the Middle East, travelers were expected to be accommodated in homes after a day of travel because there were few inns. The thin flatbread was not kept over for the next day but was baked daily as needed. By rights of hospitality, one person was expected to help meet another's needs.

The person's coming to his neighbor at midnight, asking him to rise from sleep and bake him bread, assumed that he had the right to insist that his request be honored without even apologizing for waking him. This is how we can seek, knock, and ask at God's doorway—with boldness. Through Christ's sacrifice of himself we have rights as heirs to the kingdom.

God wants to give us more than we could ever fathom, but what we ask for is limited by our humanness. Our eyes have not seen, nor have our ears heard, what God has ready for those who love him (compare 1 Corinthians 2:9). When we go to God with boldness, it is not to be for our wishes or wants but to learn of and to claim for ourselves God's willingness to help us lead faithful and fulfilled lives.

Prayer: *Generous, loving God, teach me to live according to your will. Grant me the grace to trust in your provision for my life. Never let me forget that you are always present to me and that you desire only good for me. Amen.*

RESTORATION

July 31–August 6, 1995
Monday, July 31

Frances I. Mitchell✣
Read Luke 12:13-15.

A single sin

Murder and robbery are easily recognized and easily marked off as sin. Covetousness creeps in unawares, as quiet as a cat's entrance. It can overtake us before we are conscious of it; and its forebears are envy, hatred, malice, and all uncharitableness.

In Luke's story a man from the crowd of thousands speaks up. Jesus fully understood the intent of his request and of what was happening around him. The request seemed simple and innocent: "Tell my brother to divide the family inheritance with me." In reality, it was a more complicated and delicate matter. The man was asking for something that was not his. The inheritance belonged to the brother. This man was walking on the edge of covetousness.

Jesus sees the question for what it is. His straightforward response is another question: "Who set me a judge or arbitrator over you?" He does not fall into the trap.

Our feelings of envy, hatred, malice, and uncharitableness set us up for covetousness and unhealthy pride. Our awareness of what is surfacing inside us will help us to be honest with ourselves before God. This honesty serves as an antidote to the quiet poison of covetousness seeping into our lives.

Prayer: *Lord, may today find me alert and aware of my lack of charity toward others so that I may not fall into the sin of covetousness. Amen.*

✣Clergy member, Rio Grande Conference; Agape United Methodist Church, Dallas, Texas.

Tuesday, August 1   Read Luke 12:16-21.

A greater sin

The thousands who heard the parable that day received a painful reminder of the corruption of Jewish law. Upon entering the Holy Land, their Hebrew ancestors had set up an economic system they hoped would be just and sacred. To own property was a gift from God and, thus, a sacred responsibility.

The parable gives a picture of a man who had forgotten his sacred responsibility to a law that required him to care for the land and for the neighbor. The question "Whose will they be?" also provokes the question "Whose are they now?"

According to Jewish thought the landowner must recognize God as the true owner; and, therefore, he must share the blessings from the land with those who lack food. (Remember the story of Ruth and Boaz.) The brother who was the inheritor also walked on the edge of covetousness. The nature of his life after death was in greater danger than that of the brother who had made the request of Jesus. The brother who was the inheritor had not fulfilled his sacred duty to share with the less fortunate.

The Native American traditions and beliefs also remind us of respect for the land and sharing with neighbors. There are those who say that we already produce enough food to feed the world. It is the distribution which is inadequate. "Those who store up treasures for themselves . . . are not rich toward God."

What started out as a seemingly simple request now becomes a matter of the preservation of the human race. We, too, must answer the questions "Whose are they now?" and "What is our sacred duty?"

Prayer: *Dear God, remind us today that we are responsible for our neighbor. Help us to look for ways to redistribute the food supply of the world so that all may share in its goodness. Amen.*

Wednesday, August 2   Read Colossians 3:5-10.

An atmosphere of sin

We experience the inner feelings of sin such as malice, anger, misplaced passion, unhealthy desire, and covetousness and the outward expression of these sins such as slander, wrath, foul talk, fornication, impurity, and lying. Now we are caught in a web of sin.

Today's scripture mirrors our sins and makes us aware of the mire that clings to us. These vices functioned like a net, entangling the Colossians in sin. But now, says Paul to the Colossians, it is time to rid yourselves of these sins.

Paul reminds the Colossians (and us) that conquering these vices does not happen automatically; it takes a conscious effort to eliminate them from our lives. What a challenge! New life in Christ results in ethical moral conduct. But high moral conduct is not what saves us; rather, we change our conduct because of our gratefulness for the salvation already granted us.

Dallas had an ice storm on Thanksgiving Day, and for three nights the sand trucks were out in full force. On the fourth evening I was driving home through downtown when I noticed that the air was filled with a fine dust. Traffic was kicking up the sand on the road. I thought about how sin is like that fine dust. It can fill our lives before we know it. Even when we feel justified in our anger and resentment, they can eventually choke us.

Prayer: *Help us, O Lord, to make conscious efforts to change our conduct. Make us determined to eliminate those sinful feelings and actions that entangle us like a web. Amen.*

Thursday, August 3   Read Hosea 11:2-9.

The root of sin

Israel's main problem was neglecting righteousness and justice. Their neglect was rooted in disloyalty to the God who had called them to be a nation, saved them in the wilderness, and with love had fed and nurtured them.

I often wear a clerical collar while making hospital calls or functioning in the role of advocate in public settings. It has saved a lot of words. On several occasions my 16-year-old son had witnessed the power of the clerical collar to influence issues of justice. One day, he asked me to wear the collar and go with him to return a battery he had purchased two months previously. I told him that to use the collar for justice for myself or my family, I believed, would be to misuse the collar; it would be a corruption of my efforts to advocate for justice. (I *did* accompany him as a mother—without the collar—and stood in another part of the store while he negotiated the exchange.)

In wanting justice for ourselves we often stubbornly cling to our selfish ways. But "justice" born out of self-interest results in greed, lying, covetousness, and hatred. Justice for our neighbor that grows out of our faithfulness to God is our path away from our selfish tendencies.

Hosea 11 is a reminder of who we really are and what our true relationship to God is. Our willfulness and stubbornness stand in the way. We should not corrupt justice. God's justice always advocates for others. It cannot be self-serving.

Prayer: *Thank you, God, for your persistent call of love that brings our salvation. Help us to respond to your call for righteousness and justice for the neighbor in our everyday life. Amen.*

Friday, August 4   Read Hosea 11:1, 10-11.

God calls us home

The Lord roars like a lion. The voice does not whine. It does not plead. It is neither expressionless nor full of apathy. It is not a weak and puny voice. It roars like a lion. It demands attention. It calls the children to return home.

The symbol of home is a powerful one. A real estate agent will use the term *house* when talking to the seller but will use the term *home* when talking to the potential buyer. We can detach ourselves from a house, but a home tugs at our emotions.

Home is where the heart is. Home is a place where we are truly ourselves. Home is where we laugh, cry, sing, and dance. Home is a safe place, a place of protection. Home is where we sleep in peace. Home is where we renew our strength.

Home is our natural habitat. The natural habitat of our souls is always with God. We understand the need to protect the natural habitat for wild animals. We understand that the animal thrives best in its natural habitat. We also thrive best when our souls find their natural habitat in God. In Hosea, God is calling us to the natural habitat of the soul where we regain and nourish our true spiritual self.

Hosea describes the children returning home "like birds from Egypt, and like doves from the land of Assyria," like birds returning to their nesting places even as the swallows return each year to Capistrano. When we return to our spiritual home with God, we return to the place where we belong. We are restored. We are at peace.

Prayer: *Thank you, God, for calling us to return home to the natural habitat of our spirit. Help us when we stray, when we are caught up in our own devices, and when we are deceived into believing that we are able to thrive without you. Amen.*

Saturday, August 5   Read Psalm 107:1-9, 43.

Return to the sanctuary

How do we survive the burden of our sinfulness? Where is our salvation? How do we find our way through the wilderness? Through God's steadfast love. This steadfast love is the undergirding that maintains the covenant relationship between God and the people.

Psalm 107 is considered a thanksgiving hymn that was sung by pilgrim groups on their way to Jerusalem. The sojourners experienced the hardships of the journey through the desert. They needed water and food. Maybe they were pursued by human and animal predators. Maybe they suffered physical abuse and harm along the way. As the pilgrims reached Jerusalem safely, they sang a hymn of gratitude. They knew that God's graciousness had brought them safely to their destination.

Our lives are like a pilgrimage. We experience spiritual deserts, and we are in danger of losing our way. Sin acts as a predator, often entangling us to the point that we risk losing our spiritual—even our physical—lives. We find ourselves living lives that no longer reflect God's concern for a just society.

But God's steadfast love keeps calling us back into our covenant relationship. We recognize our brokenness. God's call of steadfast love guides us, sustains us, and brings us to the sanctuary, which is an appropriate destination. We respond in an act of worship, with a song of thanksgiving and praise.

Prayer: *Divine Guide, whose steadfast love calls us, we know that it is your graciousness that brings us safely to the sanctuary. We know that while we walked through the wilderness you were there sustaining us. How can we thank you enough? Mil gracias, Señor! Amen.*

Sunday, August 6   Read Colossians 3:1-11.

The Christ of Colossians is the universal Christ, the Christ who is all in all and is able to unify the people of God.

Paul believed that Christ was fully divine. Everything was created through him and for him. We, as believers, are raised with Christ and seek our connectedness to all that Christ is connected to so that we participate in the unity.

Paul declared that in this new world order we all become equal. We become responsible. We become just. We become one. The old social order that divides us, the old ways of behaving that divide us, the sins of idolatry and apostasy are all gone. Peace and justice replace them—not just for ourselves but for the whole universe!

There are those who say that all human life is connected. We are one in our cellular makeup. Some would say that the whole universe is interrelated. The socio-economic world must be one in terms of justice for all. And finally, we are all connected spiritually as the children of the one God. Christ does away with those elements which would divide and separate us in whatever dimension.

What a journey we have made this week! How marvelous is our God! Let us sing a song of thankfulness:

> Let the shadow on our soul lift.
> Let the gloom of our sin be dispelled.
> Let the ring of self-awareness break the silence.
> Let the fire of repentance blaze hot.
> Let the cry of thankfulness bellow out.
> Let the ashes of justice fall on the neighbor.
> CHRIST IS ALL AND IN ALL.
> Amen. Amen. Amen.

THE SACRIFICES GOD WANTS

August 7-13, 1995   **David Randell Boone**✤
Monday, August 7   Read Isaiah 1:1, 10-15.

Isaiah son of Amoz addressed the word of God to the ruling classes of Judah during the latter part of the eighth century B.C.E. Because Assyria had forcibly annexed the Northern Kingdom (Israel), Judah stood alone and vulnerable. Isaiah's hearers were therefore likely to have been ruling aristocrats beset by anxiety. The destruction that had come upon Israel could visit Jerusalem and endanger the Temple.

Isaiah claimed that the rulers of Judah were no wiser than the doomed rulers of Sodom, for they supposed that Temple ritual would move God to protect Judah. Correct prayers and sacrifices by Temple priests, they imagined, would surely save the nation.

But Isaiah said not, and his preaching in God's name sought to correct this mistaken policy in the strongest terms: "I have had enough of burnt offerings . . . I do not delight in the blood of bulls . . . I cannot endure solemn assemblies . . . I will hide my eyes from you, even though you make many prayers." Why this divine loathing of Temple worship? Because Judeans had convinced themselves that God would settle for good liturgy without the doing of justice.

Prayer: *O Lord, guide planners and leaders of public worship so that our solemn assemblies may inspire us with your compassion and move us to deeds of charity and justice. Amen.*

✤Senior Pastor, Fairview Presbyterian Church (U.S.A.), Indianapolis, Indiana.

Tuesday, August 8   Read Isaiah 1:16-20.

Hoping to avert disaster, Isaiah called for the leaders of Judah and Jerusalem to chart a new course—a return from superficial liturgical propriety to an emphasis on the requirements of true religion. Judah must start "walking its talk" in the form of ministry to widows and orphans—those who had lost the economic safety net, commonly provided by father or husband.

Isaiah anticipated Christian definitions of true religion as compassionate service to others (see Matthew 25:35-36; James 1:27). Whether private or public, formal devotional exercises are no substitute compassion to the poor, hungry, sick, imprisoned. Without a constant attempt to rescue those who are without life's basics, religion becomes rotten at the core, an offense to God. If its leaders will attempt justice, God will forgive Judah's sins and make it flourish; if not, Judah will succumb to an enemy.

Authentic religion balances prayer and service, contemplation and action. Many church leaders, such as the seventeenth-century English rector George Herbert, have managed to make common worship the center of congregational life without neglecting justice. Developing a vital liturgical life and encouraging disciples of Jesus to help the poor are dimensions of church life that complement each other. Herbert wrote in "To My Successor"

> Be good to the Poor,
> As God gives thee store,
> And then, my Labor's not lost.*

Prayer: *Lord Jesus, whose praying and doing were of one piece: save us from serene hypocrisy, where beautiful words and comfortable forms can anesthetize us to the urgency of your summons. Amen.*

---

*The Country Parson, The Temple, 1633.

Wednesday, August 9   Read Psalm 50.

In Psalm 50 the Lord is dramatically portrayed as an activist Judge and righteous Prosecutor. The Mighty One comes with fire and tempest, calling heaven and earth to witness the impending divine assessment of the people of the covenant.

As a prosecuting witness, God testifies against Israel. God has been faithful to the covenant; Israel has not. In response, God brings a now-familiar charge: Israel has relied too much on ritual as a way of placating and manipulating the Holy One and has failed to cultivate spiritual affections and to fulfill the demands of the moral life.

The community has learned to tolerate stealing, adultery, and scandal-mongering; and God warns that such behavior will bring fierce and terrible consequences. Without a reversal, "I will tear you apart, and there will be no one to deliver."

In fact, God *does* desire sacrifice, but not bloody ritual sacrifices of bulls and goats, animals that in any case already belong to the Creator. Instead, the sacrifice God wants is genuine thanksgiving for divine benevolence (vv. 14 and 23). This revision of the concept of sacrifice recalls Psalm 51:17, where the penitent poet avers that the sacrifice God accepts is a "broken spirit" and a "contrite heart."

Early disciples of Jesus named the Lord's Supper the Thanksgiving, or Eucharist. In so doing, they made clear that practicing gratitude to God from the heart is the essence of the spiritual life.

Prayer: *Mighty God, my Judge, whose love enables me to bear your severity: may the sacrifices I offer you this day be heartfelt thanksgiving, genuine sorrow for my sins, and confidence in your mercy. In the name of Jesus Christ. Amen.*

Thursday, August 10   Read Hebrews 11:1-3.

The Letter to the Hebrews was written by an unknown author to a community of Christian believers who were Jews. Under persecution, these Jewish (Hebrew) Christians were being tempted to return to Judaism, a religion that enjoyed the legal protection of Roman law. Thus, the letter attempts to encourage persecuted believers in Jesus Christ to hold fast to their convictions. It does this by an eloquent portrayal of Jesus as Priest and Pioneer: the heavenly High Priest who eternally offers himelf as a once-for-all sacrifice for human sin and the Pioneer of faith who leads the faithful on their journey to the heavenly city.

For the Letter to the Hebrews, faith means an enduring, hopeful confidence that the One in whom the believer trusts is trustworthy. It means a willingness to journey onward toward a prize that one has not seen with earthly eyes. It means not losing nerve, not giving up the quest, in spite of opposition. It means loyal waiting for the realization of God's future.

Hebrews deems the Christian life a pilgrimage to "the city that has foundations, whose architect and builder is God" (11:10). In fact, the Gospel of Luke and the Acts of the Apostles also term the Christian life the road or way along which disciples walk in company with Jesus (see, for example, Luke 24:35; Acts 9:2).

This imagery reminds us that although the fulfillment of our spiritual desires has been *deferred*, the satisfaction of the soul's longing *postponed*, we will at length reach our journey's end and find ourselves at home. Until then, we walk by faith, not by sight.

Prayer: *Lord, when people challenge our commitment to you, when a shadow of doubt arises in a corner of our mind, keep us loyal sojourners whose feet are pointed homeward. Amen.*

Friday, August 11   Read Hebrews 11:8-16.

This week we have explored several dimensions of sacrifice. We considered the religious inadequacy of the ritual slaughter of animals and then moved on to other kinds of sacrificial offerings: a penitent heart, praise and thanksgiving, loyal endurance under persecution, and the cross as the High Priest's eternal offering of himself to God on behalf of sinful humanity. Today's reading suggests another dimension of the sacrifices God wants; for when God summoned Abram and Sarai from their home in Ur, their faithful response brought with it uncertainty, inconvenience, and the prospect of hard work.

From day one, Abram, Sarai, and their nephew Lot did not know where they were going (see Genesis 12). They and their descendants were to inherit a land and be a blessing. And so they set out without a map, trusting God to lead them to their destination. Second, the call of God meant for Abram and Sarai the inconvenience of a nomadic life. Sarai gave up a familiar home in Ur. Yet when she reached the land of promise to which her husband and her God had brought her, she couldn't move in. She and her family sojourned there in tents "as in a foreign land."

Finally, embracing God's call involved Abram and Sarai in hard work. Travel with servants and flocks was exhausting. And in their advanced years they faced the parenting of Isaac!

When we choose to bear the physical and emotional stressors that develop in our lives as a result of obeying God's call to service, that, too, is sacrifice!

Prayer: *Lord, when serving you stretches my physical and emotional resources to the limit, accept the spending of myself as devotion to you, and help me find the renewal I need to keep going. Amen.*

Saturday, August 12   Read Luke 12:32-34.

Here is a paradox. God gives us the gift of the kingdom, a gift that summons us to empty ourselves, to spend our energies. In this way, the Christian life is a striving to possess what is already assured, to grasp our soul's inheritance, to reach out and embrace the divine promise, to make our calling and election sure.

This process includes an assessment of the value we assign to earthly possessions. Jesus tells us that a benevolent Father takes pleasure in *giving* us the kingdom. By its nature the kingdom of God completely claims us and promises ultimately to fulfill us. Our part is to free ourselves deliberately from other allegiances, to reject entanglements with other "kingdoms." One simple way to do this is to sell our possessions and give the proceeds to be distributed among the needy, thus making a spiritual investment that cannot be worn out or exhausted or stolen or eaten up.

In Acts 4:32–5:11 Luke tells of occasions when early disciples obeyed this word of Jesus to sell and give. The story of Ananias and Sapphira shows that, while common to early Christian religious life, divestiture of property for benevolent purposes was not required by the church. Indeed, if a person could not sell and give without reservation, the practice was better avoided.

If we choose not to sell our possessions, we may be able at least to simplify our lives by *revaluing,* in the light of God's kingdom, what belongs to us. Unless we reorient our perspective on possessions, redefining *treasure*, our earthly holdings may come to possess *us*. Where our treasure is, spiritual or mundane, there the affection and commitment of our heart will be as well.

Prayer: *Lord Jesus, you are my Treasure, and my earthly resources are your gifts. May I value them as tokens of your goodness and the means by which I may share your bounty. Amen.*

Sunday, August 13   Read Luke 12:35-38.

Much like the parable of the wise and foolish virgins awaiting the bridegroom (Matt. 25:1-13), today's parable features servants of a master who is away attending a wedding banquet. The servants' role is to remain alert for the master's return, even into the early hours of the morning, so that they can promptly open the door for him when he knocks. Dressed for action with loins girded up and lamps lighted, they wait—expectant, attendant, watchful, aware.

Luke probably intended readers to understand Jesus' parable about a master and a wedding banquet as a reference to the culmination of Jesus' saving work, a time in the future often described as a messianic or kingdom banquet (see Luke 13:29 and 22:16). By the time Luke wrote his Gospel, disciples had been waiting two generations for this expected future.

Disciples still await the fullness of the messianic age. As we wait, our challenge is to stay awake and alert. We are servants keeping on the lights for the Master even when he returns late. We are ready for whatever form and timing our future with him may take.

The parable resolves in a remarkable way. When the master does return to find his servants alert and ready for him, he is so pleased that he invites them to sit at table and eat, while *he* serves *them*. For those who have known Jesus' presence in gathering around his Table, this parable not only points toward the future; it describes a joyful contemporary reality. Blessed indeed are those servants whom the Master serves.

Prayer: *Lord, keep me faithful through the long watches of the night. Keep me awake and alert to recognize the stirrings of your spirit in my life, in the lives of those around me, and in the events of my time, that I may become a servant in whom you take pleasure. Amen.*

BRING US BACK, O GOD!

August 14–20, 1995
Monday, August 14

Donald E. Collins❖
Read Isaiah 5:1-7.

Isaiah's song of the unfruitful vineyard is a powerful metaphor not only for the people of Judah who knew about vineyards from personal experience but also for those of us who buy our grapes in the supermarket!

But this is not just any vineyard. This is God's vineyard, "the house of Israel and the people of Judah." How God worked to prepare the vineyard—clearing the stones, cultivating it, "plant[ing] it with choice vines," protecting it with a wall and even a watchtower! God, Isaiah reminds us, expected Israel to yield good grapes. But instead, "it yielded wild grapes." Where God prepared the way for justice, there was bloodshed, and Israel's victims "cried out for justice" (TEV).

Thus God calls upon the inhabitants of Jerusalem, the people of Judah, and us: "Judge between my vineyard and me. Is there anything I failed to do for it? Then why did it produce sour grapes and not the good grapes I expected?" (TEV)

Suggestion for meditation: *Take a few moments to reflect on these words, which are addressed to you as surely as they are to Israel and the people of Judah. You, your family, your neighborhood, your church, your business or profession, your nation—all are part of the vineyard prepared, planted, and nourished by God. What kind of grapes have been produced?*

Prayer: *Loving God, you have prepared a place for me and nourished my growth. Thank you for your nurturing spirit. Amen.*

❖Author; Milwaukee, Wisconsin.

Tuesday, August 15   Read Psalm 80:1-3.

In the Revised Common Lectionary, the psalm for each Sunday is intended to serve as a response to the first reading of the day. Psalm 80 seems to have originated in the Northern Kingdom and was likely used as a community prayer, perhaps in response to a recent military defeat. The opening verses call upon God as the "Shepherd of Israel" to "come and save us." It is thus an appropriate response to yesterday's reading in which Isaiah's song of the unfruitful vineyard called us to reflect on the kind of fruit we have or have not produced in God's vineyard. Verse 3 is a refrain which is repeated in the middle (v. 7) and again at the end of the psalm.

In yesterday's reading Isaiah reminded us that we are the vineyard, dug, planted, and nourished by God in the hope of a good harvest. Yet the grapes we produce are sometimes sour. If we stand among those who continue to blame God, circumstances, or others for their own failure to bear good fruit, the words of the psalmist will be lost to our ears. But if we receive Isaiah's prophetic message with humility, confessing our failures, then we are ready to cry out to God with the psalmist:

Bring us back, O God!

Show us your mercy, and we will be saved! (TEV)

Suggestion for meditation: *Take a few moments now to reflect on these questions: What attitude or condition of your life is such that you need to be "brought back"? What is it in you that most resists God's attempts to "bring you back"? What do you need to do to make it possible for God to "bring you back"? Ask God to help you do that.*

Prayer: *Bring me back, O God!*
          Show me your mercy, and I will be saved! Amen.

Wednesday, August 16   Read Psalm 80:8-19.

As we read the second part of Psalm 80 we can understand why it was chosen as the psalm for this week. Its relationship to the reading from Isaiah 5 is obvious. But here the image of God's vineyard is reminiscent of the Exodus experience and Israel's occupation of the land promised by God. Yet, even within this broad sweep of history there are often temporary setbacks, such as the unspecified events and conditions alluded to in verses 5-6, 12-13, and 16.

The suffering of the people is not attributed simply to Israel's human enemies. God is asked, "How long will you be angry with your people's prayers?" Then God is blamed even more directly for the problems of Israel: "You make us the scorn of our neighbors." The psalmist goes on to blame God for breaking down the walls of the vineyard, surely a problem of human origin! This should not surprise us. Those who have suffered grief or loss know from personal experience how easy it is to blame God for what has happened. But notice in the psalm—as well, perhaps, as in your personal experience—that we are never completely without hope. In this psalm hope makes its appearance in signs of humility and responsibility: "We will never turn away from you again" (TEV).

Suggestion for meditation: *Take time to read Isaiah 5:1-7 again. Then read Psalm 80 once more. Listen to the praise offered to God, who is both Creator of the vineyard and the Shepherd of Israel. Reflect on the human condition that lets us praise God when things go right and blame God when things go wrong.*

Prayer: *Ever-present God, give us the grace to look for your presence even in the midst of suffering. Forgive us when we try to avoid responsibility by blaming you. Amen.*

Thursday, August 17   Read Hebrews 11:29-40.

Ask almost any person what he or she remembers about the Letter to the Hebrews and the response will likely be, "Chapter 11, the faith chapter." Even as we struggle to be more inclusive in our language, "Faith of our Fathers" remains one of our favorite hymns. In these and other ways we continue to praise the faith of our biblical ancestors.

Hebrews 11 provides us with an impressive overview of biblical faith, from those who passed through the Red Sea all the way to the martyrs of the early church. We marvel at those whose faith was so strong that they endured almost every conceivable form of persecution and torture for their faith.

Perhaps one reason we marvel at their faithful witness is that most of us live in a time when we can scarcely imagine being called upon to make such a witness to our own faith. Yes, there are still places in the world where Christians face persecution, but for most of us life is relatively safe and comfortable. When was the last time you were called upon to witness to your faith under threat of adverse consequences?

It may be helpful to ask ourselves what has happened to our faith in a time when it is rarely tested. Has modern religious freedom led to our spiritual decline? Has our high standard of living led to our having more faith in the stock market than in the saving power of the gospel? Has our love of comfort and convenience blinded us to Jesus' call to be the servant of others?

Prayer: *God of Abraham and Sarah, inspiration of prophets and martyrs, open our minds and hearts to the challenge and promise of faith. Make your church once more a place not only to celebrate our faith and that of our ancestors but also a place to live our faith, as servants of others. Amen.*

Friday, August 18   Read Hebrews 12:1-2.

The author of Hebrews uses a wonderful metaphor, "so great a cloud of witnesses," to emphasize the large number of those giants of faith whose witness has given shape and meaning to our Judeo-Christian tradition. That we are "surrounded" by such a cloud of witnesses is a welcome reminder that, in some mysterious way, this communion of saints remains with us even now to strengthen and encourage our own witness.

It is with the assurance of that strength and courage that we are called to cast off the burden of our own sin along with any other encumbrances that get in the way of our living as people of faith. In our time consumerism is surely such an encumbrance. How much time and energy is usurped by acquiring, sorting, cleaning, repairing, storing, protecting, insuring, and finally disposing of *things*?

Likewise, the cultural pressure to be politically, socially, and economically "correct" is a burden that weighs us down on our faith journey. How free do we feel to challenge our friends and neighbors whose idea of security is based on the possession of firearms? To what extent are we willing to risk unpopularity for the sake of principle? Are we able to put our job on the line in order to challenge injustice?

What might it mean for us to cast off the burdens of conformity and comfort in order to act freely on our faith? What private and public sins get in the way of our becoming a part of that "great . . . cloud of witnesses"?

Prayer: *Faithful God, we confess to you that many things come between ourselves and you. Help us to lay aside that which "clings so closely" so that we might be free to witness to our faith. Amen.*

Saturday, August 19   Read Luke 12:49-53.

This teaching, which many find troubling, occurs in the context of what Luke calls Jesus' journey to Jerusalem. On the journey were many who had followed him from Galilee and others who had joined along the way. They had among them varying views about the Messiah and about what would happen once they arrived in Jerusalem.

The journey in Luke's Gospel (9:51–19:27) is a time for teaching about the coming reign of God. Over and over Jesus teaches that the reign of God is not a theology of "pie in the sky by and by" but an already present reality for those who are willing to live by Christ's teachings that turn the world's values upside down. So radically different are the values of God's reign that families will be divided about which way to live. Indeed, the passage may reflect divisions in Jesus' own family (for example, Mark 3:21; John 7:5). Jesus represents a new reality, and we are called to choose for him or against him.

Unfortunately, the modern church, afraid of losing members and harmony, often glosses over the differences between gospel values and cultural values. The sad result is that our theology and spirituality have often been reduced to the lowest common denominator.

In today's reading, Jesus promises to bring fire and division because they are necessary for us to grasp the new reality of the reign of God. It is an important message for individuals and for the church, which is called not to bless the popular culture but to serve as a vital alternative to it.

Prayer: *God of wind and fire, take away our fear of division. Show us how to live in your reign and give us courage to witness to others by the integrity of our lives. Amen.*

Sunday, August 20   Read Luke 12:54-56.

The word was out that Jesus was coming on his way to Jerusalem. "Advance teams" even came to prepare the way ahead of him (Luke 10:1). When Jesus and his followers came into a town I can imagine that there must have been something of a parade atmosphere, with everyone coming out to see him. Along the way many joined the parade, but not everyone understood what it was really all about or what would happen once the throng reached Jerusalem.

Once more Jesus spoke to the crowds, trying to help them understand how little they really understood. You know how to predict the weather by reading the signs in the sky, he told them, but you don't know how to read the spiritual signs of the times.

How many of us joined in Jesus' parade as it passed through our town only to find that our enthusiasm diminished as we learned more about who and what God calls us to be? How easy it is to follow the crowds to Jerusalem if we believe that Jesus will do all the sacrificing. How easy it is for us to melt back into the fringes of the crowd when the call to follow him demands a measure of sacrifice on our part.

What do the signs of the times say about the role of the church in 1995? What do they say about the meaning of discipleship and about our role as individuals who are called to follow Christ in 1995? What is the difference between being a part of the crowd and following Jesus?

Prayer: *Gracious God, restore to us the enthusiasm we once felt for following Christ. Challenge us to follow him with increasing commitment in these difficult days, days when it is not easy to read the signs of the times. Amen.*

GOD'S PURITY AND POWER

August 21-27, 1995
Monday, August 21

Charles A. Waugaman✤
Read Jeremiah 1:4-8.

When Michelangelo accepted an irregular, rejected piece of marble, *David* was already inside. Whose vision assessed the possibilities, scheduled the skill that released the masterpiece?

When God designed the northern Arizona desert, all of the colors, crags, escarpments, and textures of the Grand Canyon were in place before the first trickle of the Colorado River bit against the upward thrust of earth's shifting crust.

God's appointment of Jeremiah as spokesman to the people of Judah was surprising only to Jeremiah. Yet the divine purpose listened to the astonishment of the prophet and tenderly answered his uncertainties. Neither the insecurity of youth nor the taint of human existence was an obstacle to God. Had God not shaped Jeremiah before his birth? Had God not phrased the first prophecy before Jeremiah had drawn breath?

We are human. We assume chance, and we assume wisdom. When the result is somehow of our own creation, we accept the wisdom and give place to pride. When we feel failure or displacement when others excel, we hug "chance" to our consciousness.

God views all as gift and as plan. What then of our reluctance and excuses?

Prayer: *Be Thou my Vision, O Lord of my heart:*
Naught be all else to me, save that Thou art. Amen.

✤Pastor, High Street Community Church, Conneaut Lake, Pennsylvania.
*Traditional Irish hymn, ca. 8th century. Tr. by Mary E. Byrne, 1905.

245

Tuesday, August 22   Read Jeremiah 1:9-10.

The goal of prophecy is not a place on the bestseller list or big royalties; it is change—change for the good. This implies that the present is wrong, weak, or inadequate. It reveals that whatever is filling our time, space, or attitude must give way.

Paul said that God is revealed in creation (Rom. 1:20) so clearly that there can be no excuse for not recognizing the fact. In creation growth demands decay. Human-made advance is no different. Human creative progress often demands that old ways must be torn down before new ways can happen.

But we human beings usually do not read nature as God intended, and *change* for us is often a bad word. It affects the emotions too immediately to assess positive and negative possibilities. Prophets are not well received.

Unfortunately, over the ages we have come to know the pattern of human reaction far too well. When God calls, one can assume human reaction. When God appoints, we can predict the reception his messages and messengers will receive. We are equally conscious of how easily we garble the most carefully practiced speeches, doubly aware of how often the audience fails to hear, or misinterprets.

When Jeremiah decried his lack of experience, God promised the necessary knowledge and words and then provided them with a touch. We can be sure that touch was as purifying and inspiring as Isaiah's was (Isa. 6:6-7). The call of the Christian is no less demanding: to pluck up and to plant . . . to break down in order to build. Be assured; God's hand still reaches out today.

Prayer: What *I have just heard is your word, O God. That I have heard is the call. Yet when my speech sounds eloquent, I feel uncertain of my motive. And when I stutter, my motives seem strong. I need your touch, again. Amen.*

246

Wednesday, August 23   Read Hebrews 12:18-24.

One is caught up short to realize that the first recorded crime took place in church. While the word may not be applicable to such primitive times, the context is given: Cain and Abel were worshipping God, one acceptably; one not. And hate, jealousy, and anger produced murder. Then blood cried out.

Abel's blood cried "Vengeance!" And to protect Cain's life, he was banished. Yet crime and murder, blood and vengeance have never left the place of worship. Religious wars are shameful enough, but we propagate and encourage bloodletting dissension within the Christian community itself. We even blaspheme by speaking of *holy* wars.

When will we learn that vengeance settles nothing? Retaliation is no solution. Possession of arms provides neither peace nor safety. No one has stated it better than our Lord in Gethsemane: "Put your sword back into its place; for all who take the sword will perish by the sword" (Matt. 26:52).

There remains but one antidote to the poisonous cry of vengeance. It is the powerful blood spilled on Calvary. Christ's blood shouts "Forgiveness" more loudly than Abel's cries "Vengeance." Yet the world settles for hate. Why? Because fear is rampant; the antidote has never been accepted.

Surely we as Christians can now shout the good news: "Enough of destruction, the time is here to build. Enough of plucking up. Christ has watered the soil with hope. Let us plant!"

Prayer: *Lord, I want to see your church free from the burden of sin. Begin with me. Exchange the blood of vengeance on my hands for the soil of loving service. Amen.*

Thursday, August 24   Read Luke 13:10-13.

It is difficult to picture breathing into a face, not to mention capturing such an image in wet plaster. Michelangelo, on his back on that high scaffolding, had work enough to limn (paint) God in human form, reaching out a finger to the gorgeous, anatomically correct but inert Adam on the earthly bank of his birth material. That initial breath transformed the clay into a living being. Is it so strange that God would continue to use touch to create and recreate today?

Jesus' touch was often what released God's power into human need. And so it was in today's reading. After eighteen years of looking at the ground, how must it have felt to scan the stars again, to trace circling swallows? And what of looking persons in the eye again after nearly two decades of speculation by many about what sin she must have committed that caused God to send upon her such an affliction. Surely grace comes with such touch, or the gift cannot be borne.

And can we miss the echoes of that other woman, stricken with hemorrhage, inching her way toward Jesus through the crowded street (Luke 8:43-48)? A dozen years of physical and monetary bleeding must sap hope as readily as vitality. But she teaches us an essential truth—with God the touch is two-way. We have the right to reach out as well as to receive.

How remiss we are to hesitate to extend compassion; how wrong in questioning the laying-on-of-hands in Christ's name! The need and the blessing are as old as breathing, as palpable as clay.

Prayer: *Thou are the Potter, I am the clay.*
            Mold me and make me after they will,
            while I am waiting yielded and still. * Amen.*

---

*From the hymn "Have Thine Own Way, Lord" by Adelaide A. Pollard, 1902.

Friday, August 25   Read Psalm 71:1-6.

We feel safer at home—not because we all enjoy disaster-proof, impregnable castles with fences and security guards but because the surroundings are familiar and negotiable. The visually impaired depend on this; the sighted feel but seldom articulate it. In the psalm appointed this week, the psalmist depends upon God in the way the visually impaired depend upon the familiarity of surroundings.

How wonderful if we could catch and share that dependence upon God! Surely it could transform our whole way of life. Having "home" and safety regardless of location or circumstance would be to know the living god.

From birth the psalmist credits the Lord with well-being. God's call to Jeremiah projected that protection of God's love back before conception. In both passages youth is encouraged and honored. Our Lord maintained that recognition: "Unless you change and become like children, you will never enter the kingdom of heaven" (Matt. 18:3).

Our God is a living God, neither old nor aging. We need to cling to that. It is part of our refuge.

A few years ago during a drive, I admitted to a poet friend that in my mind I am still 12 years old, the age I most enjoyed. He confessed to being 9. Suspecting this attitude was some poet's foible, we turned to his wife, not known to be poetic in the least. "To be honest, I still see myself as 16," Ruth confessed. "Thank goodness, youre driving," I responded. "You're the only one old enough!" To us also God says, "Do not say, 'I am only a youth.'"

Prayer: *"O LORD . . . my rock and my fortress . . . My praise is continually of you." Listen, Lord, and I will tell you of my praise for you. Amen.*

Saturday, August 26   Read Hebrews 12:25-29.

Here is a scripture that fills the mind with vivid images. The recent California earthquakes. The northern Alabama tornadoes on Palm Sunday, 1994. Hurricane Andrew. The house-wrenching summer floods of 1993. Devastating forest fires encouraged by several years of recent droughts. All "natural" ways God allows our lives to be shaken. Why? The writer of Hebrews says it is so that what can be shaken may be sifted out and the permanent revealed and appreciated.

Photographs following natural disasters or on-site inspections of the scenes often testify that it is surprising that not more loss of life results. Material things crumble. Tangible possessions char or disappear. Heirlooms vanish. And suddenly the precious-ness of human life soars in our gratitude.

Yet, too soon rebuilding or insurance demands blur the revelation. Much of religion is like that—a superstructure of habit, tradition, and culture that actually hides our faith. It is not surprising that God must periodically shake us up, crumble away, incinerate the cross and reveal the Divine Nature again in truth and honesty. Our God is, indeed, a consuming fire. But hope, as well as warning, flames in this scripture. We are assured the valuable will only be purified.

A recent performance of a *Messiah* chorus comes to mind.

> And he shall purify the sons of Levi, that they may offer unto the Lord an offering of righteousness.*

Prayer: *Free my hands and mind and heart, O God, of all that uselessly occupies my living. Thus shall I be more free to praise you wholly and purely. Amen.*

---

*Messiah, George Frederic Handel, "And He Shall Purify"

Sunday, August 27   Read Luke 13:10-17.

In Helen Barrett Montgomery's translation of the New Testament Luke 13:12 reads: "Jesus noticed her."* Of a dozen translations consulted, only Montgomery and J. B. Phillips make this clear. Perhaps it was that, for 18 years everyone who attended that synagogue *saw* this woman—yet, in all that time only Jesus *noticed* her. What a glorious distinction!

Who with similar needs in my church, in my community, or on my travels have I seen but not noticed? And if I noticed, how many did I—with a touch, a prayer, a look of compassion, a listening ear, a word of greeting—bring to Christ to be set free?

The ruler of the synagogue had eyes for the Sabbath—and for Sabbath-breakers. His passion for the law devoured his compassion for people: "Were not six days enough?" Jesus's answer was clear: "No!" Love is always timely. Love knows no Sabbath, no siesta, no vacation.

We are quick to give this ruler star position. "Look at him!" we cry. "Hypocrite!" Only parroting Jesus. Yet how many of us, by action if not word, announce the opposite: "There's one day a week assigned to God's work. If they can't come on Sunday for healing, blessing, or petition, forget it!"

Jesus set no limits on love—not of time, locale, or person. Christ gave example and promise that we would do even greater things. We recall from the Gospel, "and all the crowd rejoiced for all the glorious things that he *continually* did"* (v. 17*b*).

Prayer: *Teach me to notice. Teach me the purity to love as you do, Lord Jesus, that I may know your power. Amen.*

**The New Testament in Modern English*, translated by Helen Barrett Montgomery (Philadelphia: The Judson Press; copyright 1924 by the American Baptist Publication Society).

THE FIERCE LOVE OF GOD

August 28–September 3, 1995
Monday, August 28

Beth A. Richardson❖
Read Luke 14:1, 7-14.

A friend and colleague recently asked, "Where do you intersect with the poor?" I have not been able to shake off that question. Where *do* I intersect with the poor? At the second-hand store as I look for bargains? At 20th and Broadway as I drive by the man with the sign saying, "Will work for food"?

Somehow, I don't think that's what my colleague meant. Or Jesus, when he said, "When you give a banquet, invite the poor, the crippled, the lame, and the blind."

What does this prickly passage mean for me today? For those of us who are able to live beyond bare necessities?

The culture begs us to proclaim that "it is different now; the scripture doesn't mean *that* today." "We can't all be Mother Teresa." "Isn't Jesus talking about the 'poor in spirit'?" "The rich need ministry, too."

I live, as do many of us, insulated from those who are poor. It takes effort, a conscious choice, to step out of my place of privilege and into contact with the poor, the outcasts, the ones who cannot repay me.

And mostly, I resist going. I am afraid, awkward, and self-conscious. I am blind to opportunities. I am unwilling to take risks. But faithfulness demands taking risks. We are invited to sit at a new place at the banquet table.

Suggestion for meditation: *Where do I intersect with the poor? What opportunities do I have to follow Christ in ministry with the outcasts?*

❖Diaconal minister, The United Methodist Church; assistant editor of *Alive Now* magazine, The Upper Room, Nashville, Tennessee.

Tuesday, August 29   Read Jeremiah 2:4-6.

I wonder what it would have been like to be the prophet Jeremiah. He began his ministry during the reign of good King Josiah, the king who instituted reforms and repaired the Temple. It was downhill from there. Before the end of Jeremiah's life, he had watched the destruction of the Temple and witnessed the captivity of the people by the Babylonians. All the while, he was telling the truth about what was coming. (What a depressing job to be a prophet!)

God spoke to the people through Jeremiah, "What wrong did your ancestors find in me that they . . . went after worthless things, and became worthless themselves?" I'm no Jeremiah, but I have a sense of what it's like to witness destruction and captivity and worthlessness. I see it everywhere. In the faces of the hungry and homeless. In "ethnic cleansing" in Bosnia, Rwanda, India, Gaza, and Burundi. In inadequate housing and medical care. In children gunned down by other children. In the pursuit of wealth which has no concern for human welfare.

I also have a sense of what it is like to run after worthless things. The culture invites my participation in the abundance of materialism. It says that I can possess happiness and fulfillment through buying the latest, the best, the finest. I can have security by saving and investing. But there is an emptiness inside me not filled by possessions or a good job or a solid retirement plan.

God speaks today to me, to us, through the prophet Jeremiah: "[You] have gone after worthless things."

Suggestion for meditation: *Where are the worthless places in my life? In my world? What action can I take today to hear God's call and live in God's truth?*

Wednesday, August 30   Read Jeremiah 2:7-13.

Jeremiah proclaims God's word to Israel to repent and return to faithfulness. The words are harsh: "I accuse you . . . and I accuse your children's children." The God of Israel demands faithfulness to the covenant.

The indictment: idolatry. "My people have changed their glory for something that does not profit." God reminds the people that they were brought "into a plentiful land to eat its fruits and its good things." But the people turned away. They went after false gods.

In a vivid image, the prophet presents the crimes of the people: "They have forsaken . . . the fountain of living water, and dug out cisterns for themselves."

Imagine a hot and thirsty person choosing warm, stagnant water over fresh, cool running water. Imagine building cisterns which crack and become contaminated, when one can drink from a fountain of living water.

The God of Israel—demanding, angry, jealous, faithful—calls upon the heavens in desolation. Who are these fickle people who eat sand instead of fresh fruit, who pass up a sweet, flowing fountain to drink from putrid wells instead?

The people have been unfaithful. But God has not abandoned the people. God is frustrated and angry, but God continues to offer soothing water to a thirsty people.

We are a thirsty people today. We also have gone after "things that do not profit." We live in a culture of idolatry, drinking fetid water when we are offered the living fountain.

Prayer: *We thirst for you, O God, for your life-giving spirit. We are lost in a desert of our idolatry and cannot find the way to you. As you led your people Israel through the wilderness, lead us to your land of plenty. Amen.*

Thursday, August 31   Read Psalm 81:1, 10-11.

The theme of this psalm is familiar. God says to Israel, "I . . . brought you up out of the land of Egypt. But [you] did not listen to my voice." God reminds the people of their past: that they cried for help and God rescued them from slavery in Egypt. God led them through the wilderness and to the promised land. But still, they did not trust God and they turned away.

The Interpreter's Bible calls this psalm a "prophetic liturgy." It was most likely used in liturgies during Succoth—the Festival of Booths, a harvest festival. What a peculiar psalm to use during a celebration—it dwells so much on the people's mistakes! But it illustrates the honesty and richness of Israel's relationship with God. Even in the midst of festival worship, the people recall their history of captivity and deliverance, of freedom and unfaithfulness. All these events—the good times as well as the bad—are a part of their relationship with God.

The story of the Hebrew people is so very honest, so very human. It is an unedited version, not cleaned up for a religious audience. All the faults, quirks, and errors are there for us to see.

The story reminds us that we, also, are very human, that we make mistakes and we turn away from God. We spread hate rather than love. We hurt other people. We refuse hospitality for the strangers and the sojourners among us because they are different.

But there is hope and grace in the story. God did not turn away from the Hebrew people but remained faithful in the midst of faithlessness. And God does not abandon us, even in our failures.

Suggestion for prayer: *Write a psalm that tells your spiritual story, your failures as well as successes. Read your psalm as a hymn of gratitude to God.*

Friday, September 1   Read Psalm 81:12-16.

God says through the psalmist, "I gave them over to their stubborn hearts, to follow their own counsels." The stubborn hearts at Meribah—"Why did you bring us out of Egypt, to kill us . . . with thirst?" (Exod. 17:3) The "stiff-necked" people at Sinai—"Come, make gods for us" (Exod. 32:1).

There are stubborn hearts today. Mine is one. I identify with the people in the wilderness. I worry that there will not be enough, that I will lose my job, my security, my health. I want to do things *my* way so that I will be sure they get done and get done right.

Waiting on God, being patient and trusting that my needs will be provided for—that is not my strength. Why should I launch into a wilderness without provisions? Why should I trust a God I cannot see, a God who seems to always procrastinate until the last minute when coming to rescue me?

My stubborn heart wants to listen to God only when it fits into my plan. But God invites me to take risks, to listen to and follow God's leading. I may not be led where I thought I was going or receive the things I asked for.

Letting go of my stubborn heart means cultivating a relationship with God. It means trusting even when everything seems lost. The psalmist tells me that God will provide nourishment for those who will listen—I will be fed with the finest wheat and satisfied with the sweetest honey.

God invites me to let go of the control that creates a stubborn heart and a stiff neck in my day-to-day living.

Suggestion for meditation: *Where are the places in my life that I exhibit a stubborn heart? What would it take for me to let go of those places and receive God's nourishment?*

Saturday, September 2   Read Hebrews 13:1-6.

When I opened my Bible to this reading, I sighed with relief at the first verse, "Let mutual love continue." *At last! A positive note in this week of difficult scripture readings!*

Then I asked myself, *What's so difficult about hearing the prophetic word, being faithful to God, interacting with the poor?* Perhaps it is difficult because reading the passages reminds me of how much I am not doing. Perhaps I am afraid to pass on prophetic words, afraid others will "shoot the messenger."

But as I read the passages which challenge me, I sense that surrounding these words of challenge is a fierce love. The same God who demands our commitment also wraps us in love. The God who requires our faithfulness also sets a heavenly banquet before us: tables loaded with cool, fresh, living water; the finest wheat; and sweet honey.

The writer of Hebrews exhorts Christians to perform acts of service. Show hospitality to the strangers. Be with the prisoners and those who are tortured, *as if you were prisoners with them and being tortured.* They are acts of service based in love, love of God and love of others. *Mutual* love, love that is shared.

How else can we survive the apathy, the greed, the violence of this world? How else can we walk in faithfulness with Christ?

We are wrapped in God's love and equipped to speak and act in service to others. Christ stands with us as we prepare food for those who cannot repay us, as we call others to works of justice, as we act in mutual love for our human family and the world.

Prayer: *God of challenges, give me courage to speak and act your truth. Surround my works of justice with your fierce love. In the name of Christ. Amen.*

Sunday, September 3   Read Hebrews 13:7-8, 15-16.

Today's reading offers a simple and powerful summary for this week of reflection. We have seen images of humility and hospitality at God's heavenly banquet. We have heard the prophet's indictment of a people who have become worthless, who drink from cracked cisterns. We have examined stubborn hearts which do not listen to God. And we have glimpsed the sustenance which God offers us—living water, plentiful fruits, grains and honey.

Finally, we read words of instruction from the writer of Hebrews. The ideas are not earth-shattering but self-evident. The words convey challenge and discipleship wrapped in mutual love.

"Share what you have." What I have is a lot. I am a privileged person. I do not know exactly how to share what I have, but there are people who can teach me. Saint Francis, Mother Teresa, Gandhi, and Laura McCray (a member of my church who is an inspiration to me) —these and others are my teachers.

"Do not neglect to do good." Doing good does not have to be difficult or dramatic. Doing good is about living each moment as a sacred one and seeing each person as a child of God. It comes from an attitude of prayer, a tuned-in-ness to God's love.

"Continually offer a sacrifice of praise to God." What is a sacrifice of praise? I think it has to do with living in gratitude, acknowledging the incredible gift of life and love and presence that we have from God. It is praying, singing, and acting from the heart of grace.

Suggestion for prayer: *Reflect on God's gifts to you. Today, how will you do good and share what you have? Offer God prayers of praise and thanksgiving.*

1996

Is just around the corner!
Now is the time to order your copy of
THE UPPER ROOM DISCIPLINES 1996

Year after year, The Upper Room Disciplines continues to appeal to more and more Christians who, like yourself, desire a more disciplined spiritual life. Be sure to order your copy today, while the 1996 edition is still available.

THE UPPER ROOM DISCIPLINES 1996
$7.95 each; 10 or more $6.76 each
Ask for product number UR727.

NOT MY WILL BUT GOD'S WILL

September 4-10, 1995   **Hilda R. Davis✤**
Monday, September 4   Read Jeremiah 18:1-4.

And he reworked it into another vessel

This image of a potter working with clay is familiar to many of us. We stand with Jeremiah at the potter's house and watch as the potter shapes and forms this piece of clay. But the potter is not satisfied and re-forms it into a vessel that seems better. We wonder, *Is this vessel better?*

But even as we stand with Jeremiah watching the potter form a more fitting vessel, we know that in God's hands we are also the vessel being formed. We know that the potter creates, shapes, and forms a vessel that carries out its purpose most effectively. Just as the clay is in the potter's hands, we, too, are created, shaped, and formed to carry out a purpose unique to our talents. God molds us not to our will but to the purpose that seems the best for service to God through our community. Each time God re-forms us our efforts become more focused, our vision becomes clearer, our service is less self-serving.

Prayer: *Dear God, let us be willing to be formed for your service. Give us patience with ourselves as we are reworked to be the person that seems good to you. Amen.*

✤Editor of curriculum for children and persons with mental retardation, Church School Publications, The United Methodist Church; member, Clark Memorial United Methodist Church, Nashville, Tennessee.

Tuesday, September 5   Read Jeremiah 18:5-11.

Can I not do with you . . . just as this potter has done?

While this passage continues the analogy between God and a potter, it also continues a recurring theme found in the Book of Jeremiah: the reward of good and the punishment of evil. God delivers to Jeremiah a message that calls for the repentance of the house of Israel. If they do not repent, Jeremiah is reminded that God can destroy their kingdom just as the potter's hands are able to destroy the clay vessel.

This message tells us that all of us are responsible for our global destruction and all of us are accountable. We see natural disasters that have been caused not by nature but by greed. We have science and technology that can benefit the world, but we continue to allow politics to decide how wealth is distributed. According to this passage, unless we repent, we will see our own destruction.

We cannot repent—turn around our direction—on our own. Through this passage in Jeremiah, God admonishes us to listen to God's voice. When we are obedient to God's message of caring for the environment and for one another, we hear God's will for our lives in community. When we are open to God's plan, for us we can reap the benefits of being in service to our world. God continues to shape us into vessels that are to be used for good, not evil. God's plan is that we carry out this purpose. We can when we are willing to listen.

Suggestion for meditation: *Where in your own community do you see evidence of brokenness? What can your church do to re-form the situation to God's plan for wholeness. Ask to be able to hear God's messenger. Ask God for a vision for your church and for your community that fulfills God's plan for your life.*

Wednesday, September 6 Read Psalm 139:1-6.

O LORD, you have searched me and known me

How many people can we say really know us? We are a mobile culture and have less time to become well-acquainted with people in our community.

My daughter and I have moved from one city to another several times within the span of a few years. Whenever we were beginning to know a city—the best shops, where children could eat free, a church home—we had to move. Each move provided a better opportunity for us, but we found ourselves alone at first, having to get to know our community all over again. I sometimes regret that my daughter will not have the same experience I had growing up. I lived in the same house, went to the same stores, knew everyone's business in the neighborhood until I left for college. I miss that for my daughter.

However, the psalmist tells us that we are never really alone—even when we're strangers in a new city. We have a God who is in relationship with us. We can be assured that God knows us with the wonderful knowledge of intimacy. We are surrounded by the presence of God. God takes the time to know us. We know God through our relationships with one another.

Therefore, we are not to try to look for a God so big, so cosmic that we miss God right in front of us. If we look across at our neighbor, around at creation, and within ourselves we will discover the presence of God.

Prayer: *God who knows us, we want to know you. Help us recognize your presence in others. Allow u_ to see that how we treat our neighbors and how we treat our earth reflects our knowledge of you. Amen.*

Thursday, September 7   Read Psalm 139:13-18.

I praise you, for I am fearfully and wonderfully made

We can feel special and wonderful when we realize that we are part of God's purpose. We have a God who knows us so intimately that even before we were born he had a plan for good for our lives. Our creation was not by accident. Each of us was formed with purpose and beauty. The psalmist rejoices that we are wonderfully and fearfully made. Here the Hebrew word for *fearfully* could also be translated "with reverence." We are indeed an awesome creation.

More than one friend has told me that they have recognized that God has a plan for their lives. One seminary classmate described to me the struggle she went through as she decided to accept her call to the ministry. She would have to give up a well-paying job, leave her familiar community, and find a means of support during the three years of seminary study. Her constant prayer was, "Show me your way, Lord." She was able to find sources to finance her education as well as her living expenses. She is a willing witness to the reality of God's hand in her life.

As we become willing to trust God's will for our lives, we become free to experience the joy of being known and loved as a part of God's wonderful creation. As we try to discern God's will for our lives, we can rejoice that God continues to be with us—when we move, when we feel alone, when we are uncertain what to do. God is with us to the end.

Prayer: *God, our Creator and Sustainer, help us to trust your will for our lives. Amen.*

Friday, September 8   Read Philemon 1-12.

I . . . appeal to you on the basis of love

This passage recalls for me as an African-American woman the part of my history where slavery was justified in part by this letter of Paul. This is certainly a temptation we must be aware of today—using scripture to justify personal sin.

However, as this passage continues to speak to me, the joy and liberating power of love is the overwhelming message. Paul writes this message as a prisoner. We wonder whether Onesimus has come to Paul because he had no one else to speak for him. We wonder how Paul could help, since he is in jail. How could they become close—they were so different. Possibly the bond they shared of being imprisoned enabled them to transcend barriers of class and culture. Paul not only accepts Onesimus as a friend but embraces him as a son. When Onesimus goes back to Philemon, Paul sends his own heart. Paul is not the prisoner here; we are the prisoners when we are unable to love freely those who are different from us.

In our society we have many barriers to overcome. There are invisible barriers of doctrines, status, and politics. Add to those invisible barriers the visible barriers of race, body image, and age concerns. It can be easy for us to become locked into being in community only with people who are like us. We can imprison ourselves.

Let us allow the love of God to break down barriers of difference. Let us reach through our prison doors and speak on behalf of those who have no voice. Let us allow the joy and encouragement we have received to give us the boldness to encourage those who may not recognize their usefulness.

Prayer: *God, help us break the barriers of personal sin and embrace the joy of liberating love. Amen.*

Saturday, September 9   Read Philemon 13-21.

Confident . . . that you will do even more than I say

It appears to me that obedience has a certain amount of duty associated with it. But for Paul obedience is just the basic attitude. He encourages Philemon to move beyond obedience to free will. Free will goes beyond duty to love.

Philemon should be encouraged for what we assume will be a willing acceptance of Onesimus as a Christian brother. Paul is assuming that the community will support Philemon by helping him reach beyond the expected obedience to Paul's request. The expectation was an important one—voluntary acceptance of Onesimus with brotherly love. Onesimus and Philemon, as Christians, are part and equal in the community of Christ.

However, I wonder about Onesimus. He has no community to help him with his decision. He has to discern whether he is going back to what could be his old role as a slave or a new life of loving service in the church community. Onesimus also had a decision to make, a decision based upon faith.

Like Onesimus, we are also challenged to step out in faith with our decisions. Do we consider the support of our community a requirement to our forgiving past hurts? Or do we seek solitude and time to reflect before we make reconciliation a reality? We each have our own style of handling hurt, forgiveness, and reconciliation. However, it is not enough for us to be obedient when we welcome back those who have hurt us. We must take another step and willingly accept them as a "beloved brother" or sister.

Prayer: *God, it is not easy to return to situations where we have been hurt. Nor is it easy to accept back those who have hurt us. Give us the faith to be willing to love, regardless. Amen.*

Sunday, September 10   Read Luke 14:25-33.

So therefore, none of you can become my disciple if you do not give up all of your possessions.

Jesus begins this passage by strongly stating that those who wish to become his disciples must hate not only their families but their very life. *Hate* as used here means to "turn our backs to." Jesus issues us the challenge of turning away from what we love most in order to be his follower. This appears to be a dilemma.

Jesus himself provides a model for us in his life. He left his family, and he gained a new family in his disciples; he gave up his life, and he gained a new life in the resurrection. Jesus expects us to go into discipleship aware that there will be pain and struggle. A life of discipleship is a commitment. It is a commitment that not only requires all but gives all in return. Jesus tells us there will be struggle, there will be hard decisions; but anything of value is worth a sacrifice (see Matt. 10:34-39).

When we accept a call to discipleship, we have to recognize that sometimes we have to turn our backs on our former life. We may have to sacrifice to go to school. Or we may have to work in a church that repays us only with love. We may teach in crowded classrooms, nurse dying patients, or create a home when we could be earning a salary. God does not always give us easy choices. We cannot gain without letting go. That is the cost of discipleship.

Suggestion for meditation: *As you think back through the readings for this week, be thankful for God's will for your life. Reflect upon where you have said, "Not my will but your will be done, God." Be thankful for the challenge to live a life of discipleship.*

September 11-17, 1995   **John W. Bardsley✤**
Monday, September 11   Read Jeremiah 4:11-12.

Hopeless

A prophet is chosen to speak for God. Jeremiah realized that a spark of the divine was in him. Accepting the call to be a prophet around 626 B.C.E., he spoke to the nation of the coming judgment of God.

The political forces bearing down from the North were bringing Judah's final hour. God could no longer permit a life-style contrary to divine will. Idolatry had crept back into Temple practice. There was great and immediate danger that Judah might lose its distinctive character and no longer be a vital spiritual force in the life of its people.

God's powerful actions were described as a destructive wind sweeping down from the peaks of the wilderness, so intense and hot that it would take the breath away. The prophet had warned them again and again; but the people, royalty and commoner alike, had ignored a warning as well as the way to avoid catastrophe: "Return to me" (vv. 1-2). Now the consequences were upon them.

God is loving, merciful, and forgiving; that is true. But God does indeed judge us by our thoughts and actions.

Prayer: *O God, help us to hear your warnings and to heed them, that we may return to you! Amen.*

✤Retired United Methodist clergy of the Holston Annual Conference; Fall Branch, Tennessee.

Tuesday, September 12   Read Jeremiah 4:22-26.

Warning

The trumpet has sounded the alarm (v. 19), but Jeremiah cannot make the people take heed. He cannot convince the people to return to God instead of relying so heavily on frail, earthly means of security. At this precise moment, God gives the reason for judgment: The people are "foolish" and "stupid." They have honed their skills in evil, but they have no idea how to do good.

God is faithful, loving, long-suffering, but eventually even God's patience wears thin, and the sentence comes down. Why? Because of the Lord's "fierce anger" and "blazing wrath" (NAB) at the deeds of the people.

Jeremiah prophesies a world in upheaval. The cosmic destruction resembles the throes of early creation (see Genesis 1:2), without form and void. When the creature ignores the Creator's commands, tragedy and disappointment follow, as we see in David and Bathsheba (2 Sam. 11-12) and in Moses' not being allowed to enter the Promised Land.

A change of heart was needed!*

Prayer: *O God, help us to live as people with a new heart, a heart that knows you and desires to follow your way. Amen.*

---

*See Jeremiah 4:4; 24:7; 31:31.

267

Wednesday, September 13　　　Read Jeremiah 4:27-28.

Not listening

When Josiah's influence was removed, Jeremiah saw just how badly Judah had deteriorated. She faced two enemies really: the invasion "from the north" (v. 6) and the invasion from the "heart . . . of wickedness" (vv. 14-18). Jeremiah vividly described how God was determined to carry out the judgment (v. 28). The confrontation between God and God's people was coming soon! Time and eternity were about to cross in a memorable event. God says, "I have purposed; I . . . will not turn back." The "day of the LORD"—that fateful, awful, awesome day!

God, however, does not cause total destruction (v. 27*b*). A remnant shall remain. God had already noted that if the people had a mind (v. 1), they could return to God's ways. They needed to repent (vv. 2-3) within the heart itself (v. 4).

God was seeking justice and truth from the people, but their actions belied their words! Instead of being strengthened during difficult times and responding to those times by renewing their faith, their adversities had embittered them. How often have we, too, seen this very thing happen?

I read somewhere that "the boat in the ocean is free, but the ocean in the boat is all wrong." The chosen people of God had not learned the lessons God had for them. The utterly sinful state of the nation made it impossible for them to receive God's forgiveness. The nation simply could not activate the cure for low-grade morality.

Prayer: *O God, "Woe are we." Hear our penitent cry and restore our relationship with you. Amen.*

Thursday, September 14   Read Psalm 14.

God's victory equals joy.

The psalmist is concerned over the widespread corruption in the land. God looks to "see if there are any who are wise, who seek after God." But God could find no one: "no, not one!"

Atheism says, "There is no God!" and to the psalmist this is foolish. From the time we are taken to Sunday school and church, we are taught foundational religious principles of living. These basics keep us sensitive to the needs of other members of the family of God. The atheist, in denying the existence of God, can easily lose this sensitivity by neglect. Just as muscles atrophy from lack of use, so will the deep-seated religious and spiritual instincts atrophy from lack of application in daily life.

Studies reveal that constant viewing of violence in the media dulls our senses to the point that we are no longer shocked or disturbed by violence. When we become dulled to its consequences, violence breeds violence. Disrespect for life increases.

Does God look down today to find no one doing good, "no, not one"? Have the people moved away from God and become "perverse" and "corrupt"? (RSV)

I believe that God will withhold final judgment only for so long. In the days of the psalmist and in the days of the early church, anticipating the Messiah kept the "faithful remnant" going (see 1 John 3:1-3). The psalmist concludes with a messianic prayer of hope. Those who remain faithful today to the hope that springs from Christ's presence and his future coming can provide a basis of hope for the broader society.

Prayer: *O God, touch us and transform our lifestyles that we may be among the faithful remnant at the last day. Amen.*

Friday, September 15   Read 1 Timothy 1:12-17.

What Christ can do

In the first letter to Timothy we read the testimony of Paul to the transformation that comes to one who places faith in Christ Jesus. Paul's conversion is widely known (Acts 9:1-19) and would be familiar to most. The mentor's life is a powerful witness to the gospel that saves his fellow worker. If the gospel could save Paul, the worst of sinners, then any who came to know Jesus as Christ could be saved for eternal life.

Paul emphasizes in his pastoral letters that "this is a faithful saying" (v. 15, KJV); "trustworthy" (Goodspeed); "sure and worthy of full acceptance" (NRSV); "you can depend on this" (NAB). This emphasis appears four other times: 1 Timothy 3:1; 4:9; 2 Timothy 2:11; Titus 3:8. One who is, as King Agrippa, almost persuaded (Acts 26:28) is reminded that he or she can be absolutely certain of this, because it happened to Paul—just as he said and just as others saw!

If the "wages of sin is death" (Rom. 6:23), then Christ Jesus is the way to life! Paul is blunt as he describes how he deliberately set out to cause pain and suffering. Not content with simply fulfilling the law, he caused physical punishment and took delight in so doing. He did all of this before knowing the loving mercy of Jesus. Then, beyond all human expectations, even to the point of being surprised, "the grace of our Lord overflowed."

Paul cannot forget he is a sinner forgiven. Nor can he forget that God did it!

Prayer: *Eternal, immortal, invisible, wise God, thank you for thinking of us! Help us to think of you! Amen.*

Saturday, September 16   Read Luke 15:1-7.

Sinner loved

The moral of this moving parable is clearly that the Good Shepherd will go to any length to save the lost sheep.

Jesus rebukes the Pharisees, who neglect the most needy, but he offers encouragement and hope to the penitent. The Pharisee would ignore the sinner. Not God! The Pharisee saw no hope for the sinner. Not God!

In Alfred Soord's painting *The Lost Sheep,* for whatever reason—curiosity, adventure, eating its way from the flock—the sheep is clinging to the edge of a cliff, bleating for help. In the fast-approaching night, birds of prey circle overhead, waiting. The shepherd finds it! He hangs on to a ledge with one hand and reaches down with the other to grasp the sheep.

A couple of thoughts come to mind. God loves the sinner no matter what the sin. And there is no room for hopelessness in God's love. Every soul is precious. As the well-known poem by Francis Thompson points out so well, "The Hound of Heaven" seeks us in our lostness until we discover him! All the energy of heaven is released to find even the one poor, wandering soul.

People tried to hide from God by burying Jesus in a tomb, but God broke the lock and released him! He is still—still!—alive in our contemporary world.

In our own unique journey, we can become so intent on personal desires that we do not hear the voice of God calling our name or see the hand of God reaching out to us. Yet, in the depths of the heart there is a still, small voice that cries for help, and there is another still, small Voice that replies, "I have found my sheep!"

Prayer: *O God, I am searching for you! Find me, please! Amen.*

271

Sunday, September 17   Read Luke 15:8-10.

Rescued

In the uncertainties of a worldwide economy, one coin seems rather insignificant. The young son dropped a penny, watched it roll beneath the car, and then crawled into the back seat. His father opened the car door and bellowed, "Get out of the car and find that penny! Ten pennies make a dime; ten dimes make a dollar!"

Jesus makes a point that the lost coin is within the house. It is unlikely that the woman in the parable had excess financial resources. It is more likely (as I read between the lines of the story) that she was living on the edge—perhaps never far from poverty. The coin would have been vitally important to a person or family in such a situation. One can understand the intensity of her search. She turned the house upside-down to find the single lost coin.

That's precisely the story of humankind—being lost (sin), wishing to be found (penitent), being sought, and being found (salvation). Are there words in any of the Gospels filled with more hope? "There is joy in the presence of the angels of God over one sinner who repents."

The Pharisees never dreamed that God's nature was like that. They might have considered God's forgiving the sinner who crawled on his knees and begged, "Forgive me!" Who among the Pharisees could conceive of God's *seeking* the sinner and *offering* forgiveness? Yet, that was God's plan in Jesus Christ.

Prayer: O *God, we don't want to be lost. We know you search for us and call our names. May we look to you and accept your forgiveness and salvation, Amen.*

September 18-24, 1995 **Willie S. Teague✤**

Monday, September 18 Read Jeremiah 8:18–9:1.

When you feel weary or unfairly burdened, do you ever read one of the prophets for comfort? The prophetic books are filled with words of doom amidst calls for repentance and words of hope. Today's reading from Jeremiah is neither a prophecy of doom nor an offer of hope. Rather, these verses are a moving lament over a great calamity that has befallen the people. There is no suggestion that the calamity is punishment for some sin. The lament shows Jeremiah's great compassion for the people.

Because his grief is beyond healing, Jeremiah is moved to ask: "Is there no balm in Gilead? Is there no physician there?" The Afro-American spiritual "There Is a Balm in Gilead" seems to answer Jeremiah's question. The spiritual says that when we feel discouraged or that our work's in vain, the Holy Spirit will revive us again.

When you feel discouraged or unfairly burdened, remember Jeremiah's tears and Jesus' bidding: "Come to me . . . and I will give you rest" (Matt. 11:28). Remembering Jesus' promise in difficult times is an act of faithful living.

Devotional exercise: *Sit quietly. Relax and breathe deeply. Breathe in, remembering that Jesus not only speaks words of comfort to the weariness of your life but also promises rest and renewed strength. Hold the breath as you claim Jesus' balm. As you let your breath out, receive the rest Jesus promised. Continue to breathe slowly and rest in the Balm of Gilead.*

✤Editor of the *South Carolina United Methodist Advocate*, Columbia, South Carolina.

Tuesday, September 19   Read Psalm 79:1-9.

The psalmist, like Jeremiah, knew the pain of watching Israel suffer. The occasion for Psalm 79 is an attack on Jerusalem. This psalm of lament not only expresses compassion for Israel's suffering but also addresses God's absence in the face of her suffering. Israel's suffering presents a crisis of faith. If God has chosen Israel and if God is God, then how can God allow Israel to suffer at the hand of her enemies?

The psalmist asks, "How long, O LORD? Will you be angry forever?" Then the question: Is God not acting because of our sins? The psalmist prays that God will not hold their ancestors' sins against them and will quickly show compassion for Israel.

Have you ever had a similar crisis of faith? Have either you or someone near to you faced great suffering that makes no sense? Often such suffering results in our wondering where God is. Frequently, it results in reexamining life to justify God's absence from our suffering. *Surely*, we think, *there must be some sin that causes God to withhold compassion and healing.*

In such a crisis of faith, the psalmist did not hesitate to ask the hard question of God: "How can you allow this to happen to me?" But the psalm did not end with the question. It goes on to tell God that when the suffering ends, "we . . . will give thanks to you forever" (v. 13). Like the psalmist we all, at times, make such deals with God. God hears our plea; our doubts and questions do not negate our attempts to live faithfully.

Devotional exercise: *As you relax and breathe deeply, remember God's promise of steadfast love. Recall times when claiming that promise was difficult. Remember that, like the psalmist, Jesus had difficulty in the garden and on the cross. Rest in the knowledge that God does not flee in the face of such crises of faith.*

Wednesday, September 20   Read 1 Timothy 2:1-4.

These verses are the first of four instructions concerning public worship. We read here that "supplications, prayers, intercessions, and thanksgivings be made for everyone." The faithful are to request assistance in meeting personal needs, to intercede on behalf of others, and to give thanks for God's steadfastness.

While the instructions to Timothy have to do with public prayer in public worship, they are helpful to individuals as well. We should not separate our private prayer life from our prayers in corporate worship. Therefore, our daily prayers as well should include personal requests, intercessions, and thanksgiving.

In addition, Timothy is instructed that prayers are to "be made for everyone" because God "desires everyone to be saved." Therefore, the faithful are to pray for all sorts and conditions of humanity; and specifically are there to be prayers for "kings and all who are in high positions."

Again the instructions for public prayer make a claim upon our personal prayers. Daily we are to pray for those "in high positions"—of government as well as in our churches, schools, and other societal institutions. The result of such prayers is "that we may lead a quiet and peaceable life in all godliness and dignity." Note that the author does not say that *they* may lead but that *we* (all) may lead a life of godliness and dignity.

Devotional exercise: *Remembering God's promise of steadfast love:*

✚ *Tell God of the needs of your life.*
✚ *Pray for all sorts and conditions of humanity. (Be specific.)*
✚ *Pray God's blessing for all in authority. (Name them.)*
✚ *Pray that all may come to know Christ and may "lead a quiet and peaceable life in all godliness and dignity."*
✚ *Give thanks to God for the blessings you have received.*

Thursday, September 21   Read 1 Timothy 2:1-7.

Here, Timothy is reminded of the basis for all worship—one God, one mediator, and God's desire for all to be saved. In verse 5 the author of the letter may have been drawing upon an early church creed, the first part being a shorter form of the *Shema*, the foundation of the Hebraic understanding of God: "Hear, O Israel, the LORD is our God, the LORD alone" (Deut. 6:4).

We may not live in a time when the prevailing religions worship many gods, but many people in our society do have divided loyalties. We may not literally worship money, success, prestige, power, influence, or pleasure; but many of us do find our lives controlled by the desire to have one or more of these. How would our lives be changed if we had only one heart's desire—to worship the one true God?

The second part of the creed is the affirmation that just as there is one God, there is also one mediator, Jesus Christ. To restore peace between two estranged parties a mediator must empathize with both parties. The claim here is that because Jesus was both God and human he was the one perfect and complete mediator between God and all humanity. Many of us can accept the divinity of Jesus more readily than we can accept his humanity. Why is that so? If we know Jesus' humanity, then he may actually be able to reestablish our relationship with God.

The third part of the creed is that Jesus, the mediator, "gave himself a ransom for all." Just as there is one God and one mediator, there is also one humanity saved by Jesus' ransom.

Devotional exercise: *Read verses 5 and 6 over and over until you know them by heart. Then quietly examine the forces controlling your life. Ask God to come in and take control, that you may have peace in an abundant life in Christ.*

Friday, September 22   Read Timothy 2:1-7.

Running throughout these verses is an emphasis upon the universality of the gospel and its universal relevance. We are *not* dealing here with the doctrine of universalism (that all humanity will be saved). We are told that God desires for all to be saved and that in Christ Jesus the ransom for all has been paid.

Prayers are to be made for *all humanity*. God desires *all humanity* to be saved. Jesus "gave himself as a ransom for *all*." We hear echoes of *1)* Paul's claim that God was reconciling the *world* through Christ (2 Cor. 5:18-19); *2)* John's famous word that "God so loved the *world* that he gave his only Son . . . " (John 3:16); and *3)* Jesus' claim that if he is lifted up he will draw *all* humanity to himself (John 12:32).

If the gospel is for everyone, what effect does that have not only on our prayer life but also on how we live in relationship with others? If the gospel is intended for all, what does that say about how we receive all people into the church and into our lives? If the gospel is for Christians and non-Christians, what claim does that make on the way we relate to non-Christians?

There is no greater call to mission and evangelism than these verses. If all humanity is capable of receiving God and if God wishes all to be saved, then we who know of our salvation must go beyond praying for everyone. Faithful living calls us to love as we have been loved and to have in us the mind of Christ.

Devotional exercise: *Sit quietly. Relax and breathe deeply. Read verses 1 and 3 over and over until you know them by heart. As you come to know in your heart of hearts that God desires everyone to be saved, examine your prayer life to insure that you are indeed praying for all humanity. As one saved by Jesus Christ, examine your life. Are you honoring God's desires toward universal salvation?*

Saturday, September 23   Read Luke 16:1-9.

Few passages of scripture are more perplexing than this one, for Jesus appears to be lifting up a dishonest person as a model for righteous living. A landlord has become aware that his manager is dishonest. Upon hearing this the manager asks, "What will I do, now that my master is taking the position away from me? I am not strong enough to dig, and I am ashamed to beg." To insure that he will continue to have friends and a home, the manager decides to reduce the debts of those who rent from the landlord. The landlord commends the manager for his shrewdness.

What truth does Jesus teach by telling this parable?

In verse 9 Jesus says to his disciples, "Make friends for your-selves by means of dishonest wealth so that when it is gone, they may welcome you into the eternal homes." Note that the concern for a welcome home is the same as that expressed by the manager in verse 4. Jesus is commending not the dishonesty of the manager but his shrewdness in using money to guarantee himself a home.

Perhaps the parable's lesson is that it is possible to manage material possessions in such a way as to guarantee an eternal home. The implication is that how we manage our worldly possessions has eternal consequences. By admonishing the disciple to use money in making money, Jesus may be reminding them to minister to those in need.

Devotional exercise: *Sit quietly. Relax and breathe deeply. Focus on the role money plays in your life. Examine the ways in which you use material wealth, not only to meet your needs but also the needs of others.*

Sunday, September 24   Read Luke 16:10-13.

These verses elaborate on Jesus' understanding of stewardship. Verse 10 makes little sense in a culture in which bigger is better and success means advancement. We are impressed with large salaries. Many of us aspire to larger jobs and greater responsibilities. Jesus, on the other hand, often emphasized the little things in life. He spoke of a cup of water, the letter of the law, one talent, and the widow's mite.

Jesus says the test of how we will deal with the large issues of life is how we have dealt with the small ones. "Whoever is faithful in a very little is faithful also in much; and whoever is dishonest in a very little is dishonest also in much." Jesus calls us to a life of faithful attention to the ordinary, frequent, and familiar tasks without regard for how insignificant they may be.

In verse 13 Jesus concludes with a saying that puts wealth and devotion in perspective. Basically he says that we cannot serve two masters. Our loyalty must not be divided. Jesus reminds us that we are called to be good stewards of wealth but that we must not seek it. We are to seek only God and are to use wealth as a means of serving God and of ministering to others. If we love God, we will use our wealth as an expression of that love; but if we love wealth, we will be unable to seek God.

Devotional exercise: *Reflect on Charles Wesley's hymn "Forth in Thy Name, O Lord." Select a phrase from it to hold in your mind, allowing it to become a prayer of your heart during the day ahead.*

Forth in thy name, O Lord, I go, my daily labors to pursue;
thee, only thee, resolved to know in all I think or speak or do.
For thee delightfully employ whate'er thy bounteous grace hath given;
and run my course with even joy, and closely walk with thee to heaven.

September 25–October 1, 1995 **Peggy Ann Way✤**
Monday, September 25 Read Jeremiah 32:1-3*a*.

Where does the word of the Lord come to you? Jeremiah, as usual, is in trouble, imprisoned while perennial wars continue; and his future is in doubt. His historical situation is complex. He hears and speaks the word in less than ideal situations. What he says is not necessarily understood and does not immediately turn Zedekiah closer to God and bring peace to a troubled world.

The meditations for this week reflect on two themes. The first is that placing oneself squarely in the midst of suffering is a faithful act. You are invited to let go of the romance that is sometimes associated with being a prophet and to place a particular prophet and his faithfulness in a real prison in a real warring world. At the same time, you are invited to claim your own space—however restricted, painful, or ambiguous—as the space where God comes and out of which and to which you speak. What is your painful space?

The second theme is one of finding hope even in the spot in which you and Jeremiah find yourselves. These meditations are about claiming the suffering of the human context, persisting in faithfulness even there, resisting despair and cynicism, and finding ways to speak and to be that offer alternatives and hope.

Prayer: *In my own place, O God, come to me. Free me to give name to the imprisonment of my present context, that I may resist injustice, despair, and disillusionment, and be of hope for others. Amen.*

✤Professor of Pastoral Theology, Eden Theological Seminary; member, Church of the Open Door (United Church of Christ); St. Louis, Missouri.

Tuesday, September 26   Read Jeremiah 32:6-15.

Technology leads us to expect quick results, and a sophisticated medical culture may lead people to expect cures for all diseases. An uncritical psychological culture may seem to promise easy relief for all dis-eases of the self and our relationships. Yet from within our own imprisonments and ethos of wars, oppressions linger; grieving continues; and chronic illnesses of mind, soul, and body persist. Our theologies of crisis, problem-solving, and conflict resolution do not lead to the results anticipated. Perhaps you are now working on a distressing personal issue or are involved in convoluted relationships. Your funding may have been cut, or your job may be in jeopardy. The cultural depression of our times may have settled deep within you or your children, and survival rather than joy becomes your goal.

These ambiguous and confusing situations of history are all too real. The strength of our faith is that scripture does not avoid or sentimentalize them. They are to be neither denied nor surrendered to. Rather, in their very midst we are to make an act of hope, say a prayer that remembers joy, and count on a future that gives courage to persist toward the good that God intends. So, too, we must celebrate little things rather than major accomplishments. History changes slowly. In the meantime, let us place our hopes in vessels that may have to last for a long, long time—as did the real and suffering people of scripture. And, like them, let us find ways to affirm that God's promises will be fulfilled.

Prayer: *Be with us as we sit among our friends and companions, often tired and disappointed, yet knowing that you will bless our investments in faithful hopes. Help me to grasp that your time, O God, is for us, and that the thing for which we hunger will be in the land. Amen.*

Wednesday, September 27   Read Luke 16:19-26.

The children of Somalia. The elderly and the children in Bosnia-Herzegovena. The victims of a drive-by shooting. The little girl abducted from her home and murdered by a stranger. Natural disasters such as floods, hurricanes, and earthquakes add to the suffering. The radical suffering of the world makes no sense. Does it really help to affirm that Lazarus was carried by the angels to Abraham's bosom? For Lazarus did not get better, and making a song of his angelic end does not diminish the real and relentless pain he experienced.

Even as you read this you can image a present human torment from which there is no surcease. Strategies of response are not curative; compassionate thoughts do not diminish real suffering.

Even so, for those of us who would seek to persist faithfully in the midst of the sufferings of history there are possibilities. We do not turn away and refuse to see in order to avoid the reality of suffering without sense or ease. In our faithfulness we risk seeing radical suffering and being present to it, even to the point of recognizing our own finitude and helplessness. It is positive not to avoid such pain, just as it is positive to acknowledge that there is no instant cure for human suffering.

To refuse to see it, to turn away, to sentimentalize or place easy blame does not help. What does? Presence, persistence, and small acts of resistance in our own places count. These are the virtues of the faithful in a suffering world. Without them, we may sentimentalize, run away mad, or burn out.

Prayer: *O suffering God, we trivialize your suffering when we skim over the reality of human pain. Fill me with strength and courage to live faithfully in my own unrelieved suffering and to assuage human pain in every little way possible. Amen.*

Thursday, September 28   Read Luke 16:27-31.

The rich man wants to make it all right—at least for his brothers. Give them a clear message! Send one whose presence they can't refuse! But what is it that they—and the rich man himself—failed or refused to see? God's promises have *already* been made. Hope has *already* been offered!

At some point each person struggling to live faithfully must respond in faith even if data is unconvincing. So much theological effort is related to crisis—the crisis of faith, of disease, of conflict. Yet most of life is lived in a state of chronicity, where there are continuing and continual struggles toward health, wholeness, justice, hope. Our times of anguish demand faithfulness even when the realm of God is glimpsed rather than realized; even when Jew and Palestinian continue battling over promised lands; even when justice is experienced in its absence and promises seem far from reality.

In such times the temptation is *to wish* instead of *to hope*—to describe to God what we expect rather than to receive from God the grace offered in that strange admixture of human pain and God's grace that names human history. To await *the* sign that will convince us before we risk hope is to turn away from God's promises in the midst of everyday human experience where people hunger after presence (maybe *our* presence with them) and hope that transcends the limitations of human wishing.

Prayer: *Speak to me, Teacher, that I don't turn away from comfort by expecting my wishes to be fulfilled rather than my hopes actualized, in however small ways. In your time, O God, may my memory remember your promises, my being experience your present blessings, my actions embody my faithfulness to you. Amen.*

Friday, September 29   Read Psalm 91:1-6, 14-16.

The experience of faith's depths does not lie in the avoidance of terror, the refusal to see Lazarus, the denial that prophets are held captive, or seeing cities with violence in their streets and citizens with hope in both religion and government destroyed. Indeed, if the scriptures were about abstractions and principles, we would not be prepared for the ravages of history and the realities of human finitude. Not only do we die but we live within limitations of bodies and governments, of our own abilities and those of other persons. We are created as relational beings, and we share our existence with others who frequently have "the wrong point of view." Sometimes these "difficult persons" are within our own biological families, and they certainly co-exist with us in our various families of faith.

Probably most of us would affirm that certainly we must love one another, even as we confess that God certainly can't mean *that* particular person or *that* group of persons. We may not even use the word *terror* to describe this, yet certainly our inability to receive others without fear of losing or reshaping our own identities represents some profound resistance. The loss of self, or like-selves, or meanings that have named us is familiar in ecumenical or interfaith dialogue, as well as in ethnic rivalries and racial conflicts. We need to add a phrase to our love commandment: Love one another, but let no one underestimate the difficulties of the task! Without vulnerability in our own identities we allow holocausts, we refuse dialogue, or we seek to be victorious over rather than to be in partnership with.

Prayer: *O ever-present God, in the midst of my terrors keep afresh in me the deep knowing that you will deliver, protect, answer, be with, rescue, honor, and satisfy—even me, even now, even in this place. Amen.*

Saturday, September 30   Read 1 Timothy 6:6-10.

"There is great gain in godliness . . . with contentment."
Contentment? In the midst of what happens to Jeremiah and
Lazarus, the psalmist and the ordinary person caught up in
suffering? What a strange meditation for this week of scriptural
reflection on suffering and the depths of hope!

How difficult it is even to express what knowledge of the
presence of God offers . . . or even what kind of knowledge that
is. For the knowledge may not be the cultural knowledge of
rationality and technology; it may not be verifiable by scientific
data or always match that presented by authoritative sources. It
may indeed be more like that strange wisdom that grows out of
pain intersected by grace, or suffering that bursts forth in
inexplicable joy, or even an inner peace that sustains one in
patience and persistence.

Such wisdom may begin with a refusal to deny or avoid the
realities of suffering in human worlds, including our own. It may
be nurtured by a comparable refusal to see such suffering and
experience such pain as all that there is. Somewhere deep within
such sensibilities lies the capacity to continue, to celebrate God's
promises, and to act in hope.

Perhaps this can be viewed as the contentment of consenting
to one's own finitude as the locus of God's inordinant love—no
matter what. This is not a surrender to suffering and
meaninglessness. Rather, such a deep contentment frees one to
see the suffering of others and be present with them. It leads to
acts of faith and hope in the midst of holocaust, cultural
devastation, and irreplaceable losses.

Prayer: *I pray that my contentment may arise from a center filled with
your love and presence. I pray that such contentment is received as
grace and blessing and responded to with persistence and hope. Amen.*

Sunday, October 1   Read 1 Timothy 6:10-19.

As times change, words take on different meanings. To *aim* and to *fight* may not speak most clearly to the contemporary person struggling with issues of faith and meaning in a world filled with suffering, injustice, violence, and pain.

Yet, if by faith we seek to be participants in the kind of world God intends, we may find it helpful to name our journey in the language of moving from one place toward another. Thus, we seek to invite persons (including ourselves) from being strangers toward becoming fellow citizens in the realm of God. The movement is from brokenness toward wholeness, from estrangement toward reconciliation. The experience of a fractured human existence filled with pain and suffering is invited to move toward that redemptive existence of peace and justice that God intends.

To claim that the movement is always *toward* rather than *actual* realization places our small efforts within an historical process where they count. Within this perspective, there may be some virtues of faithfulness that need to be reclaimed rather than trivialized. Acts of resistance to injustice in our own places make us participants in the promised coming of the realm of God. And this very endurance, persistence, and resistance frees us to celebrate the ever-present and ever-promising God. And so we continue in history, in suffering and with hope, not only aiming at and claiming righteousness, godliness, faith, love, steadfastness, and gentleness but actually experiencing them in the movements of our own lives and struggles.

Prayer: *Ever-present God, grace me with endurance and persistence as I make my pilgrimage toward all you have promised. Amen.*

OUR ANCESTORS' FAITH

October 2-8, 1995   **Trudy Flenniken**✤
Monday, October 2   Read Psalm 137.

Have you ever been homesick? So desperately lonely for your former dwelling place that you actually cried?

Of unknown authorship, Psalm 137 tells of the yearning for their homeland by the Jews held captive in Babylon. We are told they wept when they remembered Zion.

Zion, one of the hills on which Jerusalem was built, became sacred to the Jewish people when the Ark of the Covenant was brought there by David. With the moving of the Ark to Solomon's Temple on Mount Moriah, "Zion" was extended to include the Temple. This was the holy place to which the people longed to return.

With taunts and jeers, the Babylonian abductors demanded the captives sing for them joyful songs of Zion. In their sadness and longing for Jerusalem, the brokenhearted exiles hung their harps, once instruments of praise and joy, on the branches of the willow trees on the banks by the rivers of Babylon.

Despite the mocking torments of their captors, the Jewish exiles remained faithful, calling down punishment upon themselves should they forget Jerusalem. Thus, far from home for seventy years, they neither forgot nor forsook their worship of the one God.

We, too, are called to be faithful wherever and in whatever circumstances we may find ourselves.

Prayer: *Dear God, sometimes I feel far from you. Help me to know that you are always with me. Amen.*

✤Active layperson in the Pacific Beach Presbyterian Church, (U.S.A.), San Diego, California.

Tuesday, October 3   Read Lamentations 1:1-6.

A popular trek for travelers in California is following the Forty-niner trail, the path taken by prospectors in the days of the Gold Rush. A few of their settlements remain, but most of them today are ghost towns. Empty streets and tumbled-down buildings give mute testimony to the bustling activity of the past.

So it was with Jerusalem following the siege and destruction of the city. Roads once filled with joyful worshipers bound for Temple feasts were deserted. The Temple itself lay in ruins. No longer did throngs pour through the city gates, now reduced to rubble. Young women had been dragged away. Priests groaned in despair. An air of hopelessness hung over the city.

Having consistently warned the people of the punishment an angry God would bestow on them if they continued in their wicked ways, the prophet Jeremiah had begged them to abandon their worship of foreign gods and idols and return to God. His warning went unheeded. Desolation resulted.

In this passage the author truly grieved for the ravaging of Jerusalem and the suffering of its people. Like the writer of Lamentations, we, too, will face times of severe affliction. But when we face adversity, we can have confidence that God will not forsake us, just as God did not forsake the people in exile.

Prayer: *Father in heaven, we lift up to you those who grieve for family and friends who have strayed from your pathways. Show us how we can comfort those who grieve and help those who have strayed find you again. Amen.*

Wednesday, October 4   Read 2 Timothy 1:1-5.

Even as a small child, I had a special affection for the pewter teapot. It had belonged to my great-grandmother whom I had never known. This lone remaining piece of what once must have been a beautiful tea service had been handed down from my grandmother to my mother and then to me.

Timothy's inheritance described in our scripture today, however, was not a material gift. It was the gift of spiritual faith passed down to him by his maternal grandmother, Lois, and his mother, Eunice. This second letter to Timothy commends their sincere faith, now living on in Timothy, a "true son in the faith" (1 Tim. 1:2*a* , NIV).

The offspring of a Greek father (Acts 16:1) and this pious Jewish woman, Timothy was nurtured as a child by his mother and grandmother as was the custom of devout Jews at that time. Thus, he became familiar with the Hebrew scriptures. Hearing the message of Christ as the fulfillment of the Hebrew prophecies, Timothy, Lois, and Eunice became Christian believers. We can only wonder what Timothy's life and that of the early Christians might have been like had not both Lois and Eunice loyally passed down to Timothy the heritage of their faith.

In a world where there is much concern about how we can best bequeath our worldly possessions to family and friends, surely the greatest gift we can leave them is our living out a strong faith in God and the knowledge of Jesus Christ.

Prayer: *Thank you, Father, for those who have gone before us, who have preserved for us an inheritance of faith. Amen.*

Thursday, October 5   Read 2 Timothy 1:6-10.

My father was not a highly educated man. His few years of formal learning took place in a one-room schoolhouse in Ohio back in the 1880s. His handwriting, though, was the most beautifully shaped script I have ever seen. Even more beautiful than the familiar handwriting on his letters to me were the messages they contained: words of love, support, and encouragement.

In the same fatherly fashion, the author of the epistle wrote tenderly to Timothy, addressing him as "my dear son" (v. 2). This letter to Timothy was likewise one of encouragement and an appeal for faithfulness, urging Timothy to persevere in his ministry. Using his own life as an example, the author testified to the richness of his experience with Christ.

Reminding Timothy of the gift of the Holy Spirit given him through the laying on of hands, the author urged him to be like Paul, unashamed of his testimony and willing as well to suffer for Christ. Timothy must not allow the gift of God within him, originally bestowed by the laying on of hands in a service of ordination, to die out. Rather, he is to act out of this gift with all the power, love, and self-discipline it brings.

This call to Timothy to "rekindle" the gift is likewise a challenge to us to continue following Christ's last command: "Go therefore and make disciples of all nations" (Matt. 28:19).

Prayer: *Dear Lord, may my life be a living letter to others, bringing them encouragement and love. Amen.*

Friday, October 6   Read 2 Timothy 1:11-14.

To the imaginative five-year-old that I was, the crude fruit and vegetable cellar beneath my childhood home was a scary place. Its entrance was a trap door in the kitchen floor. Rough and uneven steps carved from the solid earth led down into this dark cavern where provisions were stored for the winter. I thought of it as a dungeon.

How similar must have been the underground prisons in the time of the early Christians—dark, cold, and bare. Although these were places not of punishment but of confinement until trial, prisoners were nevertheless shackled in stocks or bound in chains.

It ass in such a place that Paul spent his last days. His loneliness and suffering must surely have been great. Yet to suffer for the sake of the gospel was an honor and a privilege. It was not something to be ashamed of, even when one was reduced to living as one of society's lowliest. Paul had faith that the "sound teaching" he had proclaimed would be kept safe by God until the end of the age.

The author calls on Timothy to follow Paul's example and "guard the good treasure entrusted to you." The Holy Spirit, dwelling within, would give Timothy the power to carry out this charge.

The Holy Spirit dwells within us today too. The power to proclaim and to safeguard the gospel's message is ours to accept.

May each of us discover that power within us.

Prayer: *God of Mercy, we pray for those who today are imprisoned for your sake. May their faith in you never waver, for we know you are with them. Amen.*

Saturday, October 7   Read Luke 17:5-6.

I took very literally the Bible verse I heard in Sunday school about faith moving mountains (Matt. 17:20). *Why couldn't faith, I reasoned, also move houses?* Then my best friend could live next door to me. Disappointed when my childish experiment failed, I blamed myself, saying, "I just don't have enough faith."

According to today's reading, the disciples felt the same deficiency in their faith. Why, in the midst of Christ's teaching about forgiveness, did the apostles suddenly interject, "Lord, increase our faith!" Scripture does not tell us. We can only wonder why they felt this need and what prompted their request at this particular time. We know only that they recognized their need and asked that it be filled.

In reply, Jesus compared faith to the familiar mustard seed. This tiniest of seeds "grows and becomes the largest of all garden plants, with such big branches the birds of the air can perch in its shade" (Mark 4:32b, NIV). But Jesus did not say they must wait for their faith to reach its fullest potential. Instead, he told them if they had faith, no matter how tiny it might be, their commands would be obeyed.

We can only speculate on the reason and the timing for the apostles' request. As we see them loyally carrying on Christ's ministry after his death, we realize their plea was answered: their faith did increase.

If we, like the apostles, feel our faith is weak, could it be that we have not asked Christ to strengthen it?

Prayer: *Giver of all gifts, you have said that if we will ask, we will receive.* So today, gracious God, I come asking that through you my faith will grow stronger. Amen.*

---

*Luke 11:9a.

Sunday, October 8   Read Luke 17:7-10.

In today's reading Jesus abruptly switches from talking about faith to talking about duty and unworthiness. In this parable, the servant, who has faithfully worked in the fields all day, comes home at night to prepare and serve dinner to his master before eating his own meal. The servant expects no thanks or praise, we are told, because he considered himself unworthy.

In New Testament times it was common for upper class and wealthy Jewish families to have slaves or servants. Although their well-being was protected by Jewish law, servants were nevertheless considered not as equal beings but as the property of the household. Whatever the reason for servitude, a servant had no choice but to faithfully obey his or her master.

We, however, have the freedom to choose whom we will serve. We think of the words of Joshua: "But as for me and my household, we will serve the Lord" (Josh. 24:15b). We remember the young boy Samuel as he says, "Speak, for your servant is listening" (1 Sam. 3:10). We hear Mary's humble answer to the angel Gabriel, "I am the Lord's servant" (Luke 1:38a, NIV).

Nearly two thousand years later, we, too, are called to make the choice. As would-be faithful servants of the Lord, we realize our unworthiness as did the servant in Christ's story. Yet we go forward in the footsteps of those who have gone before us, fixing our eyes on Christ, "the author and perfecter of our faith" (Heb. 12:2a, NIV).

Prayer: *God of all our days, help me to be steadfast in my journey of faith, so that at the journey's end I may hear you say, "Well done, good and faithful servant!"* * *Amen.*

---

*Matthew 25:23a, NIV.

THE AWESOME GOD

October 9-15, 1995
Monday, October 9

Judith Craig✤
Read Psalm 66:1-12.

All the earth bows down.

It's today's word, especially for youth: *"Awesome!"* If something defies comprehension, exceeds our wildest imaginations, stretches toward the impossible, it is awesome. Even the psalmist, centuries ago, used that word! The psalm for this week describes a God not just of some places or some people but our God, who roams the earth creating awe and wonder in people—even if they have not yet known the awesome One.

"All the earth bows down," says the psalmist. Why? Well, just come and see what God has done on behalf of humans. Even when the faithful thought themselves "done in" by some force or nation or natural cause that would destroy them, God was still in control, still at work, still doing that which is worthy of praise.

It isn't always easy to trace God's hand in our day-to-day circumstances, but this psalm invites us to do just that. When we are tired, when we are confused, when we are happy, when we are amazed—the psalmist invites us to look for the hand of God in all of it. No matter what the week holds for us, let us look for the presence of the God who is . . . well, A*wesome!*

Prayer: *Awesome God, give me eyes to see you in all that is around me. Amen.*

✤Resident bishop, Ohio West Area of The United Methodist Church; Columbus, Ohio.

Tuesday, October 10   Read Jeremiah 29:1, 4-7.

Do what?

Did you ever get sent out of the classroom to stand in the hall? Do you remember feeling "set apart" out there? Like exile! Being sent somewhere you didn't want to go, being stared at by those who passed by, hearing them talk about what you must have done to deserve being there —that is exile!

Our spiritual ancestors were in exile, a kind of uprooting far worse than standing in the hall. They were torn from their homes and lands and places of worship. They were sent in small groups to places where others looked at them strangely. Cut off, alienated, and frightened, they wondered what to do.

There were some who said, "It won't be long. Just wait. Don't do anything." But the word of God came to them, saying they should embrace life, make a place for themselves, join the people where they were, plant gardens, raise families. This word of God suggested that even in exile, far from anything they had known, life could be good and God would still be in it. The message still holds: for the exiles of long ago and for us in all circumstances, there is no place that is outside God's knowing and caring.

Suggestion for meditation: *Can you remember a time when you felt "exiled"? Were you aware of God's presence with you? Perhaps you are in such a lonely place right now. Can you begin to embrace life in the knowledge that God is with you?*

Prayer: *Awesome God, help me remember that you are with me in any circumstance that may come my way this day. Amen.*

Wednesday, October 11   Read Jeremiah 29:1, 4-7.

You bind us with them?

When you are far from home, lonely, cut off from all that is familiar, it is a tall order to be told that the welfare of the people where you are is as important as your own well-being. The awesome God continues to push at the edges of experience and understanding. For the exiled Israelites, first God did just that with advice to settle in fully, enjoy life where they now were. Now here is a word about seeking the peace and welfare of that place and a clear word that the prosperity of the city where they dwell is inextricably linked with their own prosperity.

These words seem to erase any sense we have that we can maintain our identity in some sort of splendid isolation from the environs and circumstances that surround us. In fact, deep involvement in the community—be it city or village or in-between—is part of what God expects of those who know the Divine Presence. Not only is the promise that we cannot be taken beyond the concern of God, the promise is also that we can find ourselves involved with surprising people we have not known and with them find a common welfare. No matter how far beyond the concern of God some places or some people seem to us—irreverent, uninterested in God, unaware of God in their midst—our well-being is intimately woven into the welfare of the larger society.

Devotional exercise: *Be aware of the people whose lives meet yours today. How is God calling you to be a bearer of the news of God's grace and steadfast love in the midst of these people's lives?*

Prayer: *God, you startle us by your reach into places we think you would not choose to be. Help us watch for you in all places and circumstances. Remind us of your care for us and for all. Amen.*

Thursday, October 12   Read Luke 17:11-14.

Working everywhere!

The young child ran ahead of his parents up the stairs of the wooden ramp built over the dunes. He reached the height of the dunes just as sunset was upon us. The huge ball of the sun seemed to touch the water of the lake. The running patter of feet screeched to a halt, and two young arms were flung wide in wonder as he said, "Wow, God!"

Over and over the response to Jesus' work of healing is reported in such phrases as "the crowd was amazed" or "we never saw anything like this before"—phrases that are like that young "Wow, God!" Much of what God does is so beautiful, so powerful, so wonderful that we are left looking for a word—like *wow!* In the case of the healing of ten persons at once, what else might have been said? While many probably reacted with wonder, there were probably those who thought lepers were not worthy of divine intervention.

The healing and encouraging work of God occurs around us all the time. Do we see it? And when we do, are we still first checking to see if the recipients are those we think worthy? The awesome God has a "worthy" list much longer than ours. Every day is a time to see where God is at work and to be ready with our "wow" regardless of our estimation of the worth of the persons or places God touches.

Devotional exercise: *What evidence of God's work do you see around you as you go about your daily routine? How do you react?*

Prayer: *Awesome and generous God, forgive us when we try to limit your marvelous works of healing and encouragement. Give us eyes to see every person, every part of your creation as an appropriate place for you to do your "wow work." Amen.*

Friday, October 13   Read Luke 17:11-19.

Saying thank you

I ate at their home often, and she indeed set out a meal with love and care, no matter how simple or elaborate the fare. But it was from him that I learned the art of remembering to say thank you for even the most routine of gracious acts. She has told me that for all the years they were married, he never left the table without saying a word of thanks for a marvelous meal.

There was nothing routine about being healed from leprosy in Jesus' time. That discovery provoked wonder in the crowds, and, one would hope, deep gratitude on the part of the one healed. Luke's story tells us that was not the case in the healing of the ten. No doubt each of the ten was elated and anxious to show others what had occurred. But only one stopped long enough to say "thank you" to Jesus. That one was a Samaritan, one the crowd would think least likely to behave in gratitude.

Every day God is graciously at work in and around us. It is probably not so dramatic and life-changing as healing—though for some it may be! But if we are alert, we discover that even the most difficult of circumstances do not block the inflow of God's gracious care for us. Are we among the nine who just go our way rejoicing? Are we gracious like the one who remembered to express gratitude?

Suggestion for meditation: *Do I move through each day with an attitude of thanksgiving? How can I become more readily thankful?*

Prayer: *Awesome and gracious God, we thank you for all the ways you will touch our lives this day with your goodness. Give us eyes to see and hearts to know you are present with us in all circumstances that will be ours. Amen.*

Saturday, October 14   Read 2 Timothy 2:8-15.

Beyond our words

Have you ever received a gift that is so beautiful or been the recipient of kindness beyond any expectation or found yourself so overcome with wonder and beauty that you were at a loss for words to express your feelings of gratitude and wonder?

When we contemplate the incredible nature of God's work of creation or the revelation of divine grace in the life and ministry of Jesus or the continuing presence of that divine initiative in the Risen Christ, what are we to say? Is there any one name, any one descriptive phrase or formula or liturgy that can catch up all there is to say about God or Jesus Christ? Is there only one acceptable way to speak about the steady presence of God in all life circumstances?

It must be part of human nature to fuss over language. Even in this early letter to Timothy we find the caution to avoid such limitation of expression as is suggested by the phrase "wrangling over words." How sad if we miss awareness of God's gracious presence with us because we are worried most about the words we use to express that presence! Surely, God is not threatened by the search for language to speak the inexpressible!

Devotional exercise: *Consider what words are most meaningful and helpful to you in expressing the reality of God's presence with you. Remember that these are* your *words; they do not have to reflect the reality of another person's experience of God.*

Prayer: *Awesome God, you are always pushing at the borders of our language's ability to express our faith. Help us stay open to whatever words or actions we can find that will speak our wonder and gratitude. Amen.*

Sunday, October 15   Read Psalm 66:1-12.

Remembering to see

We end where we began, with the psalmist of long ago stretching, as we do, to catch the wonder of God's persistent interaction with creation. One of the most common ways to recognize God is in retrospect—remembering what God has done: "Come and see what God has done: he is awesome in his deeds among mortals." That memory provokes confidence for the now and future, even when the now and future seem bleak and fear-filled. Therefore, to read again and again the psalms and their recitation of all we have seen God do is a healthy and spirit-expanding possibility for us.

As we think of the week just ending, of the days one by one, can we recognize where God has been present with us? Are there barriers of energy or understanding that we have been able to overcome—as if finding ourselves crossing a sea on dry land? (v. 6) Even if we are still feeling hemmed in by ideas or needs that limit our ability to look to the future with much hope, can we look over our shoulder and see where God has brought us to "a spacious place" (v. 12b) in spite of burdens that were holding us down and making us feel alone and unable?

It is that kind of memory—recalling what God has done—which often becomes the doorway through which we can walk toward an awareness of God in our todays and tomorrows.

Devotional exercise: *Take time to recall how God has acted and been present in your life.*

Prayer: *Awesome and patient God, we thank you for guides like the psalmists who teach us how to remember you. Help us to find you in our today by remembering where you have been with us. Thank you for memory that invokes confidence. Amen.*

IN RELATIONSHIP WITH GOD

October 16-22, 1995   **Julio Gómez**✤
Monday, October 16   Read Jeremiah 31:27-30.

This Jeremiah passage, written after the fall of Jerusalem (587 B.C.E.) when the people of God were in exile, begins with the promise to rebuild the houses of Israel and Judah. The assurance "to build and to plant" was badly needed in a time of disruption.

Today we struggle to create a sense of community. Our society is fractured by the existence of different cultures, and we hear the cry of pain as new people try to live in a new environment. After more than half a century of new immigrants, mostly from Asia and Latin America, we see that the melting pot concept no longer pertains (if it ever did) because of the lack of tolerance and understanding among the many racial and cultural groups. In view of this reality, we see people trying to organize into small cells to preserve their identity and culture.

Prior to the Exile, it was assumed that a person is part of a community. Later, when the people lost the cohesiveness that the Temple brought them, the prophets announced that the individual person could know God through obedience and prayer.

Jeremiah underlined the idea of individual responsibility. That "all shall die for their own sin" is a good reminder that ultimately we have to answer personally to God. In our relations, each of us stands as an individual responsible directly to God, who loves us.

Prayer: *Lord, make me understand that even though I live in a community, I alone am responsible for my actions. Amen.*

✤Pastor, Spanish United Methodist Church, Trenton, New Jersey; chairperson of editorial board of *El Intérprete*.

301

Tuesday, October 17   Read Jeremiah 31:31-34.

This brief text was composed when every visible evidence of the original covenant had been destroyed. The Temple was in ruins; the Ark of the Covenant was no more; and most of the people had been killed or were suffering in exile. To this sad and perhaps angry remnant, Jeremiah gave his most enthusiastic teaching: God's ultimate victory in the "new covenant."

Exile has always been an anguished interval of waiting for the day of return. Today, hundreds of thousands of Cubans await the moment of their return. They left their country because of philosophical differences. A paradise island was turned into a living hell for them. When a leader loses his humanity and his dependence upon a Supreme Being, the people suffer. Like many Cubans today, the Hebrews were anxious to return to their home.

The covenant God made on Mount Sinai had been broken. The new covenant would fulfill the old. The Sinai covenant was to be a mutual relationship of love and trust. God initiated the covenant; the people's acceptance of it was obedience. The Sinai covenant was inscribed in stone; the new covenant is to be written "on their hearts."

The Hebrews considered the heart as the source of life (Prov. 4:23). An intelligent person is a person of heart (Job 9:4). The heart as an organ of knowledge figures especially in one's knowing God.

It is said that as Sir Walter Raleigh was being led to the block, his executioner asked if his head lay right. He answered, "It matters little how the head lies, provided the heart is right."

The acknowledgment of individual responsibility is a long step toward the new covenant.

Prayer: *Father, prepare us to be participants in the new covenant, through Jesus Christ our Lord. Amen.*

Wednesday, October 18   Read Psalm 119:97-98.

In this psalm is the perfect portrait of a regenerated person and a recommendation to us about what we ought to be. Here the psalmist shows great love for the law of God. Observe the vehemence of the assertion, "Oh, how I love your law!" It is admiration, with an exclamation point! The psalmist shows affection for the whole scripture, not just the promulgated laws.

A clear demonstration of this affection is his constant meditation: "It is my meditation all day long." All the day the psalmist's heart is working on holy things, working something out of the word of God.

There is a story of Isaac Newton, the English physicist, inviting a friend to dinner but then forgetting the date. When the friend arrived, he found the scientist deep in meditation, so he sat down quietly and waited. Soon dinner was brought up —for one person. Newton continued to be abstracted. The friend drew up a chair and, without disturbing his host, ate the dinner. After he had finished, Newton came out of his dreamy meditation, looked with amazement at the empty dishes, and said, "If it weren't for the proof before my eyes, I could have sworn that I have not yet dined."

If we read the psalmist correctly, we will, out of our love for God's word, meditate on it constantly. That meditation springs out of our love for the Lord; it is not a duty we have to carry out; it is not a religious obligation. Meditation gives life to the means of grace and to that which makes those means fruitful to our souls. We need time that is spent in close communion with God.

Prayer: *Our heavenly Father, teach us to meditate on your word. May we express our love for it with a hearty affection, as we have never expressed before. In Jesus' name. Amen.*

Thursday, October 19　　　　　　Read Psalm 119:99-104.

The psalmist has spoken of his affection for the word of God and of the wisdom that word brought. Now in this text this wisdom is amplified by comparing it with the wisdom of all his "teachers" and of "the aged." The first ones excel in doctrine, and the second ones in counsel; yet, the psalmist considers that he has "more understanding" than all those because of meditation on God's "decrees" and adherence to God's "precepts."

The people of God that the Hebrew scriptures call prophets had visions and revelations. The psalmist, however, speaks of that kind of knowledge received by ordinary means, not those special revelations made to the prophets. This reliance on the scriptures helps the psalmist, who excelled by the study of the word, to put away sins.

"I hold back my feet from every evil way"; i.e., "I keep a close control over my affections, that they might not lead me to sin." Everyone faces temptation. We must resist the power of evil.

In *The Lion, the Witch and the Wardrobe*, the wicked queen entices the boy Edmund with a box of enchanted Turkish Delight. Each piece is sweet and delicious, and Edmund has never tasted anything better. There is only one problem. The more he eats, the more he wants. He doesn't know that this is the wicked queen's plan. The more he eats, the more he will want; and thus he will eat and eat until it kills him. The sweet would never satisfy his hunger; it would simply kill him. Here C.S. Lewis gives us a metaphor for sin. When we sin, we are never satisfied. A Christian must stand at a distance from sin.

Prayer: *Lord, make us conscious of the small sins as well as the great sins, and forgive us. In Jesus' name. Amen.*

Friday, October 20 Read 2 Timothy 3:14-17.

Do you remember who taught you the Christian way? Many of us cannot point out a single individual who helped us develop our faith because we grew "naturally" in the church. However, if we concentrate our memory, we may recall a particular Sunday school teacher, youth counselor, pastor, family member, or friend who aided in the Christian experience.

When I was about twelve, I lived in a comfortable home, where I was surrounded by pictures of Roman Catholic saints. These were a part of my family's religious heritage. One day a missionary invited me to the Methodist youth group. Hiding from my parents, I went to those Friday evening meetings every week. That woman was God's instrument to teach me the Bible.

Timothy had learned about the Christian faith from his mother and his grandmother. Paul advised him to resist the deceptions of those who would lead him away from the fellowship of the church. "Continue in what you have learned," and do not change your course with every changing wind of folk theology, fad, or ism. Here is the individual's obligation to think for him or herself.

Facing his death, Paul tried to prepare Timothy for the burden of impending challenges, and so recommends that Timothy study diligently the scriptures.

A person can never finally be finished with the Bible. It always has an answer in each emergent situation. Through the centuries this book has been the guide for millions of persons—always needed, always fresh, always correcting our decisions. The aim of the scripture is that we "may be complete, equipped" (RSV) to face today's challenges.

Prayer: *Father, give us grace and wisdom to teach others the truth contained in your word. In Jesus' name. Amen.*

Saturday, October 21   Read 2 Timothy 4:1-5.

In preparation for the Olympic games, the torch is passed from one faithful runner to another. Paul's life is drawing toward its end. This is his last opportunity to instruct Timothy and the entire Christian community. It is time for Paul to pass the torch.

We note a certain pessimism in this text, a solemnity placed in the context of the end-time judgment. A charge is given "in the presence of God and Jesus Christ,"—who will have the last word in history by judging the living and the dead.

We are very close to the beginning of the second millennium, and Paul's imperatives are as pertinent today as they were in the first century. Are we prepared to carry the torch of Christian faith into a new age? As we come into contact with more people than we ever thought possible through the information super-highway, are we making the word relevant to the people?

"Proclaim the message" is a command to every Christian. Our responsibility to this treasure of the gospel is not to guard it but to spread it, to make others wealthy in the knowledge of the Savior. Proclamation must continue under all circumstances, because there will be times when the people "will not put up with sound doctrine." Some people will feel that they cannot endure hearing more words of the truth. What they want is confirmation of their illusions. God's truth holds no illusion, only brightness and openness to things made visible.

Our ministry will not be judged by the church leadership, or the congregation, or friend or family, but by the One above whose judgment is sure.

Prayer: *O Lord, we see a world in convulsion, and we know that the people need your word. Give us the will to take this treasure to others. In Jesus' name. Amen.*

Sunday, October 22   Read Luke 18:1-8.

In prayer we have to exercise our own personal, individual responsibility. By our own volition, we persist in our prayers.

The text for this Sunday is about persistence in prayer. Often we turn to prayer when we are in distress. Even unbelievers sometimes utter desperate prayers in moments of great distress. There is the story of a pilot who boasted of his atheism. One day as he flew through a violent tropical storm, the copilot overheard him utter, "God, help us."

For the Christian follower, the issue is not prayer in crisis but prayer as an ongoing part of life. In the parable that Jesus told his disciples, he urged them to pray constantly so they would not "lose heart." The widow probably had a good case. She just wanted to be protected from her adversary's attacks. Her only weapon was her persistence. She was not reacting emotionally; she simply desired justice under the law. The judge was not doing his job, and the widow would not give up. This bothered the judge so much that he finally agreed to hear her case.

Perhaps the delay until the coming of the Son of man would cause the disciples to "lose heart." Could this have been a problem during Luke's times? The story instructs the disciples to continue to trust though there may be no signs.

Even when things go wrong, even when we don't seem to get the results we want, even when it seems our world is crumbling, we are to continue to pray. The widow did not give up. We receive strength in the face of difficulty when we are able to pray without ceasing.

Prayer: *Father, give us the strength to persevere when we face seemingly insurmountable situations. In your Son's name. Amen.*

WHAT GOD HAS PREPARED FOR US

October 23-29, 1995   Kellie Corlew Jones✤
Monday, October 23   Read Psalm 65.

Praise comes easily to me when I read this psalm. It reminds me that ours is a God who answers prayer, who forgives our iniquities, who brings chosen ones to live in God's house, and who redeems us by awesome deeds. The psalmist leads us in praising God as Creator, the One who out of the formless and dark chaos created an orderly world, and the One who can calm the turbulent seas and the chaotic restlessness within our hearts. The psalm culminates in reminding us that the earth has gathered God's grandeur into itself: the hills gird themselves with joy, the meadows clothe themselves with flocks, the valleys deck themselves with grain—nature itself shouts and sings for joy.

A pastor friend spent an Easter week with us. As she was leaving she said, "Do you know that you live in a paradise?" It has taken a while for me to see my surroundings as she did. From my desk I can see a small lake that glistens in the morning light; trees where cardinals, finches, blue jays, mockingbirds, and robins build their nests every spring; flowering dogwood, redbud, azaleas, iris, lilac, and crepe myrtle bloom in season.

You and I, too, were created to sing for joy because of the things God has prepared for us.

Suggestion for meditation: *Consider the wonders of God in your life. Praise God for the free gift of forgiveness, the glories of the created earth, and the benefits of earth's bountiful harvests. In what other ways is God giving us a glimpse of heaven?*

✤Prior to her death last year, the author was Professor Emeritus, University of Tennessee; Certified Lay Speaker, United Methodist Church; Martin, Tennessee.

Tuesday, October 24   Read Joel 2:23-27.

The people to whom Joel prophesies are coming out of a wasteland disaster in which crops have been eaten by locusts, all trees are dried up, seeds have not sprouted, and cattle have died of hunger. There is no water, and the people's joy has withered.

Joel has created a hymn of praise to the Lord because, with the coming of the early rains, the wasteland is about to become again a land of plenty. God will balance out the years of famine with years of plenty. Because the people have repented, God has had pity on Israel and has lifted the plagues. God's promise is also that God's people will never again be put to shame.

We all know wastelands such as those created by drought, earthquakes, flood, or hurricane. The real gift of God during such tragedy is God's own sustaining presence and the concern that people everywhere show for those who are suffering.

We also face personal wastelands during divorce as we experience betrayal from our spouse and desertion by friends; in the loss of a child; in facing a life limited by accident, aging, or disease; when told that a cancer is terminal. Worse even than these personal tragedies are the times when the light of God's love seems only darkness within us. In every troubled hour, however, the Holy Spirit is with us and will never leave or forsake us.

Prayer: *Gracious God, we turn to you in praise for your abiding love and because you walk through every dark valley with us. As we walk through a wasteland in our life, send us the "early rains," your showers of blessings. Renew us, O God, by a comforting inner vision of your presence. Amen.*

309

Wednesday, October 25   Read Joel 2:28-32.

At nine o'clock in the morning on the Day of Pentecost, Simon Peter preached, using this poetically perfect passage from Joel as his first text (see Acts 2:17-21). The Holy Spirit has come and has brought a great leap in Peter's understanding. Peter now knows that the assertion "Everyone who calls upon the name of the LORD shall be saved" is inclusive of all humankind; it is not a promise to the people of Israel only. This was what God had been saying all along; it just took a while for human ears to hear it.

The poured-out Spirit prophesied by Joel and preached by Peter is equally available for women and men, for people from all social strata, for slave and free.

Peter's sermon moved away from the material promises of Joel to the spiritual promises of Jesus. Peter had heard Jesus say, "I am the way, and the truth, and the life" (John 14:6). And Jesus said that the promise for those who believe is the promise of receiving God's Holy Spirit, which will teach, remind, comfort, and give peace through all our earthly trials (John 14:15-31).

God's promise through Joel is now a reality for us all, and we have reason to hope that the place where we can be with God is not only an earthly paradise but also the paradise to which the risen Christ has ascended and in which Christ prepares a place for us.

Prayer: *Abiding Holy Spirit, I invite you into my life to empower me to live your ways of justice and inclusiveness. Grant me the wisdom to see you in every person I see and to know that your heaven is open to everyone who calls on your name. Amen.*

Thursday, October 26   Read Luke 18:9-14.

This parable tells us that humility is one virtue which Jesus considered a requirement for entry into heaven. Matthew 18:4 reports that Jesus called a child to him and said, "Whoever becomes humble like this child is the greatest in the kingdom of heaven." In fact, Jesus said, "Unless you change . . . you will never enter the kingdom of heaven."

The young man who asked Jesus, "Good Teacher, what must I do to inherit eternal life?" (Mark 10:17) was told to give up his riches. This requirement asked too much of him.

On the mountaintop, with his disciples seated around him, Jesus first taught, "Blessed are the poor in spirit, for theirs is the kingdom of heaven" (Matt. 5:3). This theme of exalting the humble found in today's reading is the same theme in Jesus' teaching that a wedding guest should show humility by taking the less than prominent place (Luke 14:7-11).

Jesus is the only true example of the perfect life of humility, but even Jesus was tempted by Satan to give in to the human sin of pride. In his full humanity, Jesus surely saw the advantage of turning stones into bread. Because of his love for the poor, he would want to feed all the hungry people in the world. And Jesus could have been exalted without a cross if he had given in to pride and jumped unscathed from the top of the Temple as Satan suggested. Although the whole world would have worshiped at his feet, Jesus refused all self-aggrandizing tricks (Luke 4:1-13).

Prayer: *Gentle Jesus, we confess that there is a bit of the Pharisee in us even when we hunger and thirst after righteousness. Forgive us and be merciful to us. Amen.*

Friday, October 27   Read Luke 18:9-14.

Literature throughout the centuries recognizes how the human flaw of pride can cause the downfall of its leading characters, for example, Oedipus, Macbeth, Faust, and King Lear.

Too often national leaders, motivated by noble desires for justice, food for the hungry, and housing for the homeless, have seized power. But, once they have tasted power, their pride has made despots of them.

The straightforward narrative of the Pharisee and the tax collector shows two attitudes of human beings toward God and others. The Pharisee was disciplined and obedient to the law; he was legally righteous, but he had missed the point altogether. The point of a disciplined and righteous life is that it leads to a right relationship with God and with other human beings.

This self-righteous Pharisee did not understand that the realm of Christ is inclusive. He regarded others with contempt in his prayer and even named several categories of people he considered contemptible. He believed that God had created a special class for him; he refused or could not see the full community of faith that was at hand.

The tax collector humbly confessed his sinful state. Feeling that he had no righteousness of which to boast, he reached out for God's unfailing grace.

Who among us is free from prejudice and self-righteousness? Who of us can deny being like the Pharisee at times? Who of us will gain heaven if we must do so by humbling ourselves and becoming teachable as a little child?

Prayer: *Christ of the human road, let us never be separated from any of your children due to prejudice or failure to love. Let us not be separated from you because of pride. We have a long way to go. Forgive us, and strengthen us. Amen.*

Saturday, October 28   Read 2 Timothy 4:6-8.

Paul's testimony to Timothy in this letter is a well-formed psalm of assurance. It is not a self-righteous claim but an illustration of the assurance that is possible for all who are faithful to the call of Christ.

This text takes on new meaning when I remember a night my husband and I spent with Don and Jonnie, a couple who had established twenty-six different Sunday schools in Appalachia over a period of forty years. As each Sunday school grew, it would become a congregation for an established denomination, and Don and Jonnie would move on to begin anew in another place. Their work had culminated in their building a camp on a mountain for the use of all those churches.

They were grateful to God for their small retirement home on a mountainside, the only home they had ever owned. They told us how God had supplied their needs through the years when they and their children lived on the edge of hunger.

After dinner, Don brought out his violin, Jonnie her accordion; and we gathered around the piano where, accompanied by tree frogs, bullfrogs, cicada, crickets, whippoorwills, and hooting owls, we played and sang hymns into the night.

Being in the presence of humility is healing. My friends had mastered the attitude which leads to heaven, and heaven was all around us that summer evening.

Prayer: *Everlasting Christ, thank you for the faithful witness of your saints. Guide me in the paths of righteousness for your name's sake. Amen.*

Sunday, October 29 Read 2 Timothy 4:16-18.

Paul includes a poignant lament in his letter to Timothy. His trial reminds us of the trial of Jesus, who was forsaken by all his disciples. No one came forward in Paul's defense; not one friend had the courage to do so.

As Stephen had prayed for those who stoned him (Acts 7:60), and as Jesus had prayed for those who crucified him (Luke 23:34), Paul, in the same forgiving spirit, asked that all those who deserted him in his hour of trial might not have it charged against them.

Paul had, during the loneliness of standing abandoned before the Roman court, taken that opportunity for giving his Christian witness because he knew his words would be spread among the masses. His obsession was that Christ be fully proclaimed to everyone. Paul says (3:12) that all who lead a godly life in Christ Jesus will be persecuted. He recognizes, however, the joy of knowing that God will rescue the faithful from every evil attack and save them for the heaven prepared for them.

Those who during our own time have stood boldly for the equal inclusion of all people in the realm of Christ on earth have been persecuted in many ways. But there is compensating joy in seeing justice begin to prevail. Standing alone, absorbing crude jokes, and losing friends is painful, but hearing Christians use language which includes without prejudice all people, whatever their gender, ethnic background, age, or other special conditions is witness to the validity of their stand.

Prayer: *Blessed spirit of the risen Christ, sustain me with such an unfaltering trust that I will be faithful even when fear or the loneliness of death try to overcome me. Your promise for faithfulness until death is a crown of life. I do not want to miss this part of your promise to those who love you. Amen.*

October 30–November 5, 1995 **Linda Worthington❖**
Monday, October 30 Read Luke 6:27-36.

There is a special focus in October on peace with justice. The annual recognition of the work of the United Nations for peace is in October. Many churches call attention to programs in housing, hunger, and jobs at home and to disarmament, oppression, and international relations.

In this week's readings we glimpse a perspective on peace, first as nations interact in the period at the end of the Old Testament, then as Jesus instructs his disciples on their coming roles. "All the peoples and nations and languages shall serve God," Daniel says (7:14, AP). And Jesus promises, "Peace will be yours even when others hate you" (Luke 6:22, AP). He then reminds us to love our enemies and do good to them (6:35).

All Saints' Day, on Wednesday of this week, is a time to remember those who have gone before us throughout our long Christian history. Another kind of peace comes to those we remember who "heard . . . the Good News that brought you salvation" (Eph. 1:13, TEV).

Mother Teresa has embodied Jesus' teachings of bringing peace and mercy to the poor. When she came to Washington, D.C., I took a friend to meet her. We pushed through crowds of people who were trying to reach her, to touch her, to catch even a glimpse of her. She, more than anyone I know, embodies the compassion that Jesus taught us to show toward others.

Prayer: *Forgive me, Lord, that I find it difficult to be merciful and loving to those whom I do not know, and even to those I do. Amen.*

❖Freelance writer; contributing editor to *Diversity* magazine; Bethesda, Maryland.

Tuesday, October 31   Read Daniel 7:1-3.

The Book of Daniel was written during the second century before the birth of Christ by a faithful Jew to strengthen his people during a time of persecution. The writer, trying to rekindle the faith of Israel, put his message into the mouth of Daniel, the man of God, who was a great Jewish saint of an earlier age. He is the indomitable hero of the story.

Daniel was the spokesperson for God, the deliverer of a message, much like the prophets. He came at a time when Hellenism had spread throughout the known world. The Hellenistic king Antiochus IV Epiphanes, determined to destroy Judaism altogether, instituted the first religious persecution the Jewish people had known (168 B.C.E.). However, a stalwart band of devout Jews decided to fight back. "And they chose death rather than . . . profanation of the holy covenant" (1 Macc. 1:62, JB).*

One of the ways Daniel delivers God's prophetic message is through dreams and visions. In today's reading he describes the beasts that represent the great political powers who will surely rule if the people do not remain faithful to God. God's kingdom is an everlasting one for the faithful in contrast to the kingdoms of the world which, like the kingdoms described as beasts in the dream, will be destroyed in the course of time.

Daniel's message to us as a nation and as individuals is to be totally faithful to God. God keeps the covenant with those who love God and keep God's commandments.

Prayer: *O Lord, I fear for my nation and for myself, for I know that we have strayed far from your commandments. Help me, and help my nation, to be your faithful servants. Amen.*

---

*First Maccabees is one of the books of the Old Testament Apocrypha, an historical account written in the period between the Testaments.

Wednesday, November 1 Read Daniel 7:15-18.

In the midst of Daniel's vision of the beasts and destruction came "one like a son of man" (v. 13, RSV). Daniel had received this message from God, but he needed help to understand it. God sent an interpreter in the form of an angel to explain the visions so that Daniel in turn could deliver the message.

The angel indicated that the human figure among all the beasts/nations would be given everlasting and universal dominion over the holy community of Israel. The message continues that all nations shall serve God and God's dominion will not be like the beast/powers which would be destroyed. Instead, God will rule the world with a peace that will not pass away. This glimpse, through Daniel, of what the world can be shows us that in the presence of God, nations and their rulers, no matter how strong they seem, are only temporal; they will pass away.

Jesus, two centuries later, used Daniel's designation of the "son of man" to identify himself as the one whom God had chosen to judge and rule humankind forever (Mark 14:62). Jesus was convinced he was standing near the end time, that from that time forward life would never be the same.

Into his message of destruction of the kingdoms of the world, Daniel imparts a message of hope for "the holy ones of the Most High" (v. 18). To the covenant community of faith Daniel's message gives the assurance and stamina to hold fast during persecution, for God's kingdom will prevail and will come with power and glory at the end of time.

Prayer: *Help me, Lord, to remember the assurances that you have given the faithful throughout all of history. And help me to live this day as a child of yours. Amen.*

Thursday, November 2   Read Luke 6:20-23.

As Jesus' ministry began, he found these among the crowds of followers: people who were just curious; some who needed medical attention and healing; people tormented by mental illness who sought peace of mind; a few who began to realize that this itinerant preacher had words of wisdom to share. Among these followers he chose twelve as his closest confidants, his disciples, his inner circle (Luke 6:12-19).

These "chosen ones" Jesus ministered to in special ways. He expected greater responsibility and accountability from them too. Don't worry about being poor, he said; you will inherit the kingdom of God. You're hungry now, he noted, but that is only temporary. You will be satisfied.

Jesus then explained, "You are like the ancient prophets, they were persecuted, disbelieved, unheeded" (AP). Jesus urged his disciples not to give up during persecution—when that persecution was "on account of the Son of Man" (v. 22). Accept this, even rejoice in this treatment, for "your reward is great in heaven."

Most of us do not experience persecution because of our faith. Or do we? Are you one of these? A teenager who refuses to use drugs. An employee who "blows the whistle." A politician who does not accept certain campaign gifts. A farmer who doesn't use harmful pesticides. Standing fast in the faith can empower us in our daily lives to take on the tasks Christ has for us. We can stand fast, refusing to do what others are doing, withstanding any possible shunning by others. "Rejoice when that day comes and dance for joy . . . your reward will be great in heaven" (JB).

Prayer: *O Lord, help me each day as I make decisions. Help me to make the choices you would have me make. Amen.*

Friday, November 3   Read Luke 6:32-35.

Jesus continually assured his disciples that when they faced persecution they would be rewarded for their faithfulness. He also taught them that they must take a great responsibility for the welfare of others, even those who persecute them. "Treat others as you would like people to treat you," he commanded (v. 31, JB). "And you will be children of the Most High, [who] is kind to the ungrateful and the wicked" (JB).

I again saw Mother Teresa when I visited her in Calcutta in 1984 after she had been ill for some time. She looked even more frail than she had ten years earlier while visiting Washington, D.C. I came to know here at that time when, among other duties, I served as her chauffeur. On my visit with her in Calcutta, I told her how sorry I was about her recent, lengthy illness.

With her indomitable spirit and liveliness, she responded with the amazing power that she has accepted from God. "Don't worry," she said. "God is not done with me yet."

Mother Teresa has received worldwide acclaim and the Nobel Peace Prize because she has been a messenger of peace to all the nations of the world. She has accepted the responsibilities that Jesus told his disciples were theirs. She has truly done for others—the poor, the destitute, the depressed and the downcast of the world—as any one of us would want done to us even in circumstances far less challenging.

She is empowered by the Holy Spirit as God has promised to each one of us who accepts and believes in God. She serves as a modern example of one who has faithfully committed her whole life in service to God.

Prayer: *Jesus, help me to be your devoted disciple in accepting the responsibilities you place on me to care for others with compassion, even those who are my enemies. Amen.*

Saturday, November 4   Read Ephesians 1:11-23.

God rejoices in those who believe in him. We have seen that in our readings throughout this week. Paul, another of God's saints, emphasizes in Ephesians in the strongest words that God delights in those of us who call ourselves Christians. "You," he says, "became God's people when you heard the true message, the Good News that brought you salvation" (TEV). God is, has been, and always will be faithful to those who believe, and more! Paul says, "How very great is [God's] power at work in us who believe" (TEV). This power is the same that raised Christ from the dead. What more could one want!

The United Methodist Council of Bishops in 1986 wrote a pastoral letter "To All United Methodists" stating their own "clear and unconditional *No* to nuclear war and to any use of nuclear weapons." The bishops called upon the people to "receive God's gracious gift of peace . . . embracing all neighbors near and far, all friends and enemies, and becoming defenders of God's good creation; and to pray without ceasing for peace in our time."*

I am convinced that the fall of the Berlin Wall in 1989, symbolizing the end of the Cold War and diminishing the threat of nuclear war, resulted from the faithful people of God heeding the words of the bishops and others who have made similar pleas. As Paul tells us, "God chose us to be his own people... based on what he had decided from the very beginning" (TEV).

Prayer: *Help us to recognize your messengers, O Lord, and help us to heed the messages that you send us through them. Amen.*

*From "In Defense of Creation: The Nuclear Crisis and A Just Peace," a pastoral letter from the Council of Bishops of The United Methodist Church. (See *The United Methodist Reporter*, May 9, 1986, page 2).

Sunday, November 5   Read Psalm 149.

Scripture reveals a vision of shalom (peace) as God's will for all creation. Shalom is defined as well-being even in the midst of trouble. It is knowing a sense of salvation even when the world is falling around us.

The faithful have delivered to us God's messages of the path to peace. Daniel revealed that peace would come to the chosen people if they would but faithfully follow God, even if for periods of time they were under the rule of godless kings. But the faithful should have no fear because all peoples and nations and languages are expected to serve God: God's dominion is everlasting and shall not pass away (see Daniel 7:14).

Paul's message of shalom comes to those who "heard . . . the Good News that brought you salvation. You believed in Christ, and God put his stamp of ownership on you. . . . The Spirit is the guarantee that we shall receive what God has promised" (Eph. 1:13*a*, TEV).

Jesus energizes and empowers his disciples for their work after he is gone. He teaches them that "Happy are you when people hate you, reject you, insult you, and say that you are evil. . . . Be glad . . . because a great reward is kept for you in heaven" (Luke 6:22, TEV).

"The LORD takes pleasure in his people," the psalmist declares (TEV). Let *us* now sing God's praises as we reaffirm that we, too, are among those who will go into the future to do God's will. And that we, like those "who were the first to set [their] hope on Christ, might live for the praise of his glory" (Eph. 1:12).

Prayer: *O that we might find your path to peace, dear God! We know that you are ever faithful if we will but accept your precepts. Help us to faithfully follow you. Amen.*

GOD WITH US

November 6-12, 1995   **Mary Montgomery**✤
Monday, November 6   Read Haggai 1:15*b*–2:9.

In today's scripture, the prophet Haggai sees the discouragement of the people over the modest beginnings of their new temple. To encourage them, Haggai announces that he is the Lord's messenger with this word from God:"I am with you."

This scripture calls to mind the floods in the U.S. Midwest in the summer of 1993. Relentless rains turned rivers into raging torrents that devastated entire communities. Scores of people lost their homes and all their possessions. Some even lost their livelihoods when businesses were destroyed, never to be rebuilt. Why such destruction? Many felt abandoned by God.

Des Moines, Iowa, was one of the areas especially hard hit. As flood waters threatened, people came from miles around to help with sandbagging. When the city lost its water supply, thousands responded by giving bottled water, hauled to Des Moines in donated semis.

During the long weeks of cleanup, busloads of volunteers from throughout Iowa and neighboring states came to help. Many flood victims stated publicly that had it not been for the volunteers, they would not have had the strength or the spirit to go on. Were these caring people God's presence in their lives? Was this God's way of saying, "I am with you"?

Suggestion for meditation: *Think of times when you have felt that God was with you through the caring acts of others. What difference have these acts made in your life? In your belief in God's care for you?*

✤Professional writer; author of numerous books; Roman Catholic layperson and Stephen Minister; Edina, Minnesota.

Tuesday, November 7   Read Luke 20:27-38.

When my oldest son, Mark, was about five, his great-grandmother died. Upon hearing the news, he gave it a moment of thoughtful consideration. Then he said, "I'm sorry Gramma got dead, but I know where she is. She's up there with Jesus and all those other guys!"

As Christians we believe that the love of God is manifested in Jesus, who shows us that death is a passage to new life. But what happens after death? What does the new life entail? Like my young son, most of us have an opinion—but no one knows for sure.

In the scripture for today, Jesus is asked questions about life after death. He states that it will be totally different from the realm of Caesar and that in the resurrected life we will have a new nature. The answer is not as specific as we might like, and speculation about what lies beyond continues.

From time to time we hear about emergency medical procedures reviving people near death. Often these people speak of "seeing behind the closed door." They tell of light purer, more colorful, more radiant than anything known before. They speak of peace, of joy, of being enfolded in love. Their experiences cause us to pause and perhaps even to reconsider the promises of God—that death is not an ending but a new beginning wherein we enter into the fullness of life with God.

Prayer: *I need to remember, God, that you are with me wherever I travel, whenever I am lonely, whenever I am distressed. Grant me the grace to be attentive to your presence. Lead me to understand that just as you are present to me now, you will be with me when I cross over into new life. Amen.*

Wednesday, November 8   Read Psalm 145:1-5.

A man bought a rundown house on a piece of land overgrown with brush and choked with weeds. After repairing and painting the house, he turned his energies to the yard. He trimmed shrubs and trees. He raked and seeded and coaxed grass to grow. He planted flowers. Behind the house, he cultivated the soil and planted a garden that produced prized vegetables. The once-neglected property became a showplace, and townspeople frequently came by to admire it.

One woman who visited was particularly effusive. "Praise be to God for the beauty of the flowers," she said, "and the green of the grass . . . and the bounty of the garden."

The man listened for a time and then drawled, "I'm all for praisin' God and givin' him his due, but you shoulda' seen this place when he had it all to himself."

The psalm in today's reading is one of praise. Praise is part of our relationship with God. We praise God in prayer. We praise God by living out his message of love exemplified by Jesus.

Jesus promised that as we strive to live out the call to love, God will guide and sustain us; God will never reject or abandon us. God will be with us always. But as the man in the story understood so well, we can't just turn our challenges and goals over to God for God to accomplish. If we want our garden to bloom, we have to put in the toil that will make it happen.

Prayer: *Dear God, I thank you for the many blessings in my life. I ask that you be with me as I meet the challenges this day brings. If I should forget you as I go about my busy day, please do not forget me. Amen.*

Thursday, November 9   Read 2 Thessalonians 2:1-5.

The scripture for today deals with the second coming of Christ, as does much of Christian thought and writing. But isn't it possible to be so focused on Christ's coming that we fail to see that he is here with us now?

The righteous asked Jesus *when* it was that they had seen him hungry and gave him food, or thirsty and gave him something to drink, or as a stranger and welcomed him, or gave him clothing when he was in need, or visited him when he was sick or in prison. Jesus replied, "Truly I tell you, just as you did it to one of the least of these who are members of my family, you did it to me" (Matt. 25:35-40).

This scripture leaves no doubt about where we will encounter Christ. Where else might we find him? If we look at our own lives, won't we find him there as well? Is he not in the encouraging word when we're too discouraged to go on? The helping hand when we're most in need of it? The directions from a stranger when we're lost? The listening ear of a friend when we're in need of understanding and compassion?

Yet how often do we attribute receiving the help we need—when we need it—to chance? To coincidence? Is it not just as likely that we are experiencing God's action in our lives? That we are reaping the promise of our God who says, "I will not leave you comfortless; I will come to you"? (John 14:18, KJV)

Prayer: *Dear God, you have guided me through rough waters many times. Help me to remember that when I reach out to you, you take my hand in yours. Then I need not fear, for I know you will lead me to a safe harbor. Amen.*

Friday, November 10   Read Psalm 145:17-21.

When a friend of mine was going through a divorce, she said, "I never felt further from the church or closer to God." In her church community she felt judged and, at times, rejected. When she turned to God, she found understanding and unconditional love.

I have also heard people in grief support groups say that during their most intense mourning, the church was not a comfort to them. I don't believe they are saying—nor am I implying—that the clergy and their congregations lack compassion or are indifferent to the suffering among them. Sometimes the grieving do not attend church because it is too painful a reminder of the funeral and all that they have lost. Others fail to ask the church for help that would be forthcoming if they made their needs known.

Because some people who are hurting do not find solace in their church does not mean they have distanced themselves from God. Quite the contrary. During periods of emotional pain, many people say that they have never been so prayerful or felt so deeply spiritual. What they discover is the God the psalmist praises in today's reading: the God who hears their cry; the God who is just and kind; the God who is near to all who call out. However dark their thoughts, however bleak their spirit, however angry or sad or hopeless they feel, God does not condemn or judge. God listens and loves them nonetheless.

Prayer: *Dear God, grant me the grace to reach out to you in my times of need. Let me know that no matter what my circumstance, you will always be there for me. Amen.*

Saturday, November 11   Read 2 Thessalonians 2:13-15.

In the scripture for today, Paul tells the Thessalonians to "stand firm and hold fast to the traditions that you were taught by us, either by word of mouth or by our letter."

In contemporary language, Paul was telling the early Christians to get their priorities straight, to have as their highest priority the values they knew to be true and to conduct their lives according to those values.

In this connection, I am reminded of a young man who lived in a community where he was employed, had a caring family, and was surrounded by friends. But a city several hundred miles away beckoned. The young man believed that if he went there, his dreams for the good life would come true. He eventually moved to the city where he found a job that enabled him to live even better than his expectations. He had what he always thought he wanted. But after a couple of years he quit his job and returned to the community he had left. When asked why he came back, he said, "I just wasn't getting ahead. All I was doing was making money."

The story is not about the unhealthy pursuit of ambitions but rather about the part priorities play in the decisions we make. Throughout scripture we are called to see and seek God as our top priority. If we do this, and if we live our lives according to God's word, we will have our priorities straight. Who knows what blessings will then be ours!

Prayer: *Dear God, there are times when I need to reassess my values. I need to stop and consider what is most important in my life. When I get my priorities backward, turn me around and steer me in the right direction. Amen.*

Sunday, November 12   Read 2 Thessalonians 2:16-17.

One spring it rained for nine straight days. With hardly a break in the cloud cover, moods turned as gray as the weather. On the ninth day of that dreary weather, I was in the supermarket parking lot when I heard a child cry, "Look at the rainbow!"

I glanced at the leaden sky with its low-slung clouds. If there was a rainbow, it was invisible to me.

Then even more excitedly the child called, "Mama! Mama! Come and see the rainbow!"

My curiosity piqued, I turned and saw a boy about four years old with his mother as they looked down at the blacktop. "See!" he cried, pointing to an oil spot left by a car. "There it is!"

Indeed, there—in that oil slick—was a rainbow. Rain had put a shine on the black asphalt, making the violet and pink and green of the oil especially lustrous.

I drove home bemused by my experience. How easy it is to be so narrowly focused that we fail to see new possibilities. How seldom we look with fresh eyes and a mind open to new ways of relating to our environment, to others, and to God.

In the scripture for today, God is asked to comfort our hearts and "strengthen them in every good work and deed."

Recalling that rainy day reminds me of how easy it is to be overcome by the grayness of life and how, when that happens, we fail to turn to God for comfort and strength. We fail to see the rainbows.

Prayer: *Dear God, help me remember that you are always within reach. Here is my hand. Help me feel your love and strength. Help me know that with you, gray, gloomy days lead to brighter tomorrows. Amen.*

November 13-19, 1995   **Trudy M. Archambeau♣**
Monday, November 13   Read Isaiah 65:17-20.

A new creation

Into the unsettled restlessness and pain of exile, God speaks the hope-giving words: "Behold, I create new heavens and a new earth" (NKJV). The Hebrew concept of time is difficult for the modern mind to comprehend. Underscoring this difficulty, other versions read: "I will create"; "I am about to create"; "I am creating" (NIV, NRSV, TEV). Obviously, we are dealing here not with chronological time but with God's time. The Hebrew scriptures have several words that can be translated by the Greek term *kairos*, meaning God's time of fullness and opportunity. But there is no Hebrew word that adequately defines *chronos*, meaning sequential, measurable time. In God's time, God continues to design the new creation. Beyond the confines of human boundaries, God's creative action is a continuous process.

The prophetic message is set in terms familiar to the recipients: *new heavens and a new earth*. No doubt they immediately recalled the creation stories of their heritage. They could begin to sense the life-giving spirit of God hovering and brooding over the troubled, chaotic waters of their own existence. They could begin to look forward to the promised joy that would erase the memory of their pain and tears.

Prayer: *Ever-creating God, whatever unrest or confusion may surround my life, I can be certain that you are is still at work. Help me to see your new work today. Amen.*

♣Writer; correspondent, *The Michigan Christian Advocate*; worship liturgy coordinator, Christ United Methodist Church, Lansing, Michigan.

Tuesday, November 14   Read Isaiah 65:21-25.

New relationship

Whether understood in terms of restoration following the Exile or as pointing to the messianic kingdom, the eschatology expressed in Isaiah 65 anticipates a community of joy and gladness. The renewed Jerusalem will be better than the old.

Restored Security: "Like the days of a tree shall the days of my people be." Trees embody the qualities of long life, stability, and endurance (see Psalm 92:12*ff*). No longer forced to live as exiles, as homeless strangers in a foreign land, inhabitants in the restored Jerusalem "shall build houses and inhabit them; they shall plant vineyards and eat their fruit." Throughout the Hebrew scriptures prophets use similar language to create images contrasting the instability of exilic life with the approaching security of home. Insecurity and unpredictability will be replaced by safety and stability, the temporary by the permanent.

Restored Relationship: "Before they call I will answer." These words establish the reality of restored human-divine relationship. Life in exile has only temporarily broken the people's relationship with God. Alienation and separation are not final. Even sin and rebellion can be healed. Into the brokenness of fragmented and scattered lives will come the searching love and reconciling grace of God. The new relationship with God will be so intimate that God will answer even before asked.

Restored Peace: "The wolf and the lamb shall feed together." Even the natural order is reversed and restored. Echoing the words of Isaiah 11:6-9, the prophet paints a picture of God's redemptive, transforming *shalom*, undisturbed by harm or hurt.

Prayer: *O God, break the barriers and heal the wounds that separate me from a close and vital relationship with you today. Amen.*

Wednesday, November 15   Read Psalm 98:1-6.

A new song

Trumpets, fanfare, processions, and music were long associated in the history of the nation of Israel with the ascension of a king to the throne. The mood was always festive and full of rejoicing. Here, the imagery is reserved for God, who has done great and marvelous things. Psalms 94–100 were probably part of worship liturgy, written to proclaim and celebrate the reign and sovereignty of God over the whole cosmic and created order.

Remembering the saving, delivering acts of God, the Hebrews were encouraged to "Sing to the LORD a new song." Today, we, too, can join in the singing. A new song can be something that has never been sung or heard before. But it might also be the relearning and reclaiming of something eternal. What is ageless always becomes new when it becomes personal. Whenever we recognize the grace-filled intervention of God in our own lives, we compose a new song in response. Our time-bound hearts begin to move in rhythm with the Eternal, and our human spirits are tuned to sing in harmony with the music of God's spirit.

The *new song* recalls the faithfulness and constant love of God of the everlasting covenant. It summarizes God's promise-making and promise-keeping character; God's merciful and compassionate nature; and God's steadfast, unending kindness. In response to all that God is and all that God does, the invitation is issued to God's people and also to the whole earth: *To sing a new and joyous song.*

Prayer: *O God, Composer of the unfinished song of creation and the endless music of eternity, sing your song to me today, that you and I might sing a new song and make music together. Amen.*

Thursday, November 16   Read Psalm 98:7-9.

A new kingdom

Suddenly the psalmist's arena of praise expands to include the whole created order. The writer employs wonderful imagery, personifying all creation and bidding it to participate in the symphony of praise. The sea is invited to roar with resounding thunder. Rivers are encouraged to clap their hands. Mountains and hills are urged to sing together and shout for joy.

The reason for this planned and rehearsed explosion of celebration is found in verse 9: "For [God] is coming to judge the earth . . . [to] judge the world with righteousness and the peoples with equity." Such divine justice and fairness are cause for joy. Apparently looking ahead to the end times, the psalmist declares the coming of God's kingdom, where all creation will be touched and healed by God's justice and where all will live in a right relationship with God.

Looking behind and beyond the shadows of his time, the psalmist begins to see the reality of the coming age. Anticipating the coming kingdom of God, the psalmist is assured that the ultimate victory of God will not be denied or deterred. God *will* come as judge, but it will be a judgment that establishes God's purposes and sets things right. Of that, the psalmist is confident.

Clearly, the psalmist is writing not about some vague and abstract theory or theology but rather out of the depths of authentic personal experience with God, whose self-revelation is always defined by fairness and justice. Today we, too, have encountered and experienced God. Because we know God, we can share the psalmist's enthusiasm.

Prayer: *Kingdom-building God, keep us moving always in the direction of the new reign you are even now establishing. In Jesus' name I pray. Amen.*

Friday, November 17   Read 2 Thessalonians 3:6-13.

A new order

The in-breaking of God's new order requires a human response. Paul addresses the response of the Thessalonians by dealing with very practical, everyday matters. He urges them not to be lazy. Scholars disagree about the cause of their laziness. Some say the people were preoccupied with thoughts about the second coming of Christ. They apparently sensed its nearness, and living in the meantime became a chore. They gave up their regular responsibilities in order to wait for the unfolding of the kingdom. Others think that laziness had become so natural to them that it lingered on in spite of their new faith as believers. Whatever the reason, their laziness was disorderly, disturbing their own faith and disrupting the faith journeys of others as well.

It is always risky to say, "Look at me!" But Paul dared to say, "Imitate us." Though admitting on other occasions that his walk of faith was not yet perfected, here Paul states confidently that he is an example worthy of following. Look around! Today people are following us, too, as we try to be faithful. They are not searching for perfect people to model unrealistic standards, but they are looking for honest people who realize their own imperfections and admit their own failings, even as they claim the name of Christ and seek to live lives consistent with the gospel of Christ.

Finally, Paul writes, "Do not be weary in doing what is right." Living out the purposes of the new order means not growing weary of doing good. It means being willing to continue working for the right, even with no tangible or visible results.

Prayer: *Jesus, keep me close to you today, that I will not tarnish the name you have entrusted to me but will live it out with integrity. Amen.*

Saturday, November 18   Read Luke 21:5-13.

A new outlook

The disciples were dazzled by the sight of the Jerusalem Temple in all its shining white and gleaming gold. But Jesus was not impressed. Instead, he asserted with calmness and certainty, "The days will come when not one stone will be left upon another." Unthinkable! How could this be? The reconstruction of Herod's Temple would not be completed until the year 63 C.E.,* only a few years before its destruction in 70 C.E.

Jesus then went on, further unsettling his listeners. He talked about earthquakes and plagues, famines and wars. Before the end times, all will be upheaval, confusion, and chaos. Then Jesus added a personal note, "They will arrest you and persecute you . . . because of my name." The picture Jesus was painting was not a pretty one. In short, he was outlining uncertain and perilous times of fear, danger, and insecurity. Nothing would be permanent; everything would erupt in cataclysmic change.

Into this somber mood came the inevitable questions, "When? How will we know?" For two thousand years people has speculated about the end times. Conjectures about signs and warnings have abounded. We can allow ourselves to be distracted and led astray by careless curiosity and by fear and dread; or we can adopt a new outlook, realizing it is not for us to know the future. Instead, it is for us to live the present fully in the power and peace of Christ. Rather than playing eschatological mind games, we can discover what is really important. Rather than looking for signs of the end, we can look at Jesus now.

Prayer: *Steady, unmovable God, renew my outlook, that I may face this day with courage and joy, focused and centered on Christ. Amen.*

---

*C.E. is the Christian era; also known as [in the year] A.D.

Sunday, November 19   Read Luke 21:14-19.

A new self

The disciples probably expected Jesus to give them some good, sound advice on how to handle the troubling times of betrayal and persecution ahead. But, as usual, Jesus turns human thinking upside down, saying in effect, "Prepare to be unprepared" (v. 14, AP). "For I will give you words and a wisdom that none of your opponents will be able to understand or contradict." Some versions translate this as "a mouth and wisdom" (NKJV). Biblically, the mouth was an instrument of purpose and power. "I will be with your mouth and teach you [Moses] what you are to speak" (Exod. 4:12). "The Sovereign LORD has given me an instructed tongue, to know the word that sustains the weary" (Isa. 50:4, NIV).

In today's passage Jesus encourages the disciples to use their imprisonment as an opportunity for ministry, assured that he himself will supply the words and the wisdom. Jesus is discouraging worry and fretfulness over each minute detail. It is possible to be so prepared that little room is left for the movement of the Spirit. Jesus argues against restricting the Spirit by too much human effort.

Jesus knows life is not easy: "By your endurance you will gain your souls." Standing firm in the power of Christ and allowing the Spirit to guide and teach us is how we begin to discover who we really are. We begin to see the self as God sees it, and we begin to see the new self God is loving into existence. Under the daily care and direction of God's spirit the new self is formed and created and true identity is named and claimed.

Prayer: *O God, day by day help me to hear your words and learn the wisdom your spirit is teaching. Step by step on my journey, help me to grow into the new self you envision for me in Christ. Amen.*

November 20-26, 1995   **Folke T. Olofsson✤**
Monday, November 20   Read Jeremiah 23:1-4.

God, our Lord, is not a silent, passive God. God is a God who acts and speaks: "Let there be light! Let there be life! Let us make man in our image, after our likeness!" There is a basic design to be trusted, a final Word that makes all the difference, an end in which all things will be well.

Human life carries with it responsibility. God created us so that we can hear what God has to say "at sundry times and in diverse manners" (Heb. 1:1, KJV). Creation carries with it communication. God speaks and we not only can hear but also respond in words and deeds, for which we are responsible.

Jeremiah lends his voice to the word of God, and the words he brings forth contain both doom and promise. Those to whom God had given power and authority to lead and shepherd the people had, through their neglect and carelessness, failed in their response to God. For them responsibility meant doom. The other side of God's judgment is God's promise. In order to fulfill his promises, God has to deal with those who do not fulfill their responsibilities.

The promise God gave Eve, the mother of all humanity, that her seed would bruise the head of the Serpent (Gen. 3:15), is in the process of being fulfilled: If some fail in their responsibility, God will send other shepherds. Nothing can stop God from honoring his promises.

Prayer: *Lord, raise up good shepherds in church and society. Amen.*

✤Priest in the Church of Sweden, rector of Rasbo; docent in theological and ideological studies at Uppsala University, Uppsala, Sweden.

Tuesday, November 21   Read Jeremiah 23:5-6.

Leadership in church and in society means responsibility. Power and authority over people ultimately come from God. Leaders and pastors are accountable; eventually they will have to respond to God for their leadership.

Jeremiah's time and ours share the same conditions for responsible leadership: doom and promise. Doom will come for those who fail to fulfill its responsibilities: leading, feeding, keeping together and protecting the sheep. The promise once given to Abraham, the father of faith, that in his seed all nations shall be blessed, is still in the process of being fulfilled.

God judges. God gives promises to save his people, and God fulfills them. Human history, therefore, is not only a hopeless mess of aggression, oppression, and the abuse of power. There is a "line of scarlet thread" (Josh. 2:18) leading to the manger of Bethlehem, to the cross of Golgotha, to the empty tomb of the Garden, to the Baptismal font, to the Eucharistic Table. There is a Lamb of God who takes away the sins of the pastors and the people. There is a Good Shepherd, whose name reveals who he is, what he does and gives: the Lord, our righteousness.

By belonging to the people of God, I can question, criticize, and even resist devious and disastrous leadership in church and society when it is exercised against the Word of God. That is my responsibility. I can do this without resentment or despondency, because I trust God's promise that in the end every knee shall bow and every tongue shall confess that the Good Shepherd, the Fulfiller of God's promises, is the Lord.

Prayer: *Thank you, Lord, for the fulfillment of all your promises. Amen.*

Wednesday, November 22   Read Luke 1:68-75.

The priest Zechariah is struck dumb. He carries out his priestly duties in the Temple, yet he stands under the doom of God.* He did not believe that God's promises could be fulfilled in his own life and in the life of his family.

Like Abram and Sarai, Zechariah and Elizabeth had a child when nobody really believed that it even was possible. But God had promised a son, and God kept his promise.

When God first spoke to Zechariah, he responded with disbelief. Later when God kept his promise, Zechariah responded with obedience as a sign of his trust and belief in God. The first word he uttered was in praise and thanksgiving to God: Blessed, *Benedictus*. In the office of Morning Prayer the Church across the centuries has joined Zechariah in this benediction.

Why? Because there is a common experience of God, who speaks, acts, and keeps his promises; a common experience of God, who is greater than the disbelief and irresponsibility of some pastors and church leaders; a common experience of God, who fulfills his promises by creating and sustaining a people. In this action, barriers of ages, places, races, sexes, and languages are transcended.

Through faith and baptism you and I belong to this people. You and I and our families are encompassed in God's saving action. How are we to respond? "Blessed be the Lord God of Israel; for he hath visited and redeemed his people" (KJV).

Prayer: *Lord, give us responsive and responsible priests and prophets who lead your people in blessing and praise for your mercy. Amen.*

---

*By "the doom of God" the author means three possible interpretations: "imminent judgment," "a verdict," or "a threatening future." Or, we might simply say "the judgment of God."

Thursday, November 23   Read Luke 1:76-79.

The king about whom Jeremiah prophesied never came. Kings came, all right, and kings died. But no one matched the features of the One whom Jeremiah had pictured in his prophecy. Had God forgotten his promise, or failed to fulfill it? No, as always, when God acts, the fulfillment of the promise transcends its anticipated scope. The people expected a liberating king. They received a cosmic Savior.

Jesus Christ did not enter into human history like a lightning bolt out of a blue sky. He grew out of people that God had been fostering for centuries. He was connected with persons with whom God acts. John the Baptist was one of these.

In the chapel of an evangelic monastery* that I know, there are three icons behind the altar. The central icon represents Christ seated in glory on his throne, holding the Book of Life. Mary is standing to his right, pointing toward her Son. At his left, John the Baptist, head bowed, points toward Christ.

Forever pointing toward Christ—that is the office and the honor of John the Baptist. When his father prophesied about this son, he did not know that John would see with his own eyes the One about whom all the prophets had spoken and would utter the words that fulfilled all prophecies: "Behold, the Lamb of God, who takes away the sin of the world!" (John 1:29, RSV) The promise's fulfillment was far greater than Zechariah expected.

"His name is John." Finally Zechariah understood what it was all about: God's tender mercy.

Prayer: *Thank you, Lord, for all prophets who still point toward Jesus, the Good Shepherd and Lamb of God. Amen.*

*A monastery within the Church of Sweden that follows the Rule of Saint Benedict.

Friday, November 24   Read Luke 23:33-43.

The King on a cross! The Righteous Branch on the tree of curse! The Lord our righteousness crucified! There must be some mistake, some terrible misunderstanding. And yet, the sign on the cross clearly states: "This is the King of the Jews."

The religious leaders who condemn Jesus resent that claim. The soldiers (representing the political powers) who carry out the death sentence scorn it. The enemies beneath his cross, the oppressed and the oppressors, and the criminal on the cross—all unite in this scathing "if": If you are the king, then, prove it to us and step down from the cross. And he remains silent. He has already said his royal word: "Father, forgive them." All are encompassed in his prayer. The boundaries of his kingdom coincide with the boundaries of his intercession.

Two criminals representing you and me are crucified together with him. Who is this man? Who do we say he is? (See Matthew 14:16.) Christ is nailed to the cross between the only two human alternatives: revilement or repentance. There is no middle way. Revilement. Are you not one of the many, too many, powerless victims and failures in human history: executed political pretenders and religious impostors? I am sorry. Repentance. Or could it be that you, the One Who Is Here sharing our lot even on the cross, is the One who incarnates God's tender mercy? Is it true, Jesus, that the God of our mothers and fathers, the God of all the promises, is like you? *Kyrie eleison!* Lord, have mercy.

Now the King speaks, not in order to silence his tormentors but to welcome the first subject, a former criminal, into his eternal reign: "Today you will be with me in Paradise." The head of the Serpent is being bruised by the Seed, as promised.

Prayer: *Lord Jesus, remember me when you come into your kingdom.*

Saturday, November 25   Read Colossians 1:11-17.

"Why do our bodies have to rot in the grave? Why must they be burnt into ashes? Why doesn't God take us straightway to heaven?" These are the questions of a ten-year-old boy who had just lost his mother in a traffic accident. She died shielding him with her own body. Paradise is far away, indeed.

The straightforward questions of that boy, which a lot of people certainly would find tasteless in their concreteness, reveal the kind of leadership we really need.

Excellent political leaders are insufficient as are religious personalities who can guide people to a rich inner life but nothing more. We need someone who can deal with life as we know it: guilt and forgiveness, loss and death, decomposition and ashes. We need a Savior. Jesus Christ is the One who meets our needs.

Life and things are not just "there." Everything, visible and invisible, is *created*. This is the great mystery: all creation is *in*, *for*, and *through* Christ. He is the Word of God, through whom all things in the beginning were called into being. He is the Sustainer, in whom all things are held together. He is the Heir of creation, in whom all things in the end will find their consummation. In the hand of Bethlehem's newborn babe, the whole cosmos rests. In the pierced hand of the Crucified, the whole creation is contained. In the glorified body of the risen Lord, all that exists is resurrected. He is not a cosmic principle. He is a living Person.

What could I tell that little boy? That Jesus Christ is the Lord of decomposition and ashes? But holding him in my arms I said, "He is not finished yet." In the world it is still Easter Eve.

Prayer: *Lord Jesus, come soon and establish your sovereignty over all. Amen.*

341

Sunday, November 26　　　　　Read Colossians 1:18-20.

Already and *not yet*. These are the conditions under which we live as Christians. Jesus Christ has already come as the ful-fillment of all God's promises. And yet we wait for his coming. He is already the Lord of all; and still we eagerly long for that day when his sovereignty will be apparent to all.

Every time the Church is gathered on the day of the Lord's resurrection from the dead, the final victory is being proclaimed and lived in an anticipatory way. He who is the Head of the Body, the Church, is truly present as the Risen One.

Moses asked to see God's glory. He wanted to see God's face. Out of mercy, God protected Moses from seeing God's very self. Moses could only see God's back. In nature and in history we may perceive the back of God. Many people do. But the glorious face of God is only visible in the person of Jesus. In the Hebrew scriptures, God's glory killed those who came too close. In Christ, this glory heals.

What kind of world is it into which we are born, in which we live and die? It is a world reconciled to God through the sacrifice of Christ at the cross. We already live in a cosmos reconciled to God in Christ! In Christ, in his Body, which is the Church, the final consummation of all things is already at hand. In blessed water, in blessed bread and wine, we partake in Christ's final victory. Our mission to the world as Church is to live this reconciliation: a healed cosmos. The Serpent is dead; the Seed lives and reigns forever. Death is vanquished through the cross; Christ has given us new life. It is Sunday! Rejoice!

Prayer: *Glory be to the Father, and to the Son, and to the Holy Ghost, as it was in the beginning, is now and ever shall be, world without end. Amen.*

THE PEACE GOD GIVES

November 27–December 3, 1995   **Wightman Weese✤**
Monday, November 27   Read Psalm 122:1-5.

Coming to Jerusalem was a time of gladness. This psalm was to be sung as the pilgrims approached the massive East Gate of the city. The city gates, within which the judges sat, symbolized the justice drawn from the righteous statutes of Israel. The people came without fear before the judges. Their coming was, in the fullest sense of the word, to celebrate God's true shalom.

Within its three rings of walls stood the Temple, the place where the people of God came year after year to pay their tithes and to offer their sacrifices. They came to stand together as God's people to worship and praise God, to express their gratitude for God's sustenance, protection, and blessing.

The very thought of coming together with the people of God, to worship in concert within the Temple courts, brought joy to the psalmist's lips. Those who despised the company of God's people chose for themselves a double tragedy. They missed not only fellowship with God but also fellowship with other believers.

Part of the psalmist's joy came from knowing that where people praised God, there was God in their midst. As long as praises flowed from their lips and the love and reverence for God's statutes remained, God was being worshiped in spirit and in truth.

Prayer: *Dear God, may your peace rest upon us as we lift our praises to you. Amen.*

✤Minister; free-lance writer; book editor, Tyndale House Publishers; Wheaton, Illinois.

Tuesday, November 28   Read Isaiah 2:1-3.

In David's day, the people of God were exclusively the people of Israel, or so they chose to think of themselves. From all the peoples of the world, God had chosen Abraham's line. God had brought the nation of Israel to the fullness of blessing in David's throne. But from the beginning it was God's plan for a greater king to arise, greater even than David. This greater King would be the Prince of Peace to whose throne the whole world would come to worship.

It was this vision of the Temple that Isaiah saw. Jerusalem was a fearful huddle of people cowering under the threat of Assyria and rumors of war. The kingdom of Judah was in disarray, surrounded by enemies on all sides. Justice and righteousness no longer reigned within its gates, and the lamps within the Temple grew dim.

To such troubled people, the words of God's prophet came with this promise of a new Temple to which everyone could come. Isaiah's invitation was offered as David's psalm had been—as a call for God's people everywhere to come and meet the Holy One at the foot of the divine throne.

God is faithful. No matter how dark and threatening the world may be, God always makes known the place where we may find him—and the peace that only God gives.

Prayer: *O Lord, we come before you surrounded by troubles. In your presence we seek assurance and peace. Amen.*

Wednesday, November 29   Read Psalm 122:6-9.

The house of the Lord, which stood secure within the citadel of Jerusalem, was a place where believers came to meet and commune with God. It was a place where the righteousness of God was satisfied as the people brought their offerings.

Tied up in the hearts of the Israelites was the knowledge that as long as Jerusalem was secure, Israel and all it stood for and held to be sacred was secure. To prosper they must continue in the teachings of Moses. The pilgrimages undertaken by the people were for sacred transactions, physical and spiritual; to pay what was due to God; to bring God their praise as well their offerings, tokens of their thanksgiving.

The truth was there to see. But the people who came to the Temple failed to see that the One who dwelt among them—and not only in the Temple—needed no protection, but was and is the Protector. We are secure only before God's throne, safe there from all our enemies.

Jesus' once-for-all offering for sin has bought for us what the psalmist sought—peace, the privilege of coming before God without fear. The holy place has now become the throne room of our hearts. God dwelling within us is our hope of eternal life.

Prayer: *Our God, we thank you for the peace you have brought within our hearts through Jesus, the Prince of Peace, the once-for-all-time sacrifice. Amen.*

Thursday, November 30   Read Isaiah 2:4-5.

The weary, hungry laborer longs for food and rest. Troubled and tear-filled midnight hours make the joys of morning seem an eternity away. The heart is made ready for relief by the pain that it endures.

The troubled, fearful people of Judah were losing hope. Even during the reigns of the best of their kings, Uzziah and Jotham, wickedness reigned. Despite some victories over the Ammonites and the unsuccessful siege on Jerusalem by Israel and its allies, a greater threat from Assyria loomed over them. Sooner or later, judgment from God was bound to come, for God had promised peace and blessing only so long as the people continued in God's ways.

Isaiah's words were part of that great Advent story God had been preparing—the promise of a King who would judge among the nations, settle disputes for all people, and bring true peace to Israel and the whole world. But the people of Judah could not understand and fully appreciate the peace of God until they had known the terror of war, the fear of death, and the pain of loss. Those who will not accept the peace of God must accept the consequences, the constant fear of judgment. Wars make necessary the preparation for war, costly as the war itself. In all our struggles for peace both inward and outward, God's peace flows out from the mountain of the Lord's Temple, that place where we bow in worship before God. God's peace is brought by the Prince of Peace, the one before whom the whole world will one day worship.

Prayer: *Dear God, we rejoice at another Advent season, awaiting the Prince of Peace to be born anew in our lives, even as we surely await his future coming again. Amen.*

346

Friday, December 1   Read Matthew 24:36-41.

Advent season brings again deep thoughts of the Savior and King who came first as a tiny child. With the children, we count the hours till the Christ candle of the Advent wreath is finally lit. We remember with gratitude during this season the son God sent from heaven to be God-with-us. His time on earth went so quickly. It seems he spent only a few short days at his mother's knee and with his earthly father in the carpentry shop, then three short years of teaching and preaching. Finally he offered to us the ultimate Christmas gift, his sacrifice on the cross. Resurrected and ascended, the child is now the Savior King, sitting enthroned in heaven's glory.

But the story is not yet over.

Advent seasons come and go. Each year, as the season ends, the world soon goes back to its old ways of eating and drinking, marrying and giving in marriage, making no preparation for the final advent of Jesus the Lord. The world seems almost unaware of the building project that has been underway for centuries. God's realm is not being created with noisy hammers and saws but with quiet preparation, and no one knows the day or hour when it will be complete.

We who await Advent enjoy Christ's coming in truth. We see in our mind's eye beyond the Bethlehem manger to the throne he will occupy on that future day. We watch for his coming again.

Prayer: *O God, prepare our hearts for this season of Advent and Christmas, that we may again receive the gift of peace and love the Child of Bethlehem brings. Prepare us, also, for that time of his return in glory as Jesus comes again to earth. Amen.*

Saturday, December 2   Read Matthew 24:42-44.

The watchman on the city wall was the first to see the advance of attacking armies. The safety of the entire city depended on his careful vigilance. But now the waiting is not for attackers but for the return from battle of the king and his army. Soon the eyes of the watchman catch a glimpse of movement. First it is just a speck, then a column of marching people wavering on the horizon. Then the victory banners can be seen, and a mighty cheer goes up from those on the wall, anxious for their return.

We are the watchers to whom Christ was speaking. One day he will be coming back again to claim the throne he has already conquered through his victory over death and the power of evil, won on the cross and from the open, empty tomb.

The thief about whom Christ spoke gained advantage not by stealth but by speed and surprise. If the victim had been alert, he would not have been caught off guard. So it is with the return of Christ at his next coming. When it happens, the drama will unfold quickly and no one knows when, despite all the prophecies the world has heard.

We do not wait on a wall. Rather, our preparation takes the form of patience, steadfastness in good works, and unrelenting efforts to prepare a lost world to receive the gospel and the offer of citizenship into the reign of God.

Prayer: *Dear Jesus, our bodies grow weary but our hearts are aglow as we wait for your return. Come quickly and claim your throne. Amen.*

Sunday, December 3   Read Romans 13:11-14.

When the King's victory procession breaks into sight it is too late to prepare for his return. The Apostle Paul set an excellent example for the churches for whom he labored. Tracing the life of Paul through the New Testament, we see that he seems to have rested only when fatigue or illness felled him. He lived every moment as if it were his last. He truly fought the good fight.

Some say that the Christ is coming soon—any day now. Others point to certain prophecies in the Hebrew scriptures and in the New Testament that are yet to be fulfilled. But one thing about his coming is certain—it will be one day sooner than it was yesterday. Although we do not know how much sand is yet in the hourglass, we know that time will one day run out. On that day, the work we have neglected will forever remain undone. Today is the day, and now is the hour, to begin preparing. Those who await the kingdom of life and light should waste no time in works of darkness. We are children of the light.

Jesus once told a parable about a man who was unprepared, without a wedding garment, on the day the bridegroom (the king's son) arrived (Matt. 22:2, 11-14). Paul tells us here that it is the Lord Jesus Christ himself that we are to put on. That is our preparation day after day, as we await the Lord's coming.

Prayer: *Matchless Lord—king, bridegroom, and friend—grant that we may be vigilant and that we may welcome you with clean robes and with ready hearts. Amen.*

December 4-10, 1995   **Mary A. Avram**✤
Monday, December 4   Read Romans 15:4-13.

"O Israel, hope in the LORD!" (Psalm 130:7). For the Israelite true hope was always hope in God. God was the only foundation of hope.

Hope, like loving arms, encircles our Advent reading for today. The first verse gives us a way to live a life of hope through steadfastness and the encouragement that we receive from God through Holy Scripture.

When Paul says that "whatever was written in former days was written for our instruction," he is encouraging the church to read the Hebrew scriptures. In them they read the stories of God's promises to God's people, and they read that God is truthful and keeps promises. In the scriptures they, as well as we, receive encouragement to steadfastness, that "we might have hope."

In the concluding verse of the reading, God is named "the God of hope," that is, the Author, the Source, and the Supplier of hope. Hope itself is a gift of God within the community of faith and within the individual believer. For the Christian, hope binds us to God's saving action in Jesus Christ.

Advent is primarily a time of hope. We wait in hope—eager, patient, anticipatory, and active hope. Advent cannot be rushed. We wait in hope for gestation to be complete in birth. Come, Lord Jesus!

Prayer: *Come, Holy One, be hope in me this day. Amen.*

✤Spiritual director, teacher, retreat and workshop leader; member of the Wider Quaker Fellowship and of The United Methodist Church; Signal Mountain, Tennessee.

Tuesday, December 5   Read Isaiah 11:1-5.

Isaiah spoke of the future hope of Israel in these words announcing the birth or the ascension of a new king of the house and lineage of David and his father, Jesse. From this family tree would come the true king. Second Samuel 7 gave ancient Israelites the promise of a king who would be, in Isaiah's words, a "shoot" and "branch" from this tree stump.

Isaiah prophesied that the spirit of the Lord will rest upon the king and form his character. Through God's spirit he will embody the qualities of wisdom and understanding, counsel and might, and knowledge and fear of the Lord. He will not judge by appearances but will judge as God does—by looking on the heart. He will govern in the way of justice for all, even the weakest and poorest among them. And his delight will be in deep and singular reverence for the Lord. This will be God's reign for Jerusalem, Judah, and eventually the whole world. This is the hope of Israel.

In our world today there are many things, places, and persons clamoring for our hope. Where do we place our hope? On whom or what do we hang our present? Our future? On whom do we place our hope?

Hope is a foundational attitude in the life of Jews and of Christians. In biblical thought, hope is the expectation of a good future because of the promises of God.

In Advent, Christians hear the prophetic voice of Isaiah, his words repeated in today's reading, and we wait in the presence of a Bethlehem stable. We wait for the arrival of Mary and Joseph, for the birth of a child born-to-be-king.

Prayer: *God, Holy and Blessed One, cleanse me from false hope that keeps me attached to things, places, and persons other than you. May my hope always be in you alone. Amen.*

Wednesday, December 6   Read Isaiah 11:6-9.

The prophetic poem voiced by Isaiah continues in today's reading. The powerful words sing and shine. They coax a scene from our imagination that fulfills our heart's deepest longing for peace and harmony, for a world without fear and without violence. This is a world where little girls and small boys, humankind at its most vulnerable, will play and grow in serenity and safety. This is a radical transformation of life both in Isaiah's eighth-century world and in our almost twenty-first-century world.

In the conclusion of these verses the prophet gathers up the scene and centers it in "my holy mountain," God's dwelling place on Mount Zion in Jerusalem. From there, from God's house, the messianic age of God's reign through God's messiah will spread through the land and through the whole world. All the nations will seek him. The earth will acknowledge God's sovereignty as the waters cover the sea.

On the wall of my studio is a print of a woodcut by Fritz Eichenberg depicting the *Peaceable Kingdom*. On the wall of my living room is a framed, watercolor Christmas card received years ago picturing the same scene. These portrayals of Isaiah's messianic prophecy call me again and again to remember my hope in the God of hope. They also call me to remember that with humankind an ongoing peace in the midst of great differences both in kind and in commitment is well-nigh impossible—but with God all things are possible.

Prayer: *Blessed Jesus, God of hope, guide me in the way of peace and hope. Teach me, Holy One, to be peace, to be hope in the midst of life—today and tomorrow and the day after. "O come, O come, Emmanuel." Amen.*

Thursday, December 7   Read Psalm 72:1-4.

This psalm may be a prayer written by a court poet for a reigning Hebrew king. It may have been used on special occasions such as a birthday or anniversary; or the psalm may be a prayer offered at the coronation of a new Hebrew king.

We see in it, as in Isaiah 11:1-5, Israel's hope for the reign of God through their king. The community prays for the king to receive God's justice and God's righteousness so that he will judge God's people with righteousness and God's poor with justice.

In the prayer the king is reminded that God is sovereign and that the king is anointed to be God's representative. He is to defend the poor, deliver the needy, and crush those who would oppress them. The king hears again that the people he governs are God's people.

This psalm, never quoted in the Christian scriptures, is not specifically a messianic psalm. However, it carries within it the messianic hope in the idealization of the king and in the longing prayers of the Hebrew community.

We do not have kings, but we have a national leader; we have governors, senators, representatives, and mayors. Do we pray and yearn for them to govern with God's justice and righteousness? Do we pray for them and bless them continually? Do we have hope for them?

Prayer: *Gracious Redeemer, teach me again to pray daily for those in positions of power and authority in our government and governments across the world. Bless them, O God, with your justice and righteousness, that they may govern with righteousness and justice. All praise and honor and glory and hope is in your holy name. Amen.*

Friday, December 8   Read Psalm 72:5-7.

"Hebrew hyperbole" is a phrase and a way of speaking and writing that I have enjoyed since I first discovered it several years ago. The rich, grandiose, flowery, extravagant, hyperbolic language of the Hebrew court poet of Psalm 72 can waft us along on the wings of imagery and set our imaginations free.

The lyrical language of the poet lifts us out of the tedious and beyond the mundane, yet the often tedious and mundane are the very matters with which he deals. How long will the king live (v. 5); will his rule be heavy-handed or gentle, like rain on new-mown grass (v. 6); will his reign be just and peaceful for as long as it lasts? If so, may it last a long, long time (v. 7).

Reading today's verses caused me to remember an experience of a few years ago. We were living in Michigan at the time, and my husband and I had worked out a happy arrangement for yard care. He tended the lawn and I tended the flowers and shrubs. Each year I severely pruned the shrubs in front of our house. Somehow, this seemed to me to be a kind of wounding that required a compassionate response; so, each day for about a week I would use the hose to gently sprinkle the shrubs with cool water. My neighbors laughed, but this TLC was important to me.

Relating that experience to the rain falling on new-mown grass of verse 5 helps me to reach beyond the hyperbole to the yearning hope in God expressed in this psalm prayer.

Prayer: *Awaited One, may we who are the church be as gentle with the wounds of others as rain falling on new-mown grass. May we be as showers that water the earth to those persons and nations who hunger for righteousness and peace. "O come, O come, Emmanuel." Amen.*

Saturday, December 9   Read Matthew 3:1-12.

Matthew, Mark, Luke, and John all write about John, the son of the priest Zechariah and Elizabeth, but it is Matthew who names him "the Baptist."

On the eighth day following his birth, when John was being circumcised, his father was filled with the Holy Spirit and prophesied. He spoke forth that John would be called "the prophet of the Most High" and would "go before the Lord to prepare his ways." John would give "knowledge of salvation to his people by the forgiveness of their sins" (Luke 1:76-77).

In the fullness of time John appeared. His voice was one of authority like the prophets of ancient Israel. His appearance and message echoed the prophet Elijah. John knew that he was a forerunner, a herald of One so much greater than he that he was unfit even to work as his slave—but this One is not yet named.

Let us not leave John too quickly. Let us linger awhile with John as we await the advent of the One to whom he points and whose way he makes straight.

John called for repentance and confession of sins. His message carried the demand for integrity of life. Our life must bear the good fruit of radical repentance from non-faith ways and of the behavior and choices that issue from a life of faith. Our actions and declarations must be congruent, for the Awaited One will baptize us with the Holy Spirit and with fire. He stands now in the wings; he will be here soon. We are to be ready.

Prayer: *Holy Spirit of the living God, come, fill me, hold me, cleanse me. Show me my sin, that I may confess and be forgiven. Cause me to be ready for Christ to be born in me on Christmas Day. Thank you! Amen.*

Sunday, December 10

Read Psalm 72:18-19;
Romans 15:13.

Two benedictions weave themselves together in our hearts as we read and pray them on this Advent Lord's day.

The hope and faith of Israel are expressed in the glorious words of the psalmist in the praying of the benediction to conclude Book II (Psalms 42–72) of the Psalter. We find here a powerful and beautiful doxology of praise to the God of Israel.

In his letter to the Roman Christians, Paul names God the God of hope. He prays that God will fill the Christians with "joy and peace in believing," so that by the power of the Holy Spirit within them they may have a great amount, be fully supplied, have a superabundance of hope.

A few weeks ago my 98-year-old mother died, full of faith and years. Her legacy was not in material things; these only rust and soon pass away. Her legacy to all who knew her was a lifetime of hope—strong, immutable, Christian hope. Tragedy often touched her life, but her hope was firmly planted on her actual, day-by-day experience of the love of God in Jesus Christ. From her hope came courage, optimism, and gratitude. Her faith was uncomplicated. Her words were simple and clear. Her gift to all of us is expressed in the words of one sentence that she spoke in all times and places: "God's been with me all these years; God's not going to leave me now!"

This was also the hope of Paul when he addressed the God of hope. His prayer for the Roman Christians is a prayer for all of us. As we walk through Advent waiting for the One who is to come, may the God of hope fill us to overflowing with hope by the power of the Holy Spirit.

Prayer: *O come, O come, Emmanuel—God with us! Amen.*

THE ALREADY-AND-COMING KINGDOM

December 11-17, 1995   **Ariel Zambrano**✤
Monday, December 11   Read Isaiah 35:1-10.

Hope in the midst of despair

The time of Isaiah (about 740-680 B.C.E.) was fraught with dramatic events that changed the political and religious life of Judah in a drastic way. Invasions, wars, and internal political affairs kept the people in constant fear and despair.

Even though Isaiah witnessed the destruction, the pillage and plunder, in the dark night he was able to discover the stars and declare to his people: "Rejoice, I have good news for you! The time is coming when our fields will produce their crops again; be strong, fear not! The Lord is with us, the future is bright and promising!" (AP) Isaiah described a new highway that would lead to a restored New Zion, where there would be no sorrow or crying, only perpetual joy.

Like the people of Judah, we also live in very difficult days— in the world and in our communities and, perhaps, in our own lives. We are offered a new road that will take us even now to a life of peace, joy, and communion with God. Jesus said, "I am the way. . . . No one comes to the Father except through me" (John 14:6).

Suggestion for meditation: *What keeps me from walking in the way? How could I walk the road to the end?*

✤Retired minister of the California-Pacific Conference of The United Methodist Church; Claremont, California.

Tuesday, December 12   Read Psalm 146:5-7*b*.

God helps

This is the first of the last five psalms in the psalter, known as "hallelujah psalms." All of them begin and end with the words "Praise the LORD," which is the translation of the original Hebrew *haleluyah*. It is interesting to consider what prompts the sacred poet to praise God.

Here the psalmist is not praising God as Creator of the universe or as powerful Deliverer of Israel from Egypt; the psalmist's emphasis is on God as a helper who "keeps faith forever." Where we find the personal witness of the psalmist is in the fact that he declares that the Lord stands by the oppressed and the hungry. Perhaps God had helped the psalmist in some afflictive situation, and now he invites the whole congregation to sing praises to the Lord for help given in time of need.

In the secular culture in which we live, our ability to see God operating in our lives is often hampered. A good exercise would be to try to discover the different situations in which the hand of God has been manifested—helping us work out problems in the family or in our work, or God being at our bedside when we were sick, for example. The result might be that we will exclaim with the sacred poet, "Hallelujah, *my* Lord keeps faith forever!"

Suggestion for meditation: *Can you affirm with the psalmist that the Lord "keeps faith forever"? How can you express your gratitude to God for the goodness given to you?*

Wednesday, December 13 Read Psalm 146:8-10.

God at work in the world

The witness of the psalmist continues in verses 8-10 in a dynamic way. In poetic form the psalmist presents a God in action: the Lord is setting prisoners free, opening the eyes of the blind, lifting up those who are bowed down, loving the righteous, and watching over the sojourners. For the psalmist the Lord is a God who acts.

We can affirm that the sacred poet is remembering the past. As a good Israelite, the psalmist remembers the Exodus and the many ways in which the Lord's power had been manifested throughout the history of the people of Israel. The poet also remembers the tender ways in which God has dealt with them in acts of grace and love: God gave them "bread from heaven" (Exod. 16) and water from the rock in the desert (Exod. 17:1-7).

But the psalmist is talking in the *now*. He is saying that God acted like this in the past but God is also acting in the same way *now*.

In verse 10 we find that the psalmist changes to the future in a shout of faith: "The LORD will reign forever!" He is sure that the kingdom of the Lord will endure forever. Maybe the powers of this world, which are called "princes" in verse 3, are felt in a painful way, but the psalmist trusts in God and is able to finish the poem by singing in exultation, "Praise the LORD!"

Suggestion for meditation: *Can you see God working in the world now? When you read about shootings and assassinations, and television is full of violence and sex, can you affirm that God is still at the helm? Where do you find some hope for the future?*

Thursday, December 14　　　　　　　Read James 5:7.

The Lord comes!

We are now in the season of Advent. Some believe that Jesus' coming to us that first Christmas was all that was necessary, that a second coming is, therefore, unnecessary. However, the return of the Lord is affirmed in the New Testament. Jesus himself said that he will come again "in his glory" to sit on his throne (Matt. 25:31). The problem is that the New Testament offers us different ways to think about the second coming of the Lord: 1. He has already returned in the Holy Spirit on the Day of Pentecost. 2. He is constantly returning in the lives of the believers who endeavor to follow Jesus' teachings. 3. There will be a final consummation when all the peoples of the world will recognize his universal Lordship.

All these different views, and maybe more that haven't been mentioned, have a common denominator: all affirm that there will be a time when the kingdom of God will finally be established with glory and power. Or, to use Paul's words, this will happen when "all things [are] put in subjection under him" (see 1 Cor. 15:23-28).

Whatever we believe about Jesus' second coming, there is the basis to believe that what God began that first Christmas will be brought to perfect completion. God declared, "I am the Alpha and the Omega, the beginning and the end" (Rev. 21:6). This is a promise we can carry with us as we travel through troubled times.

Suggestion for meditation: *We know neither the time nor the way in which our Lord will be manifested again. How could you prepare for such an event? Christ is the center of the biblical drama, the source of our salvation. Is he the center of your life now?*

Friday, December 15   Read James 5:8-10.

Be patient!

Our meditation today begins with a note of urgency. Verse 8 affirms that "the coming of the Lord is near," and verse 9 says that "the Judge is standing at the doors." Both statements convey the idea of imminence, of something about to happen.

We know that about two thousand years have elapsed since James wrote these words, and the Lord hasn't come again. But, as we read in Galatians, the Lord came the first Christmas, "when the fullness of time had come" (Gal. 4:4), and we can be assured that his second coming will also be in the fullness of time.

Jesus exhorts us to be watchful, because nobody knows the time or the day when the Lord will come; only the Father knows (Mark 13:32). James gives us good advice for our waiting. In verses 7-10 he repeats four times the words *patience* or *patient*. He also mentions that we should behave in a loving manner toward our brothers and sisters and the members of our community. We are expected to be ready, alert, and expectant till the Lord comes.

As is commonly affirmed by the millions of Christians at the Lord's Table,

Christ has died,
Christ is risen,
Christ will come again!

Suggestion for meditation: *What do you believe about the second coming of the Lord? Do you expect his coming again? How will you occupy yourself during the "waiting"? Can you think of any aspects of your life that need to be made ready?*

Saturday, December 16   Read Matthew 11:2-6.

The establishing kingdom

John the Baptist is in prison. He is suffering physically, no doubt, but his greatest suffering is in his spirit. In his cell he has had time to ponder his ministry and the ministry of Jesus. Very important questions are now before him: Is Jesus really the "One to come"? Should we wait for someone else? John sends his disciples to ask Jesus these burning questions.

Jesus' answer is as dramatic as it is direct. According to Matthew his reply is, "Go and tell John what you hear and see," and then he enumerated a series of his miracles. Luke, in the parallel passage (7:18-23), tells us that he performed the miracles while they were there, a truly visual-aids answer. The climax in his reply is, "And the poor have good news brought to them."

Our pericope ends with these intriguing words of Jesus: "Blessed is anyone who takes no offense at me." The word translated here as "takes no offense at me" is only one word in Greek that can be translated as "sin," as we can see in Matthew 18:6-9.

John's questions reveal a struggling spirit. Jesus' answer reveals that the Kingdom has been established and, at the same time, is being established. The invitation is for everyone to enter it. The condition? Only believe.

Suggestion for meditation: *Do you have doubts or questions in your mind regarding your faith in Christ? Like John, present your plea to Jesus. Remember the words of the father of the demonic child, "I believe; help my unbelief!" (Mark 9:24)*

Sunday, December 17   Read Matthew 11:7-11.

To enter the kingdom

When John's disciples were leaving, Jesus started praising the Baptist before the crowd. He called him a prophet, "and more than a prophet." As the climax of Jesus' praising, he affirmed, "Among those born of women no one has arisen greater than John the Baptist." Then he added what seems to be a contradiction: "Yet the least in the kingdom of heaven is greater than he."

John's ministry came after the era of the Old Testament prophets and marked the beginning of the new era of the kingdom. In Jesus he saw the kingdom, but like Moses, who saw the promised land from Mount Pisgah but never entered it, he was prevented from experiencing fully the kingdom's dawning. Like Moses, he was unable to "cross the border."

I have a mentally retarded son, now an adult. When he was younger he participated in the Special Olympics in his area. Once in a race he was ahead of the other racers, but when he arrived at the finish line he made the greatest effort not to step across it. He could have won the race, but he never crossed the line. Later we learned that he had been told to get to the line, but was never instructed that he had to cross it.

If we want to arrive at the kingdom, we have to cross the line, which means to have ears that hear and eyes that see what Jesus has done on our behalf. It is Advent and very soon it will be Christmas, a good time to reflect on this matter. Let us cross the line and become citizens of the Kingdom.

Suggestion for meditation: *Are you looking at the Kingdom from the other side of the border? Are you able to recognize what Jesus did for you in Bethlehem and at Calvary?*

COME, EMMANUEL

December 18-24, 1995   **Jack L. Seymour**✤
Monday, December 18   Read Psalm 80:1-7.

Because this week ends with Christmas Eve, our reading of the texts is focused on Jesus' birth. Yet we also need to let the texts speak from their own contexts. Only after hearing their meanings can we ask why these stories were used by Christian authors to interpret the faith.

Psalm 80 is a community lament. The people remembered their captivity in Babylon and daily experienced their weakness as a nation. Their prayers begged for God's comfort and salvation. The proclamation of the psalm is that, even in pain and weakness, the people may stand before the divine one. God is the One whose face shines on them. Salvation is God's gracious act, not something earned by strength. What a blessing to be reminded each week of God's grace!

As we enter this season of celebration, we need to remember that life and grace are rooted in God's acts. Who may enter the presence of the divine one? Anyone! God's grace is freely extended.

Suggestion for prayer: *Each week the Hebrew people brought to God the needs of the people. In our prayers, let us remember some of the needs in our world. As we do, repeat, "Restore us, O God of hosts; let your face shine, that we may be saved."*

✤Professor of Religious Education, Garrett-Evangelical Theological Seminary; Chicago, Illinois.

364

Tuesday, December 19   Read Matthew 1:18-25.

God's grace, and God's grace alone, enables us to stand in God's presence. Matthew repeats this promise as he tells the story of Joseph. The acts of God are always greater than the people's expectations.

A story about Joseph's discovery of Mary's pregnancy becomes an occasion for Matthew to proclaim how God fulfills promises. The word to Joseph and to us is "Do not be afraid." Note how the story of Joseph and the angel is preceded by the genealogy of Jesus. This genealogy proclaims God's grace. Even before, God has had to intervene to keep the line of Abraham and David alive (Tamar, Rahab, Ruth, and the "wife of Uriah"). God has to act again.

Joseph is a righteous man, but his righteousness does not aid him in recognizing God's act. He has mercy but not wisdom. In his shame, he has planned to dismiss Mary. Under the law Joseph could have had Mary tried for adultery, and she could have been stoned to death. Instead, Joseph plans a merciful compromise. Yet God confronts the compromise. "Do not be afraid," the angel proclaims. The message to Joseph is to take Mary as his wife and care for her and the child. This baby will save the people.

As God has intervened before, God intervenes again as he calls Joseph to a new vocation. Jesus' destiny is preserved by Joseph's response to God's grace.

Suggestion for meditation: *God surprises us. God calls us to new actions that we do not expect. Our anger, our shame, our righteousness, and even our mercy are not guarantees that we understand God's will. As you meditate on God's call to you today, repeat to yourself several times the words "Do not be afraid." To what new vocation is God calling you that lies beyond your fears?*

Wednesday, December 20   Read Matthew 1:22-23;
Isaiah 7:10-17.

Matthew turns to the texts of his day (to Isaiah) to understand the surprising and miraculous transforming power of Jesus. *Emmanuel* is a distinctive name to apply to Jesus. This name is not used elsewhere in Matthew or in the New Testament.

Several times in the Gospel, Matthew uses the phrase "so that what had been spoken through the prophets might be fulfilled" or a similar phrase. At each of these points, Matthew announces that the fulfillment will be greater than the promise. Here Matthew extends the meaning of a passage from Isaiah.

For Isaiah, the Emmanuel could have been any child. King Ahaz and the Hebrew people shook in fear as "trees . . . before the wind" (v. 2). The Assyrian king had moved against Syria and Palestine. Because Ahaz refused to join his neighbors in defense, they in turn direct their armies at him. While the people quake in fear, Isaiah calls Ahaz to trust in God rather than in human intrigue. The king refuses. Nevertheless, Isaiah provides a sign from God. Isaiah turns to a woman with child and proclaims that this child is God's sign. God is with the people. Who is the child? Ahaz's son? Isaiah's son? Or simply a woman at court? It does not matter. For Isaiah, the birth of a child is a promise that God will restore the people.

God acts in our ordinary time and ordinary experiences. For Isaiah, an ordinary birth becomes the sign of God's actual presence with the people.

Prayer: *Holy God, open our eyes to see your gracious presence in the ordinary events of life. Help us to focus on you and seek to understand your call through those events in our lives. Amen.*

Thursday, December 21   Read Psalm 80:1-7, 17-19.

Ahaz could not read the signs of the times. He could not see God in the aspects of daily life. Do we, too, refuse to look for God's actions in everyday life? How do we read the signs of the times? Ahaz preferred his advisers. Joseph trusted his righteousness. Many of Jesus' contemporaries missed the power of his incarnation because they expected a political king. Yet, Isaiah saw the sign of God in the seeming ordinariness of an impending future birth.

Psalm 80 provides insight into reading the signs of the times. The psalmist shares the people's pain with God, describing how their tears feed them and how they are scorned by their neighbors. The return to Jerusalem after the Babylonian captivity was filled with confusion—joy at the return, despair at the ravaged land, and fear at their national weakness. Recognition of God's activity begins in honestly sharing one's experiences with God. Secondly, the psalmist reminds the people of God's gracious gifts. God "brought a vine out of Egypt" (v. 8). And, thirdly, he encourages them to question God: "Why then have you broken down its walls?" (v. 12).

How do we prepare to see the signs of the times? We reveal our pain to God, we ask questions, and we remember God's gifts. Like Ahaz and Joseph, we are too often blinded to God's presence because we do not expect it. The psalmist and the people plead for God's restoration, they expect it, and they are open to it.

Suggestion for prayer: *Ask God to open your eyes to God's gracious presence in your midst. Take time to share your experience of the day with God, ask any questions you have, and thank God for gifts received.*

Friday, December 22   Read Romans 1:1-7.

Paul opens the letter to the churches at Rome, churches that he had not visited, with his typical greeting: "Grace to you and peace from God." Also included in this introduction are a statement of his authority as an apostle, a call for the Roman churches to be faithful, and reference to an early confession of faith that must have circulated among churches. The good news, the confession says, is that the one whom God promised through the prophets is present. Jesus Christ is the Son of God. Jesus is God's presence.

This early creed is very specific, as is Paul, about Jesus' humanity. Jesus was "descended from David according to the flesh." Jesus "was declared" Son of God by "resurrection from the dead." Jesus is the presence of God within human history. Jesus was born to a woman, lived life as we do but with a special vocation, died a cruel death, and was raised within human history.

God is with us in the concreteness of every day. Paul discovered God is daily life. He here uses a creed of the church to announce himself to a new group of people. Within their histories, too, they have encountered the presence of God. Within our histories, we encounter the presence of God. Grace and peace are not just polite greetings. Grace and peace are proclamations of what God is in fact doing within human history. The rest of this letter seeks to assist the churches in Rome to live out the proclamation of God's presence.

Suggestion for meditation: *Repeat Paul's salutation to the churches in Rome. "Grace to you and peace from God." As you repeat this phrase, again focus on the presence of God. Seek to discern where grace and peace are present.*

Saturday, December 23   Read Romans 1:1-7.

Paul defines his vocation as an apostle. Through Jesus Christ he has received grace "to bring about the obedience of faith among all the Gentiles." Paul, like Joseph, has a crucial vocation for the saving presence of God. So do the Roman churches, which are called to faithful obedience. They are called "to within history belong to Jesus Christ." We are called to that same vocation. We recognize that God is present within history and that we can seek to read the signs of the times. We take this bold step because we follow the Presence we have discerned.

The Epistle to the Romans is written to a diverse group of churches. Some were house churches where wealthy patrons provided a Eucharistic meal and church leadership (e.g., Phoebe, Prisca, and Aquila). Some of these house churches transcended cultural and class backgrounds as diverse people gathered to seek to live out the gift of Jesus Christ. Other churches were "tenement churches" meeting in overcrowded apartment buildings. People with little economic resources shared what they had to provide a Eucharistic meal and to support and care for each other (16:1-16). In the midst of this diversity, Paul calls the churches to pursue "what makes for peace and for mutual upbuilding" (14:19).

Through discovering God's presence in human history, we are called to the obedience of faith. Across our differences we celebrate the meal of thanksgiving, share our lives, care, and pursue mutual upbuilding. The presence of God is to be lived in obedience and faith.

Suggestion for prayer *God's gift of grace and peace is a concrete gift within history. The churches of Rome learned this even in their diversity. Recognizing our diversity, pray for faithfulness to work for peace and mutual upbuilding.*

Sunday, December 24

Read Matthew 1:18-25.

Today is Christmas Eve. With Matthew we look to the prophet Isaiah and proclaim, "They shall call him Emmanuel." God is with us. God is with us in the life and ministry of Jesus. Jesus is to save the people and to be God's presence with us. In Matthew, Jesus is more than anyone expected: Jesus is called by God, beloved by God, and well pleasing to God. Jesus is healer, liberator, teacher, giver of new life, prophet, companion to those in pain, challenger of the traditional religion, storyteller, miracle worker, savior restoring the people, and the one who sends disciples to the ends of the earth. In each of these acts, Jesus makes God present in the world. Through each of these, God calls us to discipleship.

We began the week with the question asked every week by the Hebrew people: When would God restore the people? Who could approach the mighty throne of God? The answer is that not only is God approachable but that God is already ahead of our pleading. God is present in the world. Jesus is a reminder of that presence. Prayerfully we seek to read the signs of the times and see God's gracious love. Seeing God's grace, we are then called to our own vocations of service and obedience.

Suggestion for meditation: *As you prepare to celebrate the birth of "God is with us," meditate on the name of Jesus (Yehoshua). This name is a shortened form of Joshua, meaning "Yahweh helps, Yahweh saves." As you close your prayer looking forward to Christmas, repeat several times: "Yahweh helps, Yahweh saves."*

THE GLORY THAT HAS COME NEAR

December 25-31, 1995
Monday, December 25

John Killinger♣
Read Luke 2:8-20.

Christmas Day

Today most people's notion of glory is of Hollywoodish power and glamour. But the shepherds in this story discerned an infinitely more important kind of glory, a transcendent glory centered in the God of all creation.

Yet even the shepherds were not permitted to look nakedly upon this glory; it was too high and wonderful for that. So they received it through an angel, a heavenly emissary of God who communicated God's glory to human beings.

The shepherds were appropriately awe-stricken by this message and its proclaimers. They may even have thought they would die as a result of the encounter.

But the angel said, "Fear not" (KJV). The visitation was intended only to announce the favor of God, who was at that very moment drawing near to the human predicament in the form of a messiah. And the messiah was appearing in the most incredible way—as a baby born in a stable.

The shepherds were thus privileged to witness the greatest mystery of all time—the glory of the unspeakable God made visible in a newborn child. Life on earth would never again be the same.

Prayer: *Help me, O God, to catch even a glimpse of the glory beheld by these simple folk so long ago. Then let me return to my ordinary life as they did, worshiping and praising you for the stupendous thing you have done. Amen.*

♣Author; Distinguished Professor of Religion and Culture, Samford University, Birmingham, Alabama.

Tuesday, December 26   Read Psalm 148.

We don't know the particular inspiration that triggered the composition of this psalm. Perhaps the writer had just become a father or mother, or had recovered from a dire illness, or was saved from an untimely death by flood or fire. Whatever the reason, the author was certainly caught up in a mood of admiration and called on everything in existence, including creation itself and the angels above creation, to join in a great symphony of praise to God.

The praise is invoked in an interesting order. First the writer calls·upon the heavens themselves to voice their adoration. Then the focus is turned upon creation. And finally everything in creation is invited to join the chorus.

No one is exempt from this trumpet call to praise. Even the kings and princes are to lift their voice to God, along with "young men, and maidens; old men, and children" (KJV).

This is an appropriate psalm, therefore, to read in connection with the visit of the Magi, who, according to some legends, were themselves royal figures. Their search for the Christ child reminds us again of the glory that drew near to earth in his coming.

One can almost hear the jangle of their camels' bridles and bits as they crossed mountains and valleys and plains. Some deep mystery was drawing these wise ones inexorably toward a majesty and power beyond their own. It was an extraordinary moment in history, when all creation might well praise the God who was shaping our future.

Prayer: *Heaven and earth are praising you, O God. Tune my heart to join in their chorus of voices and acknowledge you as the Maker and Sustainer of everything. Through the Child of the mystery. Amen.*

Wednesday, December 27   Read Psalm 97.

What unusual incident had given voice to the psalmist? Had some natural catastrophe occurred? The imagery in verses two to six suggests as much: a great storm had probably toppled the trees of the forests and sent swollen streams cascading through sleepy villages, or perhaps an earthquake had caused the very mountains to tremble and shift!

As always happens at such times, people had become freshly aware of the power of God and the feebleness of human resistance. All the earthly things they had prized so highly—wealth, power, comfort, even their families—were revealed as mere idols, powerless to save them.

Nothing compares with God and the heavenly glory. Nothing in all creation!

The real Zion—the true believers—rejoice and worship when they behold the judgment of God, even in moments of threat or terror; for they know that the Almighty One reigns over everything and is merely exerting the divine power. They gasp with excitement and bow down. They lift their hearts in adoration. They take pleasure in being children of the light, whose deeds do not condemn them in the presence of the heavenly glory.

Again we are considering an important theme for Christmas. Christ's entry into the world has lit the dark places and challenged the forces of evil. His coming was a judgment on the crooked and ungodly ways of the people. Justice and love came along with retribution. We should all worship and bow down.

Prayer: *The light of Christ has revealed our brokenness and need, O God. Enable us to repent and receive your grace, which is always cause for praise and rejoicing. In the name of the One who came among us. Amen.*

Thursday, December 28   Read Isaiah 62:6-12.

What beautiful promises lace this speech of Isaiah! And what disappointment we would have in them if we thought they had already been fulfilled and then broken.

But many scholars believe the prophet was foretelling the eventual triumph of heavenly rule when all history is consummated and Christ reigns supremely over all. "See, your salvation comes!" says the text, bringing both reward and recompense in his hands.

Christmas is a time for looking far beyond the familiar scene at the manger, where the infant Messiah lies wrapped in swaddling cloths. It is a judgment on our failed sensibilities as Christians if we lose our vision in the glitter and gaiety of the season and are not deeply moved by the promise of the power that will transform all life and history.

For ancient Israelites, most of whom had never known anything but war and desolation, the most idyllic part of this promise was about peace. When the great Day of the Lord arrived, they could look forward to raising grain and making wine that would not be devoured by strangers (vv. 8-9).

Was it a mere accident, in light of this glorious expectation, that Jesus took bread and wine as the symbols of his own body and blood? That he gave them to his disciples at the last meal and told them to remember him this way until he met them again?

Prayer: *What deep and wonderful mysteries abound in this text, O God, and how they stir my heart! Let me ponder them for days to come, and feed my hungry heart with them. Amen.*

Friday, December 29　　　　　　　　　Read Isaiah 63:7-9.

One of the most tender pictures of God in the Bible, this passage is filled with such words as *steadfast love* and *mercy.* The writer knew how much God had always cared for Israel.

God had shown trust and compassion to Israel, expecting the people to behave as sons and daughters of the heavenly favor. Whenever they were distressed about anything, God was also distressed, and "the angel of his presence saved them" (KJV).

What a lovely, intriguing image this is—"the angel of his presence." We alluded in an earlier reading to God's unspeakable glory and the fact that no human being could look upon it bare, so that glory was mediated through angelic beings. This phrase is a poetic metaphor for the way God overcame the great chasm between the divine nature and human existence. The glory drew near to Israel even in olden days.

But love often sets itself up for betrayal. It is in the very nature of love that it is vulnerable. And the Israelites betrayed the love of the One who sent the angel of divine presence so many times.

As we read these words now in the Christmas season, they should remind us of how easily we ourselves can disappoint God. They should remind us of how the One who finally did not merely send an angel but who, in Jesus Christ, came in person to be with us and teach us to be on our guard lest we behave as the ancient Israelites did.

Prayer: *Forbid, O God, that I should forget all your benefits to me and thus frustrate the love you have shown me in Christ Jesus. Keep my heart faithful at all times, and let me praise you with the saints and angels forever. Amen.*

Saturday, December 30   Read Matthew 2:13-23.

More angels! The glory that has come near continues to mediate itself in ways that veil human eyes from the too-bright majesty of God. And dear Joseph, the bit player in this drama, is sensitive to the glory; he perceives it even in his dreams.

Dreams are an important part of true spirituality, for to be spiritual means being attuned to God and God's actions at all times—even when we sleep. Some people measure spirituality primarily by behavior. But the fact is that it occurs whenever we allow the holy to penetrate our inmost citadels and direct our hearts and wills from within. It has to do with conversion at the very center of who we are.

When we really experience the glorious presence of God, we begin to see God everywhere—in the faces of people we meet, in the skylines of cities and stretches of countryside, in books and movies and elevators and offices, and wherever we go. The flowers are brighter. Even the grass and trees seem to be lit from inside by some special glow.

And when we sleep, and dream, we are alert to "messages" that come to our psyches, symbols and actions that speak to the deepest parts of who we are and what God wants for our lives. Like Joseph, we are prepared to respond in an instant, following God's leadership wherever it takes us, whatever it requires of us.

Prayer: *Make me sensitive, O God, to the many ways your presence surrounds me and seeks to commune with me even now. School me in how to respond with awareness, and I shall rejoice in your glory forever. Amen.*

Sunday, December 31   Read Hebrews 2:10-18.

We should really begin reading this text at least one verse earlier: "But we see Jesus, who was made a little lower than the angels, now crowned with glory and honor because he suffered death, so that by the grace of God he might taste death for everyone" (NIV).

Jesus was made human, "a little lower than the angels," the heavenly messengers of God's glory. As the only begotten Son of God, he brought that glory even more strikingly into our midst. And by bringing it into the very valley of suffering and death, he transformed the nature of suffering and death for all time. They are no longer the terrible enemies they were. Now we can endure them with hope and expectancy, knowing that God has overcome them in Christ.

This is an appropriate text for consummating our week's thoughts, which have been centered on the glory that has drawn near us. The presence and holiness of God have been mediated in One whose special purpose was to break down the barriers between the divine and the human. Because of him, the very veil of the Temple has been rent in two. His sacrifice has enabled us to enter the heart of mystery and relate directly to the Presence that for centuries both haunted and eluded Israel. Now our salvation is complete in him.

Prayer: *We praise you, O God, for the love that has wooed and drawn us even when we were hostile and indifferent. Even now, when our hearts are attracted to idols and our minds are filled with vain thoughts, you continue to hold and guide us. Lead us by your Son and holy angels into perfect union with you, for your name's sake. Amen.*

The Revised Common Lectionary* 1995
(*Disciplines* Edition)

January 2-8
Isaiah 43:1-7
Psalm 29
Acts 8:14-17
Luke 3:15-17, 21-22

January 9-15
Isaiah 62:1-5
Psalm 36:5-10
1 Corinthians 12:1-11
John 2:1-11

January 16-22
Nehemiah 8:1-3, 5-6, 8-10
Psalm 19
1 Corinthians 12:12-31*a*
Luke 4:14-21

January 23-29
Jeremiah 1:4-10
Psalm 71:1-6
1 Corinthians 13:1-13
Luke 4:21-30

January 30–February 5
Isaiah 6:1-8
Psalm 138
1 Corinthians 15:1-11
Luke 5:1-11

February 6-12
Jeremiah 17:5-10
Psalm 1
1 Corinthians 15:12-20
Luke 6:17-26

February 13-19
Genesis 43:3-11, 15
Psalm 37:1-11, 39-40
1 Corinthians 15:35-38, 42-50
Luke 6:27-38

February 20-26
  Transfiguration
Exodus 34:29-35
Psalm 99
2 Corinthians 3:12–4:2
Luke 9:28-36

Year C – Advent/Christmas Year A
*Copyright © 1992 by the
Consultation on Common Texts
(CCT). Used by permission.

February 27–March 5
First Sunday in Lent
Deuteronomy 26:1-11
Psalm 91:1-2, 9-16
Romans 10:8*b*-13
Luke 4:1-13

Ash Wednesday lections
Joel 2:1-2, 12-17
(*or* Isaiah 58:1-12)
Psalm 51:1-17
2 Corinthians 5:20*b*–6:10
Matthew 6:1-6, 16-21

March 6-12
Second Sunday in Lent
Genesis 15:1-12, 17-18
Psalm 27
Philippians 3:17–4:1
Luke 13:31-35 (*or* Luke 9:28-36)

March 13-19
Third Sunday in Lent
Isaiah 55:1-9
Psalm 63:1-8
1 Corinthians 10:1-13
Luke 13:1-9

March 20-26
Fourth Sunday in Lent
Joshua 5:9-12
Psalm 32
2 Corinthians 5:16-21
Luke 15:1-3, 11*b*-32

March 27–April 2
Fifth Sunday in Lent
Isaiah 43:16-21
Psalm 126
Philippians 3:4*b*-14
John 12:1-8

April 3-9
Passion/Palm Sunday

Liturgy of the Palms
Luke 19:28-40
Psalm 118:1-2, 19-29

Liturgy of the Passion
Isaiah 50:4-9*a*
Psalm 31:9-16
Philippians 2:5-11
Luke 22:14–23:56
(*or* Luke 23:1-49)

April 10-16

Selected Holy Week lections
Monday
Isaiah 42:1-9
John 12:1-11

Tuesday
Isaiah 49:1-7
John 12:20-36

Wednesday
Isaiah 50:4-9*a*
John 13:21-32

Maundy Thursday
Exodus 12:1-4, (5-10), 11-14
1 Corinthians 11:23-26
John 13:1-17, 31*b*-35

Good Friday
Isaiah 52:13–53:12
Psalm 22
Hebrews 4:14-16; 5:7-9
John 18:1–19:42

Holy Saturday
Lamentations 3:1-9, 19-24
Psalm 31:1-4, 15-16
John 19:38-42

Easter (April 16)
Isaiah 65:17-25
Psalm 118:1-2, 14-24
1 Corinthians 15:19-26
John 20:1-18
  (*or* Luke 24:1-12)

April 17-23
Acts 5:27-32
Psalm 150
Revelation 1:4-8
John 20:19-31

April 24-30
Acts 9:1-6 (7-20)
Psalm 30
Revelation 5:11-14
John 21:1-19

May 1-7
Acts 9:36-43
Psalm 23
Revelation 7:9-17
John 10:22-30

May 8-14
Acts 11:1-18
Psalm 148
Revelation 21:1-6
John 13:31-35

May 15-21
Acts 16:9-15
Psalm 67
Revelation 21:10; 21:22–22:5
John 14:23-29
  (*or* John 5:1-9)

May 22-28
Acts 16:16-34
Psalm 97
Revelation 22:12-14,
  16-17, 20-21
John 17:20-26

(*Or* use **Ascension Day**
  lections for May 28)
  Acts 1:1-11
  Psalm 47 (*or* Psalm 110)
  Ephesians 1:15-23
  Luke 24:44-53

May 29–June 4
  Pentecost
Acts 2:1-21
Psalm 104:24-34, 35*b*
Romans 8:14-17
John 14:8-17, (25-27)

June 5-11
  Trinity
Proverbs 8:1-4, 22-31
Psalm 8
Romans 5:1-5
John 16:12-15

June 12-18
1 Kings 21:1-21*a*
Psalm 5:1-8
Galatians 2:15-21
Luke 7:36–8:3

June 19-25
1 Kings 19:1-15*a*
Psalm 42 and 43
Galatians 3:23-39
Luke 8:26-39

June 26–July 2
2 Kings 2:1-2, 6-14
Psalm 77:1-2, 11-20
Galatians 5:1, 13-25
Luke 9:51-62

July 3-9
2 Kings 5:1-14
Psalm 30
Galatians 6:(1-6), 7-16
Luke 10:1-11, 16-20

July 10-16
Amos 7:7-17
Psalm 82
Colossians 1:1-14
Luke 10:25-37

July 17-23
Amos 8:1-12
Psalm 52
Colossians 1:15-28
Luke 10:38-42

July 24-30
Hosea 1:2-10
Psalm 85
Colossians 2:6-15, (16-19)
Luke 11:1-13

July 31–August 6
Hosea 11:1-11
Psalm 107:1-9, 43
Colossians 3:1-11
Luke 12:13-21

August 7-13
Isaiah 1:1, 10-20
Psalm 50:1-8, 22-23
Hebrews 11:1-3, 8-16
Luke 12:32-40

August 14-20
Isaiah 5:1-7
Psalm 80:1-2, 8-19
Hebrews 11:29–12:2
Luke 12:49-56

August 21-27
Jeremiah 1:4-10
Psalm 71:1-6
Hebrews 12:18-29
Luke 13:10-17

August 28–September 3
Jeremiah 2:4-13
Psalm 81:1, 10-16
Hebrews 13:1-8, 15-16
Luke 14:1, 7-14

September 4-10
Jeremiah 18:1-11
Psalm 139:1-6, 13-18
Philemon 1-21
Luke 14:25-33

September 11-17
Jeremiah 4:11-12, 22-28
Psalm 14
1 Timothy 1:12-17
Luke 15:1-10

September 18-24
Jeremiah 8:18–9:1
Psalm 79:1-9
1 Timothy 2:1-7
Luke 16:1-13

September 25–October 1
Jeremiah 32:1-3*a*, 6-15
Psalm 91:1-6, 14-16
1 Timothy 6:6-19
Luke 16:19-31

October 2-8
Lamentations 1:1-6
Psalm 137
2 Timothy 1:1-14
Luke 17:5-10

October 9-15
Jeremiah 29:1, 4-7
Psalm 66:1-12
2 Timothy 2:8-15
Luke 17:11-19

October 16-22
Jeremiah 31:27-34
Psalm 119:97-104
2 Timothy 3:14–4:5
Luke 18:1-8

October 23-29
Joel 2:23-32
Psalm 65
2 Timothy 4:6-8, 16-18
Luke 18:9-14

October 30–November 5
Habakkuk 1:1-4; 2:1-4
Psalm 119:137-144
2 Thessalonians 1:1-4, 11-12
Luke 19:1-10

All Saints Day (November 1)
(Or use these lections for
Sunday, November 5)
Daniel 7:1-3, 15-18
Psalm 149
Ephesians 1:11-23
Luke 6:20-31

November 6-12
Haggai 1:15b–2:9
Psalm 145:1-5, 17-21
2 Thessalonians 2:1-5, 13-17
Luke 20:27-38

November 13-19
Isaiah 65:17-25
Isaiah 12 (*or* Psalm 98)
2 Thessalonians 3:6-13
Luke 21:5-19

November 20-26
Jeremiah 23:1-6
Luke 1:68-79
  (*or* Psalm 46)
Colossians 1:11-20
Luke 23:33-43

Begin Year A with Advent.

November 27–December 3
 First Sunday of Advent
Isaiah 2:1-5
Psalm 122
Romans 13:11-14
Matthew 24:36-44

December 4-10
 Second Sunday of Advent
Isaiah 11:1-10
Psalm 72:1-7, 18-19
Romans 15:4-13
Matthew 3:1-12

December 11-17
  Third Sunday of Advent
Isaiah 35:1-10
Psalm 146:5-10
  (*or* Luke 1:47-55)
James 5:7-10
Matthew 11:2-11

December 18-24
  Fourth Sunday of Advent
Isaiah 7:10-16
Psalm 80:1-17, 17-19
Romans 1:1-7
Matthew 1:18-25

Christmas Eve Readings
  Isaiah 9:2-7
  Psalm 96
  Titus 2:11-14
  Luke 2:1-14 (15-20)

December 25-31
  First Sunday after
    Christmas
Isaiah 63:7-9
Psalm 148
Hebrews 2:10-18
Matthew 2:13-23

Christmas Day Readings
  Isaiah 62:6-12
  Psalm 97
  Titus 3:4-7
  Luke 2:(1-7), 8-20

Gracious God,

*for the unexpected moments of joy
that the world can neither give nor take away,
we give you thanks.
Amen.*

Catherine Gunsalus González
Disciplines 1992